2008-2009

Economic Survey of Latin America and the Caribbean

Policies for creating quality jobs

UNITED NATIONS

ECLAC

The *Economic Survey of Latin America and the Caribbean* is issued annually by the Economic Development Division of the Economic Commission for Latin America and the Caribbean (ECLAC). This 2008-2009 edition was prepared under the supervision of Osvaldo Kacef, Director of the Division; Jürgen Weller was responsible for its overall coordination.

In the preparation of this edition, the Economic Development Division was assisted by the Statistics and Economic Projections Division, the Division of International Trade and Integration, the ECLAC subregional headquarters in Mexico City and Port of Spain and the country offices of the Commission in Bogota, Brasilia, Buenos Aires, Montevideo and Washington, D.C.

Part I, entitled "The Latin American and Caribbean economy in 2008-2009", was prepared by Osvaldo Kacef, with input from Claudio Aravena, Omar Bello, Fernando Cantú, Rodrigo Cárcamo, Juan Pablo Jiménez, Luis Felipe Jiménez, Rafael López-Monti, Roberto Machado, Sandra Manuelito, Sarah Mueller, Andrea Podestá, Claudia Roethlisberger and Jürgen Weller. The chapters of part II of the report draw upon material written by Roxana Maurizio, a consultant, as well as documents prepared by Juan Chacaltana, Guillermo Cruces and Andrés Ham, Andrew Downes, Stefano Farné, Patricio Frías, Andrés Marinakis, Lucas Navarro, Víctor Tokman and Mario Velásquez, which were discussed at a workshop held in April 2009 in Santiago. The Spanish Agency for International Cooperation for Development (AECID) helped to finance this workshop and a number of contracts.

The country reports are based on studies conducted by the following experts: Olga Lucía Acosta and María Alejandra Botiva (Colombia), Omar Bello (Plurinational State of Bolivia), Rodrigo Cárcamo (Ecuador), Stefan Edwards (Suriname), Álvaro Fuentes (Uruguay), Sarah Gammage (Honduras and Panama), Randolph Gilbert (Haiti), Michael Hendrickson (Bahamas and Belize), Daniel Heymann and Adrián Ramos (Argentina), Luis Felipe Jiménez (Chile), Beverly Lugay (Eastern Caribbean Monetary Union), Roberto Machado (Trinidad and Tobago), Sandra Manuelito (Bolivarian Republic of Venezuela), Jorge Mattar (Mexico), Armando Mendoza (Barbados, Guyana and Jamaica), Sarah Mueller (Paraguay), Carlos Mussi (Brazil), Ramón Padilla (Costa Rica and Nicaragua), Igor Paunovic (Cuba), Juan Carlos Rivas (El Salvador and Guatemala), Francisco Villareal (Dominican Republic) and Jürgen Weller (Peru). Claudia Roethlisberger revised the reports on the Caribbean countries.

Alejandra Acevedo, Vianka Aliaga, Leandro Cabello, Jazmín Chiu and Hans Fricke were responsible for the processing and presentation of the statistical data.

Notes
In this publication, the term "country" is used to refer to territorial entities, whether these are States as understood by international law and practice or simply territories for which statistical data are maintained on a separate and independent basis.
The word "dollars" refers to United States dollars, unless otherwise specified.
The following symbols have been used in the tables shown in the Survey: Three dots (...) indicate that data are not available or are not separately reported. A dash (-) indicates that the amount is nil or negligible. A point is used to indicate decimals.

United Nations Publication
ISBN: 978-92-1-121711-7
ISSN printed version: 0257-2184 ISSN online version: 1681-0384 ISSN CD-ROM: 1811-6191
LC/G.2410-P
Sales No.: E.09.II.G.2

Printed in Santiago, Chile

Contents

Tables

Part 1

Part 2

Figures

Part 1

Boxes

Foreword

The publication of the sixty-first edition of the *Economic Survey of Latin America and the Caribbean*, corresponding to 2008-2009, comes at a critical point in the economic development of the Latin American and Caribbean region. A growth phase whose nature and duration is unequalled in the region's recent history has come to an abrupt end and output is contracting. The toll this state of affairs is taking on the well-being of the population will inevitably be reflected in setbacks in social variables.

The first part of this edition of the *Economic Survey* looks at the channels through which the crisis is affecting the economies of the region and its impact on variables such as economic growth, employment and external-sector indicators. It also discusses the strengths and weaknesses of the countries in dealing with the fallout from the global crisis and the economic policies they have deployed to this end. The analysis covers the performance of the region's economy in 2008 and the first semester of 2009 and concludes with a discussion of the outlook for the second half of the year. This chapter draws on the data contained in an extensive statistical appendix.

The nature of the recovery will depend greatly on developments in the world economy, but also on the way the countries prepare for the challenges of the future. Macroeconomic management of the crisis is crucial, but so, as ECLAC has emphasized on many occasions, is laying the foundations for sustainable growth based on growing systemic competitiveness, greater social cohesion and environmentally sustainable production and consumption structures. A key task for the countries of the region is therefore to develop institutions that can help achieve those objectives. The second part of this year's *Economic Survey* examines the fabric of labour institutions which, in the recent past, have been at the centre of polarized confrontations and hotly contested debates.

The first chapter of this second part of the report reviews the historical development of labour institutions in the region, the great variety of institutions among countries and the role of their main components. The second chapter looks at recent changes in a number of specific institutions, the minimum wage, trade unions and collective bargaining, as well as unemployment protection systems. The evidence of their effects on the operation of the labour market is examined, along with alternatives for improving them. The third chapter is devoted to active labour-market policies, specifically training and skills-building, public sector employment services, direct and indirect job creation and the promotion of own-account work. The fourth chapter discusses policy choices for promoting productive labour-market integration for young people and women, who often face exclusion and discrimination in the labour market. The fifth chapter of this part of the *Economic Survey* sums up the conclusions regarding the challenges surrounding labour institutions and mechanisms for moving towards achievement of the objectives discussed.

Lastly, the individual performance of each economy in 2008 and in the first half of 2009 is analysed in the country notes, which include tables setting out the main economic indicators. These notes, together with the statistical appendix providing data on all the countries, are contained in the CD-ROM that accompanies the printed publication and are also available on the ECLAC website (www.eclac.org). The tables presented in the statistical appendix provide ready access to data for recent years and support the creation of spreadsheets. This CD-ROM also contains the electronic versions of the first and second parts of the printed publication.

The statistical information presented in this publication reflects the data available up to 30 June 2009.

Summary

After growing continuously for six years, the GDP of Latin America and the Caribbean will fall by 1.9% in 2009, which will bring about a reduction in per capita GDP of some 3%. Unemployment in the region, meanwhile, is expected to climb to around 9%.

The region's fastest growth stretch in four decades was broken by a worldwide crisis that originated in the financial systems of the developed countries. The impacts were transmitted to the region mainly through the channels of external trade and export prices, which both slumped heavily between the last quarter of 2008 and the first quarter of 2009. Although some of this downturn was reversed in the first half of 2009, terms of trade are estimated to have deteriorated by around 12% for the region overall. Some countries will feel an additional impact through the channel of services exports as a result of falling tourism revenues, which in many cases have been further eroded by the outbreak of A(H1N1) influenza.

Other factors, albeit harder to quantify, have also come into play, such as the destruction of wealth resulting from falling asset values and the impact on demand for goods and services of poorer expectations on the part of households and businesses. Growth in public consumption, on the other hand, has quickened, which may be attributed to the countries' active use of fiscal policy to cushion the impact of the crisis. Private consumption has been undermined in some cases by a reduction in the remittances sent home by migrant workers.

This time, the region is on a better footing than in previous crises with more room to deploy countercyclical measures, thanks to external deleveraging, improved fiscal accounts, the build-up of international reserves and its greater integration into international financial markets. As a result, despite projected deteriorations in the balance-of-payments current account in the region and declines in foreign currency inflows in the form of FDI, the Latin American countries are not expected to face difficulties in meeting their external obligations in 2009. A number of Caribbean economies are in a very different position, however, which has left them rather more exposed to the crisis.

Notwithstanding the seriousness of the international economic situation, some indicators support a moderately optimistic analysis and offer grounds to suppose that the worst of the crisis may be over. Accordingly, the second half of 2009 may bring the beginnings of a recovery, albeit slow and not without risk. The gradual improvement in external conditions should firm up in 2010, when the region could post growth of as much as 3.1%, though this rate falls short of those seen in the past few years and will not sustain a rapid reversal of the indicators recorded this year.

The pace of recovery in the region will depend on the extent to which the governments are able to deploy policies to offset the effects of the crisis. This, in turn, will depend on the availability of resources for the purpose. Hence the need for the international financial institutions to play an active role in financing countercyclical policies and measures to counteract the crisis.

Beyond the current economic context, the crisis provides an opportunity to reflect upon the sort of labour policies and institutions that would help to underpin sustained and equitable growth. The second part of this edition of the *Economic Survey* is devoted to an analysis of labour institutions in the region.

Labour institutions have been the subject of heated debate, both in the Latin American and Caribbean region and further afield. Given the profound transformation and growing integration of markets, together with the rapid pace of technological change, it is necessary to take a fresh look —as each case dictates— at the labour institutions developed at a time when economies were less integrated into the global economy. It is also essential to deal with the weaknesses of the existing institutions, which leave broad sectors of the population unprotected and do little to improve the employment conditions of excluded groups, especially women and young people with little education. The region needs to make progress with improving its labour institutions in order to offer better protection for workers, promote productivity, help bring about fairer working conditions and endow institutions with greater social legitimacy.

Part 1

The economic situation in Latin America and the Caribbean in 2008-2009

Chapter I

Regional overview

A. Introduction

ECLAC estimates that, after growing continuously for six years, the gross domestic product (GDP) of Latin America and the Caribbean will fall by 1.9% in 2009. This fall will bring about a reduction in per capita GDP of 3.1% and will take its toll on the labour market. As a result of falling demand for labour, the region's unemployment rate is expected to climb from the 7.5% observed in 2008 to around 9% in 2009.

Table I.1
LATIN AMERICA AND THE CARIBBEAN: GROSS DOMESTIC PRODUCT
(Percentages)

Country	2004	2005	2006	2007	2008	2009 [a]	2010 [a]
Argentina	9.0	9.2	8.5	8.7	7.0	1.5	3.0
Bolivia (Plurinational State of)	4.2	4.4	4.8	4.6	6.1	2.5	3.5
Brazil	5.7	3.2	4.0	5.7	5.1	-0.8	3.5
Chile	6.0	5.6	4.6	4.7	3.2	-1.0	3.5
Colombia	4.7	5.7	6.9	7.5	2.6	0.6	3.5
Costa Rica	4.3	5.9	8.8	7.8	2.6	-3.0	3.0
Cuba	5.8	11.2	12.1	7.3	4.3	1.0	3.0
Dominican Republic	1.3	9.3	10.7	8.5	5.3	1.0	2.0
Ecuador	8.0	6.0	3.9	2.5	6.5	1.0	2.5
El Salvador	1.9	3.1	4.2	4.7	2.5	-2.0	2.5
Guatemala	3.2	3.3	5.4	6.3	4.0	-1	2.5
Haiti	-3.5	1.8	2.3	3.4	1.3	2.0	2.0
Honduras	6.2	6.1	6.3	6.3	4.0	-2.5	2.5
Mexico	4.0	3.2	4.8	3.3	1.3	-7.0	2.5
Nicaragua	5.3	4.3	3.9	3.2	3.2	-1.0	2.5
Panama	7.5	7.2	8.5	11.5	9.2	2.5	5.0
Paraguay	4.1	2.9	4.3	6.8	5.8	-3.0	3.0
Peru	5.0	6.8	7.7	8.9	9.8	2.0	5.0
Uruguay	11.8	6.6	7.0	7.6	8.9	1.0	3.5
Venezuela (Bolivarian Republic of)	18.3	10.3	9.9	8.9	4.8	0.3	3.5
Subtotal Latin America	6.1	4.9	5.7	5.8	4.2	-1.9	3.2
Caribbean	4.6	4.0	7.0	3.4	1.5	-1.2	0.5
Latin America and the Caribbean	6.1	4.9	5.8	5.8	4.2	-1.9	3.1

Source: Economic Commission for Latin America and the Caribbean (ECLAC), on the basis of official figures expressed in constant 2000 dollars.
[a] Projections.

The region's fastest growth stretch in four decades was broken by a worldwide crisis that has brought an abrupt end to a boom phase of unusual intensity and scope and has affected almost all the world's economies, whether developed or developing.

The period of global growth which spanned from 2003 to mid-2007 began to show signs of weakening when liquidity and solvency problems, which had arisen in the subprime mortgage market in the United States, spread further afield. The shock waves were felt in financial systems around the world and had a significant impact on goods and labour markets; this effect has worsened since September 2008. This became a global disturbance of unwonted seriousness, and its similarities with the Great Depression of the 1930s prompted comparisons with that event.

This crisis clearly originated in the developed countries, from where it spread to the periphery, particularly Latin America and the Caribbean. As has been noted by ECLAC, with the exception of some Caribbean economies, the present crisis finds the region much better prepared than in the past. About two years since financial turmoil began, it is clear that the nature of the impact and the capacity of the Latin American and Caribbean countries on this occasion differ from the position during the recurring episodes that afflicted the region from the debt crisis of the 1980s until the early years of the present decade. There have been no financial panics or debt crises and, in general terms, the countries of the region have room for manoeuvre which, subject to individual disparities, enables them to implement policies to moderate the impact on production and employment.

The region will not, however, escape unscathed. The abovementioned contraction of GDP and rise in unemployment will probably be accompanied by increasing informality. Consequently, unlike the situation in 2003-2008, poverty is likely to rise and new stumbling blocks will appear on the road towards achievement of the Millennium Development Goals. This represents the end of a period of improvement in social indicators in which poverty came down by over 10 percentage points,[1] but one still marked by great inequality resulting from a development model that failed to correct —and in many cases worsened— the structural disparities typical of the region's economies.

Accordingly, in addition to this chapter devoted to the current economic situation and the outlook for Latin America and the Caribbean, the thematic chapters in this edition of the *Economic Survey* will look at the labour institutions in the region, to assess how ready the countries' labour markets are to deal with the crisis and what medium capacity they have to follow a strategy of inclusive development in the medium and long terms.

The next section of this chapter looks at the world economy. It then considers recent trends in the economies of Latin America and the Caribbean and the features of the macroeconomic space for anti-crisis policymaking and comments on the measures announced by the countries of the region. The last section considers the prospects for the short term and examines issues whose importance goes beyond the present situation.

B. The global economy

The region is faced with a crisis comparable in depth and scope to the crisis of the 1930s. A further element of coincidence: both crises began in the United States financial system and spread outward from there; they both began with the bursting of an asset price bubble and led to insolvency problems in the financial system.

In that comparison, the current crisis stands out for the huge volume of the financial assets involved, the level of interconnectedness of credit markets and the combination of great sophistication and opacity of a large number of instruments and transactions. This time, however, the economic policy response was quicker and more focused, partly owing to the experience derived from the Great Depression in terms of the need to contain the financial crisis as soon as possible and implement expansionary monetary and fiscal policies in order to stave off the risk of economic depression. Subject to the great differences resulting from varying capacities and the particularities of each case, this is what the countries have generally been doing since 2008.

1 See Infante and Sunkel (2009).

Another major difference regarding the events of the 1930s is that there are now a number of international coordinating institutions on the regional and multilateral levels, many of them set up following the Great Depression and the Second World War, others more recently, like the Group of Twenty (G20). Despite their limitations, they have some capacity to backstop the policies that countries implement individually in order to avoid, or at least restrict, predatory practices which can harm international trade —which has already been quite badly hit by the crisis— through the channel of trade or exchange-rate policies.

Thus, although it is hard to forecast the depth and duration of the current global recession, this episode could be limited to an economic contraction that, however abrupt and severe, may not be as damaging for the world economy as a whole as the Great Depression in terms of unemployment, contract breaches and destruction or prolonged underutilization of productive resources.

Figure I.1(a) shows the seasonally adjusted monthly evolution of industrial GDP in the United States during different recessionary periods. Each line begins in the first month of GDP contraction and continues until a period of two successive months of rising activity levels. As the figure shows, no recent period of recession matches the current one in terms of duration or depth. This episode is undeniably milder than the depression of the 1930s, however.[2]

Figure I(b) reproduces and updates the rate of growth in world industrial GDP as presented in a work by Eichengreen and O'Rourke. They argue that the comparison between the early stages of the Great Depression and the current situation is clearer with economies which have contracted even more steeply than that of the United States. Indeed, the pattern of industrial GDP is very similar in the early months of both crises. If the contraction had already bottomed out, however, the fall this time would be much smaller than in the 1930s.

The financial crisis which broke out two years ago was rapidly transmitted to real variables and spread worldwide, owing mainly to four factors:

- The credit squeeze caused by the financial system's fragility led banks to demand more liquidity, given the uncertainty over the renewal of their liabilities and the need to rebuild their capital, on the one hand, and doubts as to the solvency of potential borrowers, on the other.

Figure I.1

INDUSTRIAL GDP IN THE UNITED STATES AND THE WORLD

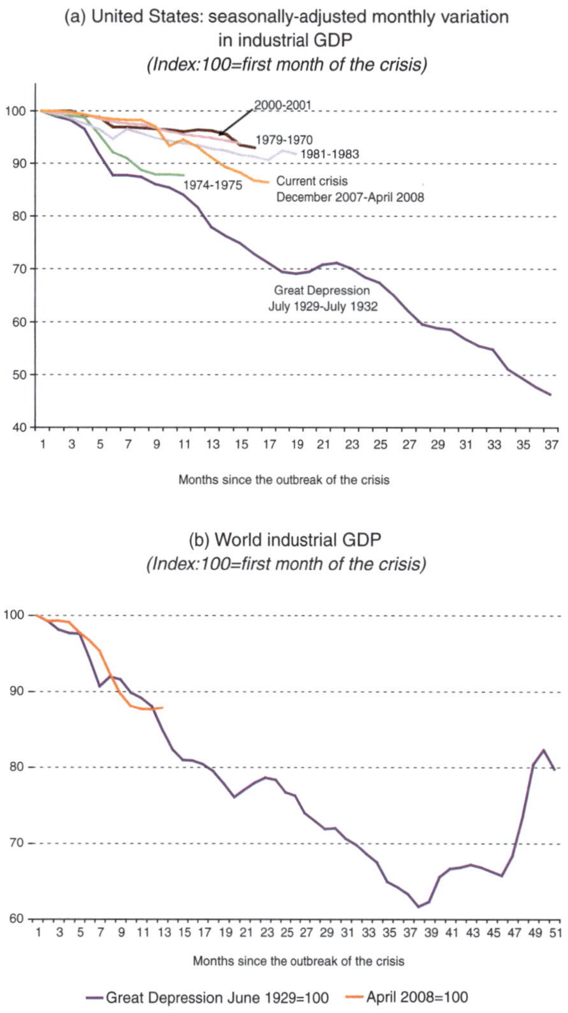

Source: Economic Commission for Latin America and the Caribbean (ECLAC), on the basis of figures provided by the Federal Reserve of the United States; B. Eichengreen and K.H. O'Rourke, "A tale of two depressions", June 2009; and International Monetary Fund.

- The destruction of wealth, both financial and non-financial, caused by losses of value in real-estate property and in shares and other assets.
- Worsening expectations regarding economic activity, affecting households' consumption decisions and businesses' investment decisions.

[2] See Krugman (2009).

- The decline in world trade between July 2008 and January 2009, as shown in figure I.2, although this seems to have slowed in recent months.

As shown in table I.2, projections agree that GDP will shrink at the global level, driven basically by GDP contractions in the developed economies. The GDP of the United States is expected to fall by around 3% in 2009, with a larger drop in Europe and a still greater one in Japan. For the emerging and developing countries as a whole, GDP variation is expected to be positive, though much less so than in recent years. The continuing growth in this group is largely due to the expected trend in the Chinese economy, although other Asian and African economies should expand too, albeit at much lower rates than in recent years.

Figure I.2
INDEX OF WORLD EXPORT VOLUME

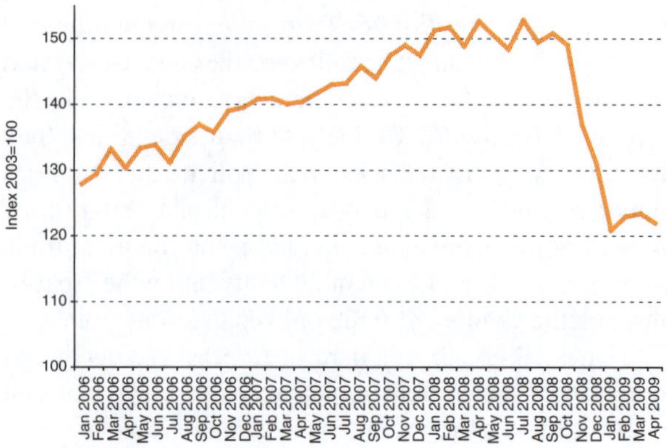

Source: Economic Commission for Latin America and the Caribbean (ECLAC), on the basis of CPB Netherlands Bureau for Economic Policy Analysis.

Table I.2
ESTIMATED WORLD GROWTH RATES, 2008-2010
(Percentages)

	IMF			World Bank			DESA		
	2008	2009	2010	2008	2009	2010	2008	2009	2010
World (exchange-rate aggregates)	2.0	-2.6	1.7	1.9	-2.9	2.0	2.1	-2.6	1.6
World (PPP aggregates)	3.1	-1.4	2.5	3.0	-1.7	2.8	3.3	-1.0	2.7
Developed countries	0.8	-3.8	0.6	0.7	-4.2	1.3	0.8	-3.9	0.6
United States	1.1	-2.6	0.8	1.1	-3.0	1.8	1.1	-3.5	1.0
Euro area	0.8	-4.8	0.3	0.6	-4.5	0.5	0.9	-3.5	0.0
Japan	-0.7	-6.0	1.7	-0.7	-6.8	1.0	-0.6	-7.1	1.5
Emerging and developing countries	6.0	1.5	4.7	5.9	1.2	4.4	5.4	1.7	4.3

Source: Economic Commission for Latin America and the Caribbean (ECLAC), on the basis of official figures from the International Monetary Fund, World Bank and the Department for Economic and Social Affairs of the United Nations.

C. Hallmarks of recent trends in the Latin American and Caribbean economies

1. Channels of transmission of the crisis

One feature that sets this crisis apart from previous episodes concerns the channels through which it has been transmitted to the economies of the Latin American and Caribbean region. Unlike in similar episodes, the strongest impacts have come through the real economy. As discussed later, there are a number of reasons why this time around export volumes and prices, remittances and other elements directly related to economic activity, combined with the deterioration in consumer and producer expectations, have been the factors behind the abrupt cessation of growth in the region in the fourth quarter of 2008.

Box I.1 describes the shocks which have hit the region recently. Only three of the 14 cases analysed (Brazil, Chile[3] and Peru) show evidence of a sudden stop in capital flows associated with the crisis, whereas in 7 cases the data appear to indicate a trade shock caused by a much greater fall in exports than would be expected in the usual cyclical movement.

The fact that the Latin American countries have in recent years reduced their levels of indebtedness, in some cases renegotiating loans with improved maturities or interest rates, while simultaneously building up their international reserves, helps to explain why the region has not, unlike other occasions, experienced a financial crisis. A number of Caribbean economies are in a rather different position in this regard, as discussed in box I.2.

Box I.1

REVERSAL OF EXPORTS AND CAPITAL FLOWS

The financial crisis has taken its toll on both trade and capital flows into the region. Two methodologies were employed to estimate these effects. The first focused on the reversals that the Latin American countries' exports have experienced as a consequence of changes in global demand. This exercise looked at the deviation of the detrended export series from its long-term trend, calculated using the Hodrick-Prescott filter. A reversal of trade was defined as any reduction in exports of more than one and a half standard deviations.

The second method was employed for episodes in which capital flows dropped sharply. This series comprises the detrended investment flows obtained from the difference between accumulated reserves and the basic balance.[a] A drop in capital flows is defined as an episode in which these flows fall more than one and a half standard deviations below the average for the period.[b]

LATIN AMERICA (SELECTED COUNTRIES): REVERSAL OF EXPORTS AND CAPITAL FLOWS

(Number of countries)

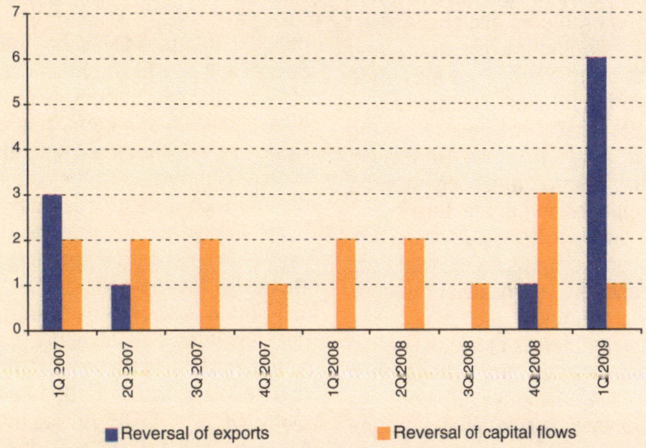

Source: Economic Commission for Latin America and the Caribbean (ECLAC).

As shown in the figure below, in 14 Latin American countries, up to the first quarter of 2009 the impact of the international financial crisis was stronger in terms of reversal of exports than in terms of a sudden capital flow reversal.[c] Seven countries experienced a heavy drop in exports between the fourth quarter of 2008 and the first quarter of 2009: Argentina, the Bolivarian Republic of Venezuela, Brazil, Chile, Ecuador, Mexico and Peru. Of the region's seven largest economies, Colombia alone did not show such a reversal. An export slump of this magnitude had not been seen in the region since the Asian crisis. Notably, the South American countries felt the brunt of this decline.

Three capital flow reversals occurred in the last quarter of 2008,[d] in Brazil, Chile[e] and Peru, as well as one in the first quarter of 2009 in the Bolivarian Republic of Venezuela.[f] In sum, since the outbreak of the international financial crisis, there have been seven episodes of export reversal and four of capital flow reversal.

Source: Economic Commission for Latin America and the Caribbean (ECLAC).

[a] The basic balance is the sum of the current account and net foreign direct investment.

[b] Includes from the first quarter of 1995 to the first quarter of 2009.

[c] Sufficient data were available for exercises to be conducted for the following countries: Argentina, the Bolivarian Republic of Venezuela, Brazil, Chile, Colombia, Ecuador, El Salvador, Guatemala, Honduras, Mexico, Panama, Paraguay, Peru and Uruguay.

[d] There were capital flow reversals in other countries in 2008 —including Argentina (second quarter), the Bolivarian Republic of Venezuela (first three quarters) and Ecuador (first quarter)— that are not attributable to the crisis.

[e] Chile shows a reversal of capital flows when public sector flows are discounted from the analysis.

[f] Like the reversals experienced in the first three quarters of 2008, this one was not attributable to the crisis.

[3] If public-sector flows are excluded from the analysis, Chile shows a reverse in capital flows. In the case of the Bolivarian Republic of Venezuela, a reversal is apparent in the balance-of-payments capital account in the first quarter of 2009, but this cannot be attributed to the crisis since the same occurs at times in 2008 before the crisis deepened.

Box I.2

MACROECONOMIC IMBALANCES AND EXCHANGE-RATE SUSTAINABILITY IN THE CARIBBEAN

Unlike the majority of Latin American countries, which maintain a dirty floating exchange-rate regime, all the member countries of the Caribbean Community (CARICOM), except Jamaica, use fixed or quasi-fixed exchange-rate regimes. The Bahamas, Barbados, Belize and the eight members of the Eastern Caribbean Currency Union (ECCU) have their currencies pegged to the United States dollar, while Guyana, Suriname and Trinidad and Tobago have an exchange-rate system in which the central bank intervenes actively to contain fluctuations in the nominal exchange rate.

While exchange-rate stability has provided these countries with a valuable instrument for anchoring expectations and reducing inflation, the situation has involved some problems and challenges: for example, significant and sustained appreciations of the bilateral real exchange rate owing to the inflation differential with the United States. As can be seen in the figure below, aside from the Bahamas, the countries have experienced marked currency appreciations in real terms.

CARIBBEAN COMMUNITY: REAL BILATERAL EXCHANGE RATE

(Index 2003=100)

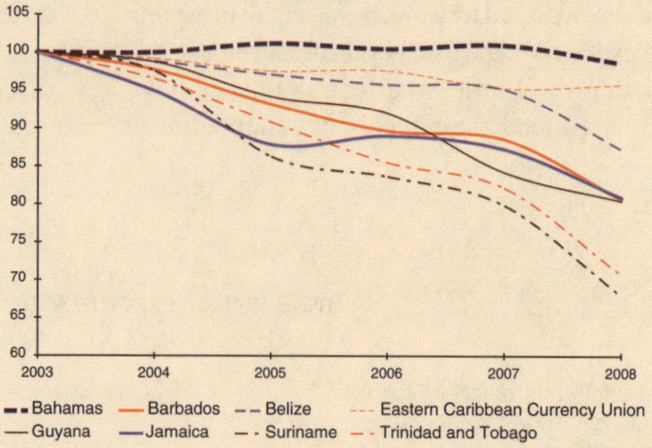

Source: Economic Commission for Latin America and the Caribbean (ECLAC), on the basis of official figures.

The currency appreciation, together with large current account deficits, high levels of public debt and low international reserves in most of the countries, add up to a very difficult situation in terms of sustaining the exchange-rate regimes, and this has been worsened by the current world economic crisis. Table 1 shows the twin deficits between 2006 and 2008 as percentages of GDP. In 2008, the ECCU countries averaged a current account deficit close to 35% of GDP, while the figures for Guyana and Jamaica exceeded 20% of GDP. It is noteworthy that in all those countries, the current account deficit is substantially higher than the fiscal deficit (between 15 and 30 percentage points of GDP), showing that private sector's excess of spending over income has been huge. Countries with abundant natural resources, such as Suriname and Trinidad and Tobago, have in recent years posted surpluses on both the fiscal and external accounts, so they were better placed to sustain their quasi-fixed exchange-rate regimes.

Table 2 shows the figures for public debt and international reserves at the close of 2008. Most of the countries have very high levels of public debt–in some cases over 100% of GDP. As for international reserves, with the exception of Barbados, Guyana and Trinidad and Tobago, at the end of 2008 none of the countries could cover over 3.3 months of imports.

Given the difficulty of access to external financing, the current state of the world economy represents a threat for most of these exchange-rate regimes. The reversal of capital inflows, or even a reduction in their quantity, would put downward pressure on the currencies which might lead to exchange-rate crises. A different outcome would be a substantial reduction in the current account deficit, which could cause a collapse of the real economy, as has been seen from various such experiences. This is not to mention the inflationary consequences, the damaging effects upon entities which experience a mismatch of currencies on their balance sheets, and the rising cost of servicing external debt. Consequently, the Caribbean countries are facing a major economic policy dilemma. Regardless of the preferences of the respective authorities, this is an issue that must be tackled urgently.

Table 1

CARIBBEAN COMMUNITY: TWIN DEFICITS, 2006-2008 [a]

(Percentages of GDP)

	Fiscal deficit			Current account deficit		
	2006	2007	2008 [b]	2006	2007	2008 [b]
Average [c]	**2.5**	**1.3**	**1.8**	**5.3**	**3.1**	**5.8**
Bahamas	1.6	1.3	1.4	20.9	17.5	13.9
Barbados	2.0	1.8	5.8	8.6	5.3	10.4
Belize	1.9	1.2	-1.1	2.1	4.1	10.8
Guyana	13.1	7.4	6.3	27.4	17.6	25.8
Jamaica	4.6	4.2	7.2	11.4	15.8	22.5
Suriname	-1.4	-5.7	-2.1	-6.8	-14.2	-14.5
Trinidad and Tobago	-6.3	-3.7	-6.5	-25.1	-24.6	-27.6
Eastern Caribbean Currency Union [c]	**4.6**	**3.9**	**3.5**	**29.8**	**34.8**	**34.4**
Anguilla	-1.0	2.1	4.0	66.3	67.9	76.2
Antigua and Barbuda	7.9	6.4	8.5	30.9	32.9	31.3
Dominica	-1.5	-1.0	-0.8	15.7	25.0	30.8
Grenada	6.4	6.7	6.4	35.1	42.9	45.3
Montserrat	3.3	6.4	9.8	17.7	22.8	35.1
Saint Kitts and Nevis	2.4	2.4	-0.4	17.4	21.5	24.2
Saint Lucia	6.3	2.2	0.2	32.1	34.1	26.9
Saint Vincent and the Grenadines	3.9	3.6	1.2	23.7	34.2	36.5

Source: Economic Commission for Latin America and the Caribbean (ECLAC), on the basis of official figures.

[a] A minus sign denotes a surplus.

[b] Preliminary figures.

[c] Simple average.

Box I.2 (concluded)

Table 2
CARIBBEAN COMMUNITY: PUBLIC DEBT AND INTERNATIONAL RESERVES, 2008 [a]

	Public debt (*Percentages of GDP*)[b]			International reserves[b]	
	External	Internal	Total	Percentages of GDP	Import cover (*months*)
Average [c]	**35.8**	**37.6**	**73.4**	**20.9**	**5.1**
Bahamas	5.7	42.0	47.7	...	...
Barbados	26.7	72.0	98.7	21.3	5.5
Belize	68.9	12.0	80.9	12.4	2.8
Guyana	72.0	31.8	103.8	26.9	5.0
Jamaica	48.7	58.2	106.9	13.1	2.8
Suriname	12.7	20.8	33.5	16.2	3.3
Trinidad and Tobago	5.8	20.3	26.1	35.3	11.0
Eastern Caribbean Currency Union [c]	**45.6**	**43.9**	**89.5**	**16.0**	**2.5**
Anguilla	6.4	16.6	23.0	15.0	1.7
Antigua and Barbuda	38.9	49.1	88.0	13.0	1.9
Dominica	66.6	26.7	93.2	16.0	2.6
Grenada	78.5	27.8	106.4	16.0	3.1
Montserrat	6.8	1.4	8.2	26.0	3.1
Saint Kitts and Nevis	57.2	113.1	170.3	16.0	2.9
Santa Lucia	37.1	33.0	70.2	13.0	2.1
Saint Vincent and the Grenadines	39.4	29.9	69.2	13.0	2.3

Source: Economic Commission for Latin America and the Caribbean (ECLAC), on the basis of official figures.
[a] End of the period.
[b] Preliminary figures.
[c] Simple average.

Source: Economic Commission for Latin America and the Caribbean (ECLAC).

Figure I.3
EMERGING MARKET BOND INDEX: EMBI+ AND EMBI+ LATIN AMERICA
(Basis points)

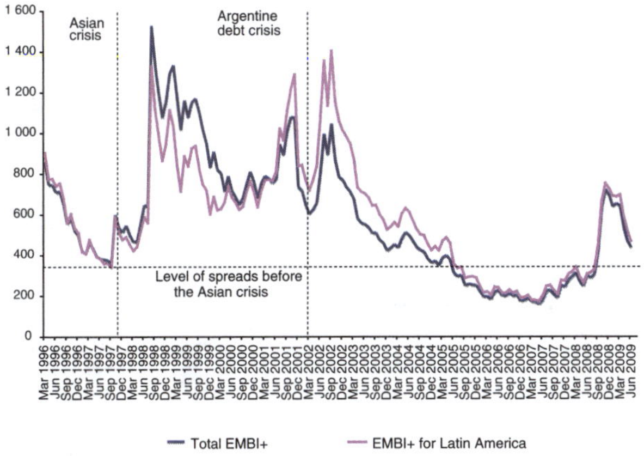

Source: Economic Commission for Latin America and the Caribbean (ECLAC), on the basis of figures from JP Morgan.

Even at the worst point of the crisis (September-October 2008), the jump in risk premiums implicit in sovereign debt yields was smaller than during other crises. Risk premiums have since trended sharply downwards, similarly to those of the emerging economies in general.

The region's financial systems have relatively low external exposure, so the domestic credit supply is not as sensitive as it might be to external conditions, especially by comparison with the emerging economies of Asia and Eastern Europe, as shown in figure I.4.[4] Section C5(b) and section D examine these issues in greater depth, as does box I.2, which looks at the main differences exhibited by most of the Caribbean economies in this regard.

Figure I.4
NET EXTERNAL POSITION OF THE FINANCIAL SYSTEM, DECEMBER 2008
(Percentages of GDP)

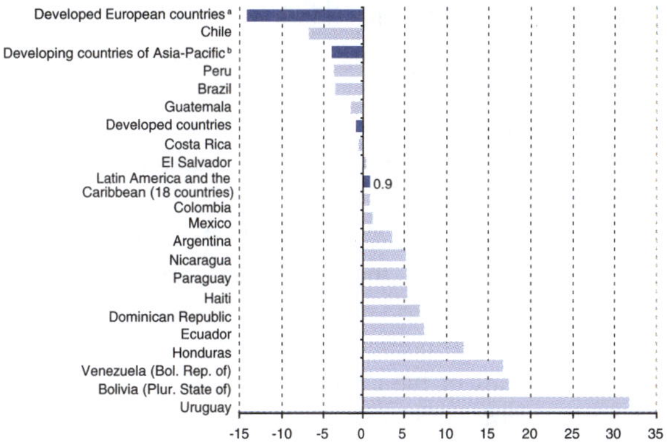

Source: Economic Commission for Latin America and the Caribbean (ECLAC), on the basis of figures provided by the Bank for International Settlements (BIS).
[a] Excluding the Russian Federation.
[b] Excluding China.

4 This figure shows the net external positions (assets minus liabilities) of banks located in the country and which report to the Bank for International Settlements (BIS).

The impact has been felt more strongly through the channel of trade, as can be seen from the slowdown of export volumes. The global recession and the drop in world trade are hurting commodity prices, which have plummeted from the highs reached in 2008. This pattern has been partially reversed in the last few months but this has not made up for the falls experienced between late 2008 and early 2009.[5] Accordingly, the region's terms of trade have worsened, following a period of significant gains. The terms-of-trade loss is estimated at up to 10.8% for the region as a whole and even more for exporters of hydrocarbons and metals.

Some countries, especially Mexico and the countries of the Caribbean and Central America, will feel the additional impact of falling tourism revenues, which in many cases have been further eroded by the outbreak of the A(H1N1) influenza. These issues are examined more closely in section C5(a).

2. Macroeconomic aggregates

As mentioned above, in addition to the international repercussions that the crisis in the United States has caused across financial markets and external trade, other factors, albeit harder to quantify, have also come into play, such as the destruction of wealth resulting from falling asset values and the impact on demand for goods and services of poorer expectations on the part of households and businesses. These factors are particularly significant in countries with larger domestic markets that influence economic activity more heavily.

Aside from declining export volumes, the macroeconomic impact of the crisis in the region has been reflected in shrinking investment and a heavy slowdown in private consumption. Growth in public consumption, on the other hand, has quickened, which may be attributed to active fiscal policies; this will be discussed further below.

In some countries, private consumption has also been eroded by a dip in migrants' remittances, the amount of which fell by 5%-10% in year-on-year terms between the fourth quarter of 2008 and the first quarter of 2009. The fall in investment, meanwhile, has reflected smaller inflows of foreign direct investment (FDI), which slipped by around 40%.[6] This effect has been particularly apparent in the countries of the Caribbean and Central America where FDI flows represent a high proportion of GDP.

In the fourth quarter of 2008, after rising at rates of at least 5% over the previous 14 quarters, regional GDP gained a mere 1.3% in year-on-year terms; in seasonally-adjusted figures, this represented a fall of 1.9% in comparison with the third quarter of 2008. This was the first drop in the region's GDP in almost six years. The slowdown intensified in the first quarter of 2009, with a contraction of 2.1% with respect to the first quarter of 2008 and 2.4% against the fourth quarter of 2008, also in seasonally-adjusted figures.

Figure I.5
LATIN AMERICA: YEAR-ON-YEAR VARIATION IN AGGREGATE DEMAND, 2008-2009
(Constant 2000 dollars)

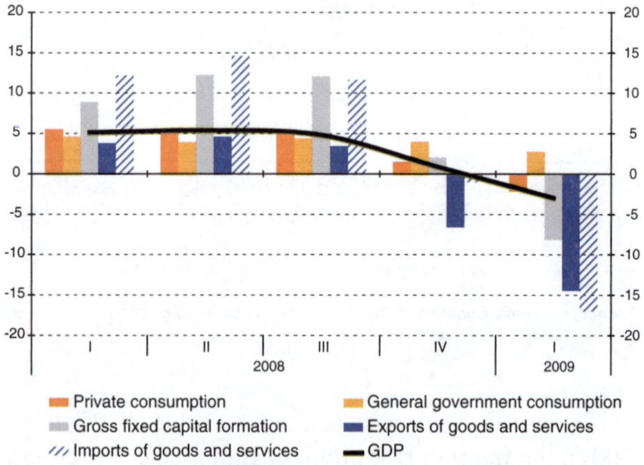

Source: Economic Commission for Latin America and the Caribbean (ECLAC), on the basis of official figures.

5 There is also no certainty regarding the duration of these price rises.
6 See ECLAC (2009a).

3. Labour market and wages

Recent developments in labour markets have reflected the performance of the region's economy. In the great majority of the countries, the strong job creation that was a hallmark of the recent high-growth period continued in the first part of 2008, but this began to change in the last quarter of the year and the employment situation took a sharp turn for the worse.

With the considerable slowing of economic growth, the employment rate began to record year-on-year falls, which steepened in the first quarter of 2009, marking the end of a five-year stretch (2004-2008) of strong improvements in labour-market indicators during which regional unemployment had come down from 11.0% to 7.4%.

In early 2009, the sharp fall in the employment rate led to a year-on-year increase of 0.6 percentage points in the unemployment rate, which reached 8.5% in the first quarter of 2009. This translated into an increase of over one million in the number of urban unemployed. Particularly badly affected were Chile, Colombia, Ecuador and Mexico, whose urban jobless rate rose by more than one percentage point between the first quarter of 2008 and the first quarter of 2009. The rise in unemployment would in fact have been steeper had it not been for a downtrend in the labour participation rate at the regional level, which softened the impact of falling employment on unemployment statistics.

For 2009, the unemployment rate is forecast to rise by more than one percentage point, which would bring it to around 9%, representing an additional three million people joining the ranks of the unemployed.[7]

Figure I.6

LATIN AMERICA (9 COUNTRIES): EMPLOYMENT AND UNEMPLOYMENT RATES, FIRST QUARTER 2006-FIRST QUARTER 2009

(Percentages)

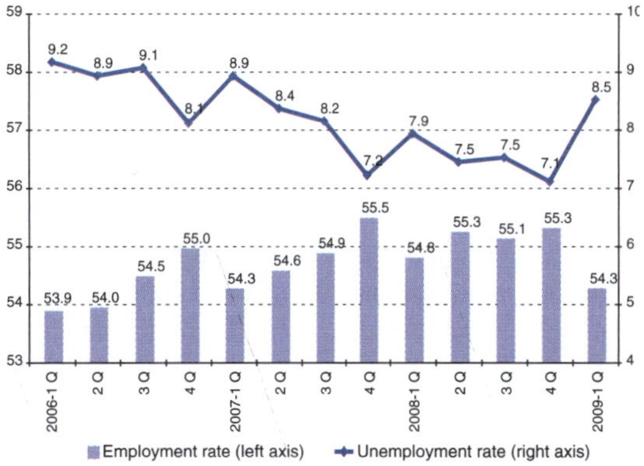

Source: Economic Commission for Latin America and the Caribbean (ECLAC), on the basis of official figures.

4. Inflation

Inflation in the region stood at 8.4% in 2008 (6.4% in 2007). The inflationary surge ran from mid-2007 until September 2008, affecting the countries of South America, as well as those of Central America and the Caribbean.

Beginning in September 2008, the pace of inflation began to slow considerably following a sharp plunge in world prices for food and fuels (which had been the main drivers of price rises in the region) and the toll taken by the international crisis on domestic demand. This trend continued into the early months of 2009. In the 12 months to May 2009, average inflation in the region fell to 6.1% (a simple average of 5.7%), with the largest decreases occurring in the countries of Central America.

Figure I.7

LATIN AMERICA AND THE CARIBBEAN: CONSUMER PRICE INDEX AND CORE INFLATION

(Percentages)

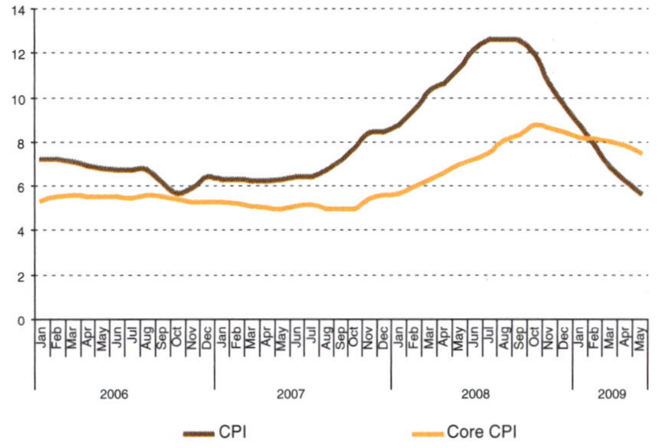

Source: Economic Commission for Latin America and the Caribbean (ECLAC), on the basis of official figures.

7 See ECLAC/ILO (2009).

5. External accounts

(a) The balance-of-payments current account

The region ended 2008 with a current account deficit equivalent to 0.6% of GDP, compared with a 0.5% surplus in 2007. This marked the end of a five-year period of consecutive current account surpluses. The trade surplus narrowed to 0.3% of GDP (1.3% in 2007) and the current transfers surplus shrank to 1.6% of GDP (1.8% in 2007). The income balance was only slightly less negative than the previous year's figure.

The deterioration in the region's balance-of-payments current account is expected to deepen in 2009. A deficit of 2.3% of GDP is projected, mostly because the anticipated downturn in the region's terms of trade will sharply worsen the trade balance, which is expected to go into deficit. Falling remittances will also contribute to the current account deterioration, though to a lesser extent. These factors will, however, be partially offset by a narrowing of the deficit on the real services balance and, above all, a smaller deficit on the income balance, in keeping with expectations of reduced profit remittances by foreign companies operating in the region.

Figure I.8
LATIN AMERICA AND THE CARIBBEAN: STRUCTURE OF THE CURRENT ACCOUNT BALANCE, 2003-2009 [a]
(Percentages of GDP at current prices)

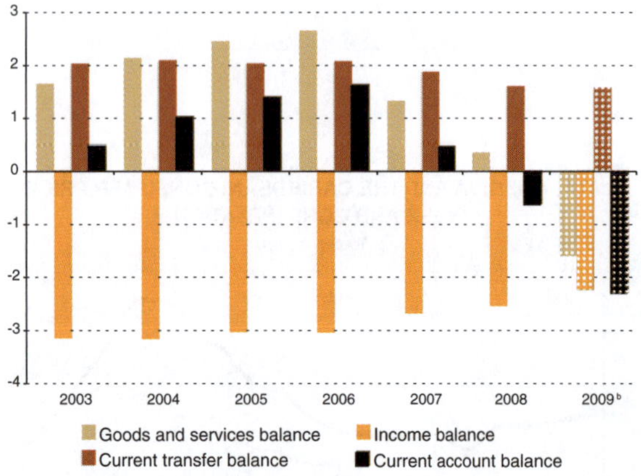

Source: Economic Commission for Latin America and the Caribbean (ECLAC), on the basis of official figures.
[a] Not including Cuba.
[b] Projection.

(i) Goods and services balance

There were two clearly distinct stages in 2008. As figure I.9 shows, trade in goods, both exports and imports, increased strongly in the first three quarters of the year. Quarterly figures for export values climbed at an average rate of 26.5%, although volumes increased more slowly. Quarterly import figures traced a similar pattern, with an average increase of 28.5%. The impact of the international economic crisis began to be felt in the fourth quarter. Exports shrank by 10.4% in the last quarter of 2008 owing to slowing external demand, which dragged down both volumes and prices. As was to be expected, Central America and Mexico were the worst hit by the contraction in external demand, since their economies are more open and they export much of their merchandise to the United States. This trend carried over into the first quarter of 2009, when export volumes suffered a year-on-year fall of some 7%.

Thus far in 2009, falling world demand has been reflected in the imports of the region's main trade partners (China, European Union, United States). Figure I.10 shows that in April 2009, the imports of the United States from the Latin American and Caribbean region were 30% below their level 12 months earlier; over the same period, those of the European Union plunged by 25% and those of China were down 22%. In the latter two cases, however, the contraction has slowed in recent months.

The real services balance has followed a similar pattern. The services deficit grew from 0.4% to 0.6% of GDP. The economies that rely most heavily on the services sector, particularly tourism, are those of the Caribbean (where, in many cases, services represent around 20% of GDP) and, to a lesser extent, Central America (where the proportion is around 6% of GDP). South and Central America saw slower growth in tourist arrivals in 2008, but this was not the case in the Caribbean.[8] In the first four months of 2009 tourist arrivals declined 3.7% in Central America and 6.5% in the Caribbean (UNWTO, 2009).Tourist arrivals rose 0.2% in South America in the same period, however.

Another feature of recent trade performance is the downturn in the region's terms of trade in 2009, resulting from falling commodity prices, as shown in figure I.11. ECLAC forecasts that Latin America's terms of trade will slide by 10.8% in 2009, following a 3.0% rise in 2008. For South America and the MERCOSUR countries, decreases of 15.7% and 5.9% are expected, respectively. The worst affected countries will be exporters of metals and petroleum and energy, whose terms of trade will fall by 20.6% and 28.3%, respectively.

The variation in commodity prices has had the opposite effect in Central America and most of the Caribbean economies, which suffered major terms-of-trade losses in recent years and witnessed a slight upturn in 2009 (see figure I.11 and box I.3).

8 Growth in South America was 3.9% (6.5% in 2007), in Central America 7.2% (12% in 2007) and in the Caribbean 2.4% (1.6% in 2007).

Figure I.9
LATIN AMERICA: TRADE PERFORMANCE BY SUBREGION
(Percentages)

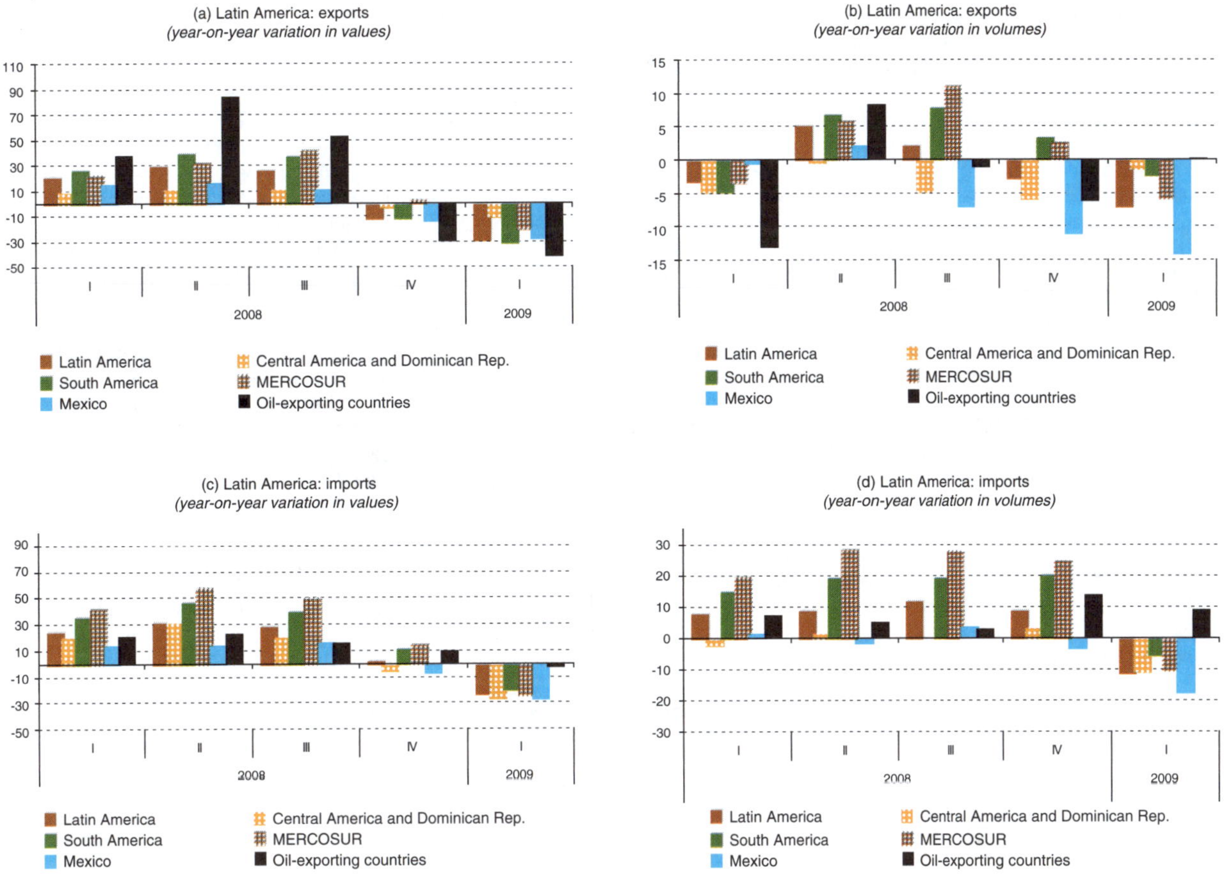

Source: Economic Commission for Latin America and the Caribbean (ECLAC), on the basis of official figures.

Figure I.10
YEAR-ON-YEAR VARIATION OF IMPORTS FROM LATIN AMERICA AND THE CARIBBEAN, BY DESTINATION
(Three-month moving averages, in percentages)

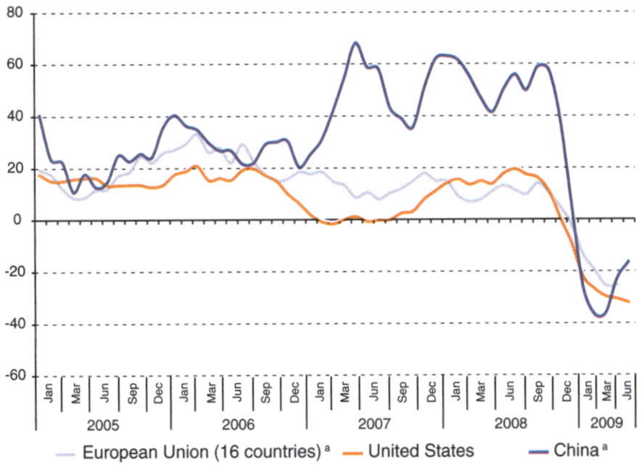

Source: Economic Commission for Latin America and the Caribbean (ECLAC), on the basis of figures from Bloomberg, the Statistical Office of the European Communities (EUROSTAT) and the United States International Trade Commission (USITC).

a Does not include imports from the Caribbean.

Figure I.11
LATIN AMERICA (19 COUNTRIES): ESTIMATED YEAR-ON-YEAR VARIATION IN TERMS OF TRADE, 2008-2009
(Percentages)

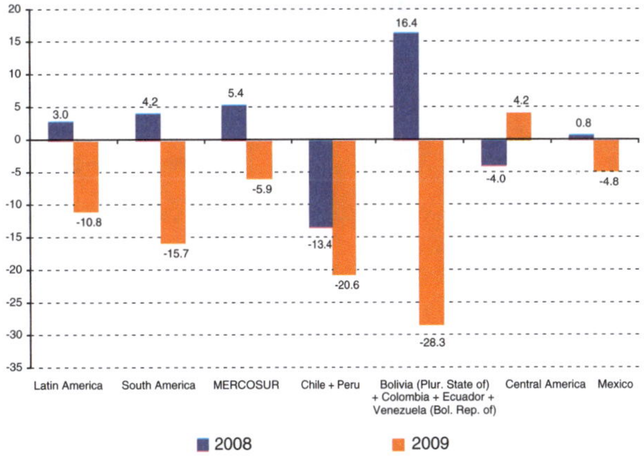

Source: Economic Commission for Latin America and the Caribbean (ECLAC), on the basis of official figures.

Box I.3

TERMS OF TRADE IN THE ENGLISH-SPEAKING CARIBBEAN

The region's trade balance was severely affected by volatility in international commodity prices. For the English-speaking Caribbean countries (the vast majority of which are importers of oil, petroleum products and food), the rise in prices in 2008 and their subsequent fall significantly altered the terms of trade.

With a view to developing a preliminary assessment of the impact of international commodity price fluctuations on terms of trade in the subregion, ECLAC estimated the variation of this aggregate in 2008 and 2009. This calculation is based on the most recent data on export and import structure available in the Commodity Trade Database (COMTRADE), as well as on trends in international prices of the goods exported and imported by the countries analysed. The data for Belize was corrected as of 2006, since the country began exporting oil in that year. In the case of Grenada, the exercise controlled for the 2005 effects of Hurricane Ivan (which badly hit banana exports) by using the previous year's figures.

Weighted indices were calculated using the commodity price indices from the United Nations Conference on Trade and Development (UNCTAD) database, as a proxy for the export and import commodity price index. These therefore do not include the effects on the unit value of imports and exports of preferential price agreements, such as Petrocaribe, and the impact of prices preset in trade agreements. A weighted index for measuring changes in manufacturing prices was calculated using the unit value indices of manufacturing exports by developing and developed countries prepared by the Department of Economic and Social Affairs (DESA).

The figure below portrays the terms-of-trade downturn experienced by the majority of countries in the English-speaking Caribbean in 2008. For the subregion as a whole, the decline is estimated at 3.3%. However, this result is heavily influenced by the terms of trade in Trinidad and Tobago, the largest country of the group. When Trinidad and Tobago is excluded from the calculation, the drop reaches 9.6%. High prices in international markets, particularly for food and energy products, played a significant role in this negative result. The exception to the trend was Belize, where oil represented 45% of total exports in 2008.

More favourable terms of trade are projected for most of the countries in 2009, thanks to markedly lower commodity prices. For the region as a whole, not including Trinidad and Tobago, an improvement of around 11.4% is expected. Terms of trade will worsen, however, for commodity-exporters such as Trinidad and Tobago (which exports natural gas, oil and petroleum products) and Belize (which exports oil).

The large terms-of-trade variation in the English-speaking Caribbean countries can also be attributed to these countries' export composition. Most of these countries have a highly specialized export structure based on only a handful of products (especially raw materials). As a result, they are much more affected by highly volatile international commodity prices than countries that export a larger proportion of manufactured products.

ENGLISH-SPEAKING CARIBBEAN: ESTIMATED YEAR-ON-YEAR VARIATION IN TERMS OF TRADE, 2008 AND 2009 [a]

(Percentages)

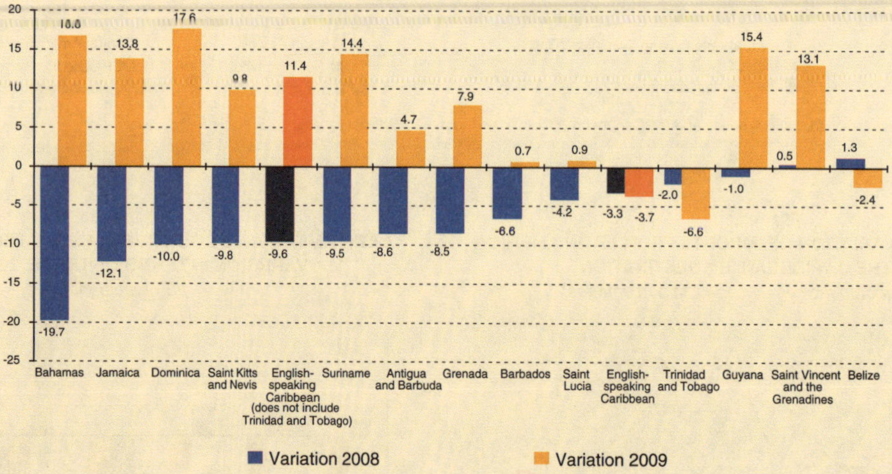

Source: Economic Commission for Latin America and the Caribbean (ECLAC), on the basis of official figures.

[a] Includes Suriname.

(ii) Income and transfers balance

The deficit on the income balance widened by 9.6% in 2008, mostly owing to an increase in payments of profits and dividends. In absolute terms, Brazil, Mexico and Chile showed the largest outflows, followed by Colombia, Peru and Argentina. Most of the region's FDI is concentrated in those countries: exporters of commodities, on which production profits rose in 2008.

Current transfers dipped from 1.8% to 1.6% of GDP in 2008 as a result of the fall in remittances sent home by workers resident abroad.[9] Inflows of remittances began to decline in the third quarter of 2008 and this trend steepened in the first quarter of 2009. Partial data available for the second quarter of 2009 show a contraction of between 13% and 19% in Colombia, El Salvador, Guatemala, Jamaica and Mexico between May 2008 and May 2009.

Figure I.12
LATIN AMERICA (8 COUNTRIES): YEAR-ON-YEAR QUARTERLY RATES OF GROWTH IN REMITTANCES
(Percentages)

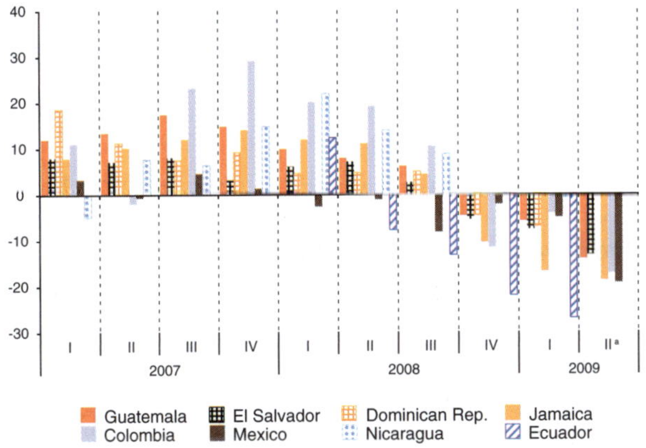

Source: Economic Commission for Latin America and the Caribbean (ECLAC), on the basis of official figures.
[a] Includes April and May.

(b) The capital account

Although the first signs of the onset of the crisis were seen in the United States in mid-2007, its effects took over a year to reach the securities markets of emerging countries. It was not until the Lehman Brothers failure that volatility and risk premiums rose in relation to earlier patterns in a way that was comparable to events in the developed countries' financial markets. Up to that point, the emerging economies had continued to enjoy normal access to world financial markets.

This episode crystallized expectations that the developed countries' financial markets and economies would slide into a deep recession which, though of highly uncertain magnitude at that time, would certainly lead to a contraction in the world economy. This drastically changed expectations regarding the performance of the emerging economies, their capacity to service their debt obligations and the potential yield of investments in those economies. The anticipated capital losses of the developed countries' financial institutions —seemingly limitless amid the wave of bankruptcies and hurried mergers then taking place— were expected to trigger a deleveraging that would constrain the supply of credit both within those countries and for emerging economies.

In October 2008 risk premiums for emerging countries rose steeply in international markets and they remained high until late 2008 (see figure I.3). During this period, investors sought to liquidate their positions in those countries' domestic markets, leading to a flight of foreign exchange which was at times quite substantial. At the same time, short-term external borrowing facilities for emerging countries' banks were not renewed, which exerted further pressure on foreign-exchange markets. Those facilities are crucial for maintaining the momentum of external trade, which therefore suffered an additional impact in a context in which world trade was already shrinking, as noted earlier. Events in the financial systems of the developed countries thus had a direct and unusually rapid impact on the emerging countries' exports and activity levels.

Figure I.13, which shows patterns in lending to emerging-country banks by international banks which report to the Bank for International Settlements (BIS), clearly shows that credit contracted during the last quarter of 2008, following a long uptrend that began in mid-2002 after the impact of the Asian crisis had eased. As a result of that change, the capacity of emerging-country banks to support lending, such as credit for external trade, was heavily curtailed. As the figure shows, the most exposed regions (emerging economies in Asia and the Pacific and in Europe) were the worst affected. Latin America and the Caribbean, whose banking systems are generally less integrated into world markets than those in the aforementioned areas, faced a smaller, although still significant contraction (10.5% in the last quarter of 2008) in external bank credit.

Within the Latin American and Caribbean region, the South American countries encountered the greatest difficulties in access to external bank credit in the last quarter of 2008, as measured by total external liabilities (public and private) owed to banks reporting to BIS. The largest falls, in GDP terms, were experienced by Brazil, Chile and Peru, as noted in box I.1 as well as the Dominican Republic and Uruguay.

[9] Current transfers are most significant in the countries of the Caribbean and Central America: in Guyana they make up 28.4% of GDP, in Haiti 23.9%, in Honduras 21.1%, in El Salvador 17.3%, in Nicaragua 16.8%, in Jamaica 14.4% and in Guatemala 12.9%. In absolute terms, Mexico accounts for the largest share of regional remittances —almost 40% of the regional total.

Figure I.13
EXTERNAL LIABILITIES OWED BY EMERGING-COUNTRY BANKS TO BANKS REPORTING TO THE BANK FOR INTERNATIONAL SETTLEMENTS
(Millions of dollars)

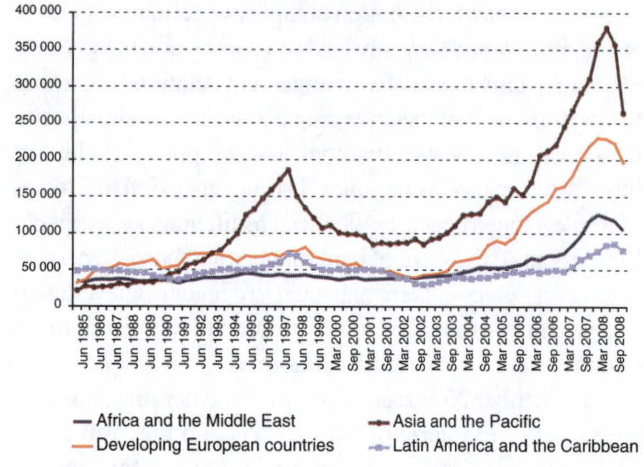

Source: Economic Commission for Latin America and the Caribbean (ECLAC), on the basis of figures provided by the Bank for International Settlements (BIS).

In response, as discussed in section D1 the central banks of several countries of the region took steps to ensure liquidity in local currency and foreign exchange in order to support their banks. To the same end, the United States Federal Reserve entered into agreements with the central banks of Brazil and Mexico.[10]

Figure I.14
LATIN AMERICA: CHANGE IN TOTAL EXTERNAL LIABILITIES OWED TO BANKS REPORTING TO THE BANK FOR INTERNATIONAL SETTLEMENTS, SEPTEMBER TO DECEMBER 2008
(Percentages of GDP)

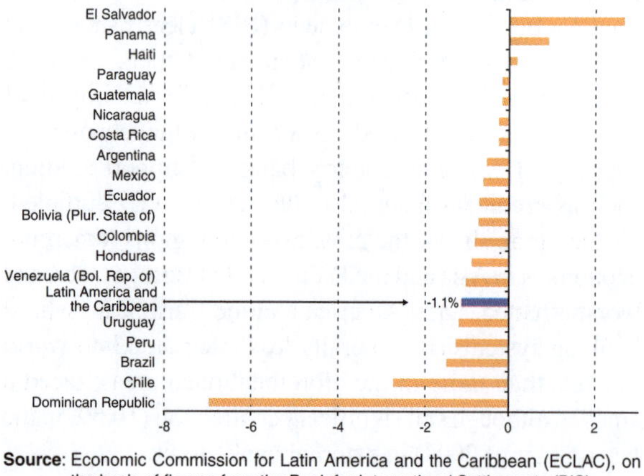

Source: Economic Commission for Latin America and the Caribbean (ECLAC), on the basis of figures from the Bank for International Settlements (BIS).

Sovereign and corporate bonds in global markets ceased to be issued in the countries of the region during the period of higher risk premiums, as shown in figure I.15.

Figure I.15
SOVEREIGN AND CORPORATE BOND ISSUES IN GLOBAL MARKETS
(Billions of dollars and basis points)

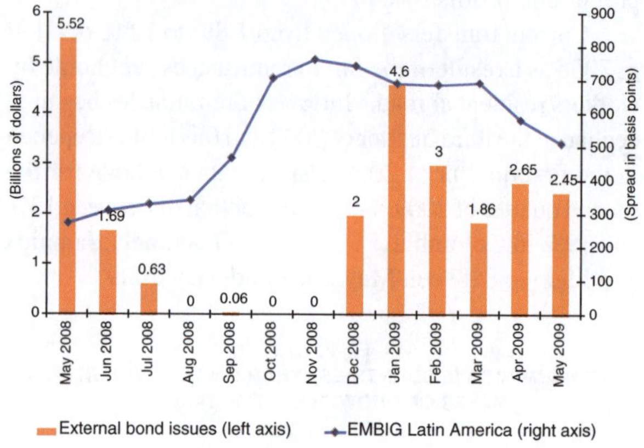

Source: Economic Commission for Latin America and the Caribbean (ECLAC), *Capital Flows to Latin America: Recent Developments* (LC/WAS/L.97), Washington, D.C., May 2008; and figures provided by JP Morgan.

Balance-of-payments figures show —as was to be expected in an uncertain environment— that investments abroad by residents increased by 47%, while investments in the region by foreigners rose by 11%. This rate of growth is far below that of previous years, as several investment projects were cancelled in late 2008.

This set of factors has clearly had an impact on international reserves, which fell back after reaching a record level of some US$ 500 billion in September 2008. In the first four months of 2009, reserves in the region had fallen by approximately 9%, or US$ 48 billion, from their September 2008 level. This was strongly influenced by the drop in reserves in the Bolivarian Republic of Venezuela, Brazil, Ecuador, Mexico and Peru, as shown in figure I.16. Some Caribbean countries, including Jamaica, have also seen a major drain in international reserves.

In the first few months of 2009, the conditions for a gradual improvement of this adverse situation began to emerge. With the entry into office of a new administration in the United States, new programmes to avoid a financial meltdown began to take shape, in addition to those inherited from the previous government, while

---

[10] See ECLAC (2009b).

banks were being taken over in a number of European countries. This bolstered the expectation that, apart from isolated bankruptcies, all possible steps would be taken to prevent the failure of institutions which were of systemic importance. Meanwhile, monetary policy in several countries sought to re-inject liquidity by lowering interest rates to close to zero, as well as to restore the flow of credit by offering guarantees on interbank lending.

The risk perception regarding emerging countries began to wane in the first quarter of the year, although it remained higher than in the preceding three years. The region regained access to international capital markets, and issuance of sovereign and corporate bonds resumed (see figure I.15). Pressure on the foreign-exchange markets eased, resulting in a certain appreciation of some currencies. In turn, share prices began to recover, and in several countries of Latin America, the stock-market gains largely reversed the losses seen at the height of the crisis.

Figure I.16
LATIN AMERICA AND THE CARIBBEAN: INTERNATIONAL RESERVES VARIATION, SEPTEMBER 2008 TO APRIL 2009 [a]
(Percentages)

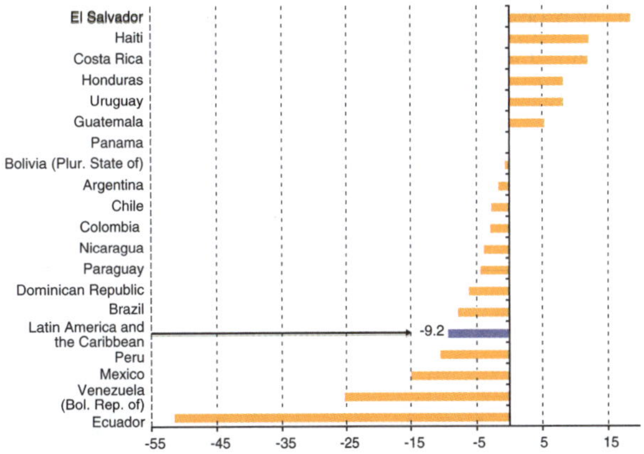

Source: Economic Commission for Latin America and the Caribbean (ECLAC), on the basis of official figures.
[a] Preliminary figures for Haiti, Panama, Paraguay and the Plurinational State of Bolivia.

D. Macroeconomic space and policies to deal with the crisis

As ECLAC has noted on several occasions, macroeconomic behaviour in the region has changed, although to varying degrees in the different countries. In contrast with previous periods of growth, countries have recently promoted a rise in savings rates, decreasing the reliance on external financial resources and, in many cases, reducing the absolute value of obligations owed to the rest of the world. This trend has been marked by a decline in governments' external liabilities that more than offset the private sector's greater reliance on international lending.

Sounder public finances have translated into a large decrease in the ratio of total non-financial public sector debt to GDP. In several cases, this resulted from higher government revenue and economic growth as well as changes in some relative prices.[11] Public-sector finances in Honduras, Nicaragua and the Plurinational State of Bolivia were also strengthened by benefits received in the framework of the Heavily Indebted Poor Countries (HIPC) Debt Initiative.[12] In other cases, debt reduction resulted from renegotiations after crisis episodes.

In several countries the composition of public debt changed considerably, in terms of ownership (with a larger share being held by residents) and denomination (with an increase in debt denominated in local currency). These changes reduced the vulnerability to exchange rate fluctuations of governments that depend mainly on domestic economic activity for their revenue.

In sum, the countries of Latin America generally paid down their debt over the last decade. This was especially true of the public sector and left the region in a better position than in previous crises, since there was less need to turn to the markets to roll over external obligations. As discussed in box I.2, however, the converse is true in many of the Caribbean countries, several of which have built up debt levels equivalent to over 100% of GDP.[13]

The region's external position was also bolstered by the accumulation of significant international reserves. In the wake of episodes such as the Asian crisis, various developing countries had decided to build up their external

[11] Government revenue improved largely because of economic growth, higher commodity prices and tax reforms implemented in many countries.

[12] Conversely, indebtedness levels rose in Guyana, which also participates in the HIPC Debt Initiative.

[13] In late 2008, external debt was equivalent to 170.3% of GDP in Saint Kitts and Nevis, 106.9% of GDP in Jamaica and 106.4% of GDP in Grenada.

assets, reducing their reliance on borrowing in the event of liquidity constraints. This type of self-insurance reflected the decision to pay a price —equivalent to the opportunity cost of the external resources accumulated— in recognition of the procyclical nature of the international credit supply and out of a desire to avoid the conditionalities associated with multilateral agency financing.

Figure I.17
LATIN AMERICA AND THE CARIBBEAN: NON-FINANCIAL PUBLIC SECTOR DEBT
(Percentages of GDP)

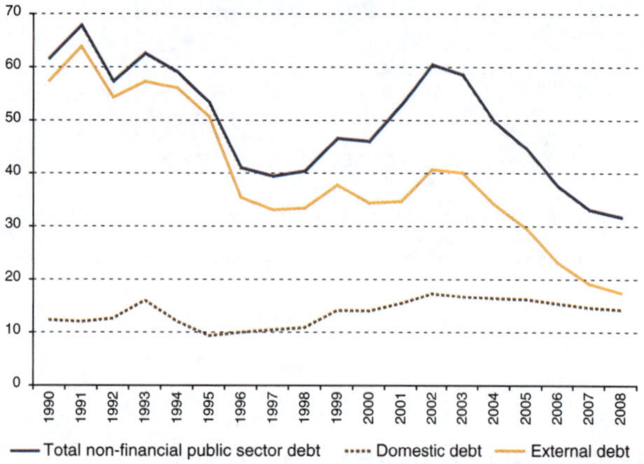

Source: Economic Commission for Latin America and the Caribbean (ECLAC), on the basis of official figures

The countries of Latin American and the Caribbean were no exception to this global trend and they built up their international reserves significantly, especially when export prices began to climb. As shown in figure I.18, since 2002 the pace of accumulation of net reserves had accelerated. When the current crisis broke out, those international reserves, both in absolute terms and in proportion to imports, were at historic highs and far above the levels seen during previous crises.[14]

Despite projections of a deterioration in the balance-of-payments current account in the region and of a decline in inflows of hard currency in the form of FDI, the countries of Latin America are not expected to face difficulties in meeting their external obligations in 2009. As shown in figure I.19, the sum of the foreign currency required to cover the projected basic balance (current account balance plus the balance of direct investments) and estimated external obligations that fall due in 2009 is fully in line with the available external assets of the countries, even in the event that only a very small portion of external liabilities can be refinanced. As analysed in box I.2, a number of Caribbean economies face a far different situation in this regard.

Figure I.18
LATIN AMERICA AND THE CARIBBEAN: NET INTERNATIONAL RESERVES
(Percentages of imports and billions of dollars)

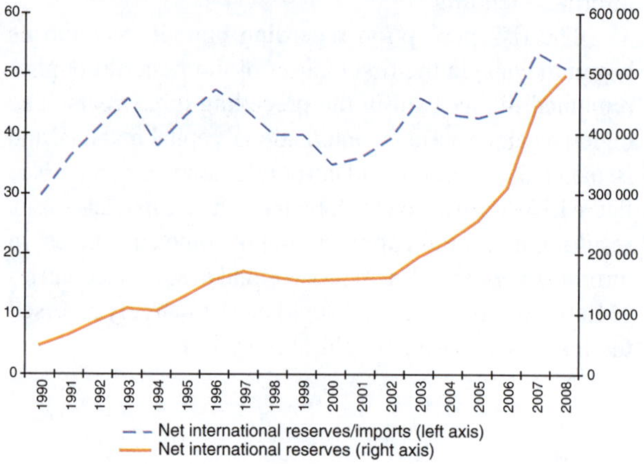

Source: Economic Commission for Latin America and the Caribbean (ECLAC) and the International Monetary Fund (IMF).

Figure I.19
ESTIMATES OF BASIC BALANCE, INTERNATIONAL RESERVES AND EXTERNAL DEBT OBLIGATIONS FOR 2009
(Percentages of GDP estimated for 2009)

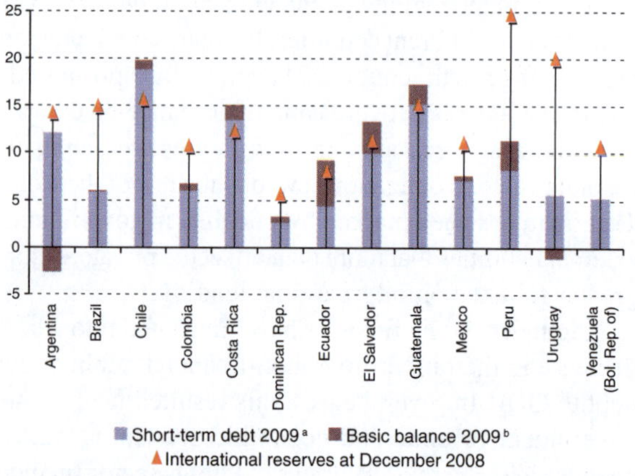

Source: Economic Commission for Latin America and the Caribbean (ECLAC), on the basis of figures from the Bank for International Settlements (BIS) and International Monetary Fund (IMF).
[a] Preliminary estimate; includes payment of short- and medium-term debt.
[b] Positive values indicate a basic balance deficit.

14 The perceived effort of the countries of the region would appear even larger if calculations of international reserves included the sums saved by a number of countries in sovereign funds, fed by fiscal surpluses. This has, however, implied a substantial sacrifice in terms of the opportunity cost of resources that the countries of the region and emerging economies in general have had to incur to offset the flaws of the international financial markets against which they had little defence during other crises.

The stronger footing of several of the region's countries not only distinguishes the current financial difficulties from those they have faced in previous episodes of crisis, but it also has created additional space to implement policies to mitigate the effects of the crisis. Manoeuvring room was provided by reserves accumulated by the public sector as well as by the lower levels of indebtedness, making it possible for countries to borrow without jeopardizing their financial sustainability. Nevertheless, the recent repercussions of the crisis have narrowed the macroeconomic space for implementing policies to spur domestic demand and have underscored that choices must be made regarding instruments and resources available to governments for fulfilling competing objectives.[15]

The crisis has been accompanied by a gradual deterioration in macroeconomic indicators. It is estimated that, for the region overall, the balance-of-payments current account and the public sector's financial balance will show a deficit of more than two percentage points of GDP (with much variation among countries, as some, especially in Central America and the Caribbean, are running high external and fiscal deficits).

In addition to the constraints that changes in public accounts and external accounts may impose on the resources available for countercyclical interventions, the characteristics of the economies of the region place other limits on the efficacy of macroeconomic policy. Specifically, irrespective of the importance of maintaining liquidity levels that allow financial systems to operate smoothly, the effectiveness of monetary policies in countries with low levels of monetization may prove to be limited. Highly uncertain situations may hamper the mechanisms by which expansionary monetary policies expand the credit supply, and those by which increases in the credit supply lead to an effective use of available financing to raise demand for goods.

In crisis situations, when credit markets tend to become segmented, fiscal policy may play a key role in maintaining aggregate spending levels. Nevertheless, the countries of the region often face institutional constraints and limitations on the public sector's capacity to implement policy. This restricts the manoeuvring room for using fiscal policy flexibly for macroeconomic stabilization. In particular, although tax cuts are relatively simple to implement, they may have only a limited effect in countries in which taxation is low to begin with. Furthermore, in conditions of uncertainty, increases in disposable income do not necessarily spur demand, especially if the beneficiaries of tax cuts belong to the upper income groups. In addition, increases in public spending place greater burdens on institutions and public administrations. Increasing public investment takes time, especially because the countries do not normally have a stock of pre-assessed projects standing ready to be implemented. Targeted subsidies can be highly effective, but not all countries have developed mechanisms to identify and reach the potential beneficiaries of social programmes.

Figure I.20

LATIN AMERICA AND THE CARIBBEAN (19 COUNTRIES): CURRENT ACCOUNT AND FISCAL BALANCE, 2001-2009

(Percentages of GDP)

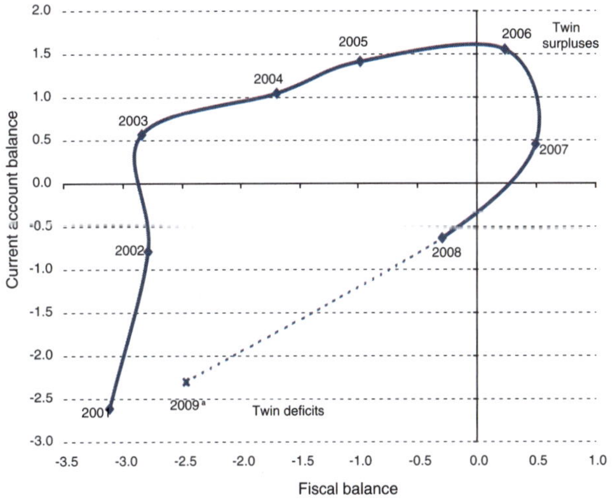

Source: Economic Commission for Latin America and the Caribbean (ECLAC), on the basis of official figures.

ª Data for 2009 are preliminary estimates.

In any event, given the opportunities for and constraints on macroeconomic policy, the countries of the region have implemented such policies quite actively. These efforts are discussed below and in box I.5.

15 See Fanelli and Jiménez (2009).

1. Monetary and financial policy

Faced with the changing international outlook in the last four months of 2008, in which credit in the developed countries tightened and the inflationary pressures that had prevailed for much of the year eased, the region's central banks took steps to ensure that there was sufficient liquidity for domestic financial markets to function.[16] To this end, the legal reserve was reduced, terms were shortened or liquidity absorption operations were reversed, and special mechanisms for rediscount or repurchase operations were established or broadened. At the same time, central banks held monetary-policy interest rates almost unchanged, with the expectation that lower raw-materials prices would lessen inflationary pressure. Since the final months of 2008, inflation has tended to decline in most of the economies of the region and has remained within the target ranges set by the monetary authorities, at least those that set explicit inflation targets. Inflation is expected to continue downward during 2009.

In early 2009, the central banks of most countries in the region lowered their monetary-policy rates to spur economic recovery, in coordination with their fiscal measures. The easing of inflationary pressure and expectations of a lower rate of inflation have created the space to change the orientation of monetary policy.

Examples include the steps taken by the central bank of Brazil, which lowered the basic interest rate of the Special System of Clearance and Custody on four occasions between December 2008 and April 2009, with a total reduction from 13.66% to 11.66%. Similar measures were taken in the same period by the central banks of Colombia, Guatemala, Mexico and Peru. The central bank of Chile slashed its interest rate by seven percentage points, from 8.25% in December 2008 to 1.25% in May 2009, and the central bank of Honduras also sharply cut its rate, from 9% to 4.5% between November 2008 and March 2009. Central bank monetary-policy rates are expected to continue to slide in some of these countries, where they are still quite high in real terms.[17]

Nevertheless, expansionary monetary policy proved unable to prevent the credit market from slackening, especially once the international crisis worsened. Year-on-year growth in total lending, in real terms, has continued to slow thus far in 2009 in Argentina, the Bolivarian Republic of Venezuela, Brazil, Mexico and Peru, although the Venezuelan economy was the only one to see a fall in absolute terms. A common element in the seven largest economies of Latin America is that, as with monetary aggregates, the performance of credit differed between April 2008-October 2008 and November 2008-April 2009. During the first period total lending increased in Argentina, the Bolivarian Republic of Venezuela, Brazil, Chile, Colombia, Mexico and Peru, whereas from October 2008 to April 2009, lending was stagnant in Brazil, Chile, Mexico and Peru and contracted in Argentina, the Bolivarian Republic of Venezuela and Colombia. Consumer credit, which provides an early warning of worsening economic expectations, decreased in this period in the Bolivarian Republic of Venezuela, Colombia, Mexico and Peru, while it rose slightly in Argentina, Brazil and Chile.

An important indicator of the soundness of the financial systems of the region is the ratio of non-performing loans to total lending. Since the last quarter of 2008, this ratio has risen moderately in the seven largest economies of the region, although without taking the non-performing portfolio to levels far different to those of the last four years.[18] In addition, in all of these economies, portfolio provisions are higher than or similar to the amount of non-performing loans. Nevertheless, the continuous rise in this indicator since September 2008 requires both central banks and bank oversight agencies to remain vigilant.

[16] The spike in inflation in 2007 and the first half of 2008 complicated the management of monetary policy and hindered the achievement of inflation targets set by the central banks. Inflation remained over-target during this period in Chile, Colombia, Mexico, Paraguay and Peru. Brazil was the only country whose inflation rate remained within the target range (which is broader than that of the other countries), but there too inflation rose and hovered above the middle of the band. Although the climbing inflation was driven mainly by supply shocks triggered by food and energy prices, most of the central banks raised their monetary policy rates in order to anchor inflationary expectations. Although inflationary pressure eased in the second semester of 2008, real interest rates remained very high at the end of the year.

[17] Argentina constitutes an exception to this trend, since developments in the currency markets there have limited the central bank's scope for lowering interest rates.

[18] For example, in March 2009 this ratio was less than half of its March 2006 value in Argentina, and less than half of its March 2005 value in Peru; in Chile and Mexico, it was similar to its values in July 2005 and September 2005, respectively; in Brazil, the April value was similar to the value in September 2006; and in the Bolivarian Republic of Venezuela and Colombia, its value was slightly above that recorded in the previous four years.

Figure I.21
LATIN AMERICA (SELECTED COUNTRIES): INFLATION TARGETS AND INFLATION RATE
(Percentages)

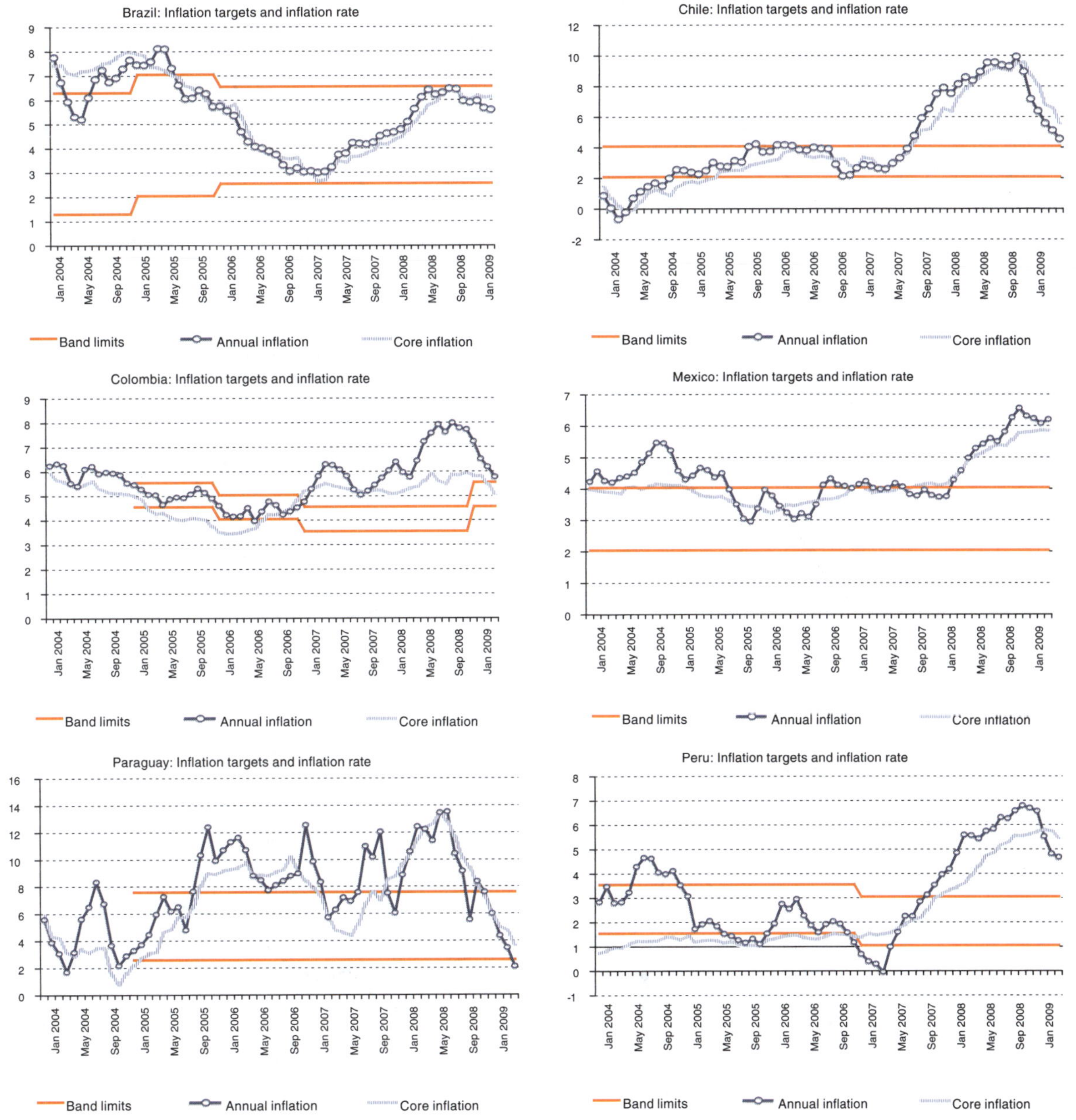

Source: Economic Commission for Latin America and the Caribbean (ECLAC), on the basis of official figures.

2. Exchange-rate policy

The reaction of exchange-rate policies to the crisis varied across Latin America and the Caribbean. Beginning in the third quarter of 2008, when the international financial crisis broke out, seven Latin American countries saw their currencies depreciate against the dollar in nominal terms. In some countries, including Mexico, the depreciation was significant. One notable exception was the Plurinational State of Bolivia, whose currency appreciated by 1.9% from July to December 2008 as part of the anti-inflation strategy implemented by the central bank.

Figure I.22

LATIN AMERICA (SELECTED COUNTRIES): EXCHANGE-RATE INTERVENTION AND NOMINAL EXCHANGE RATE

(Billions of dollars and respective currencies)

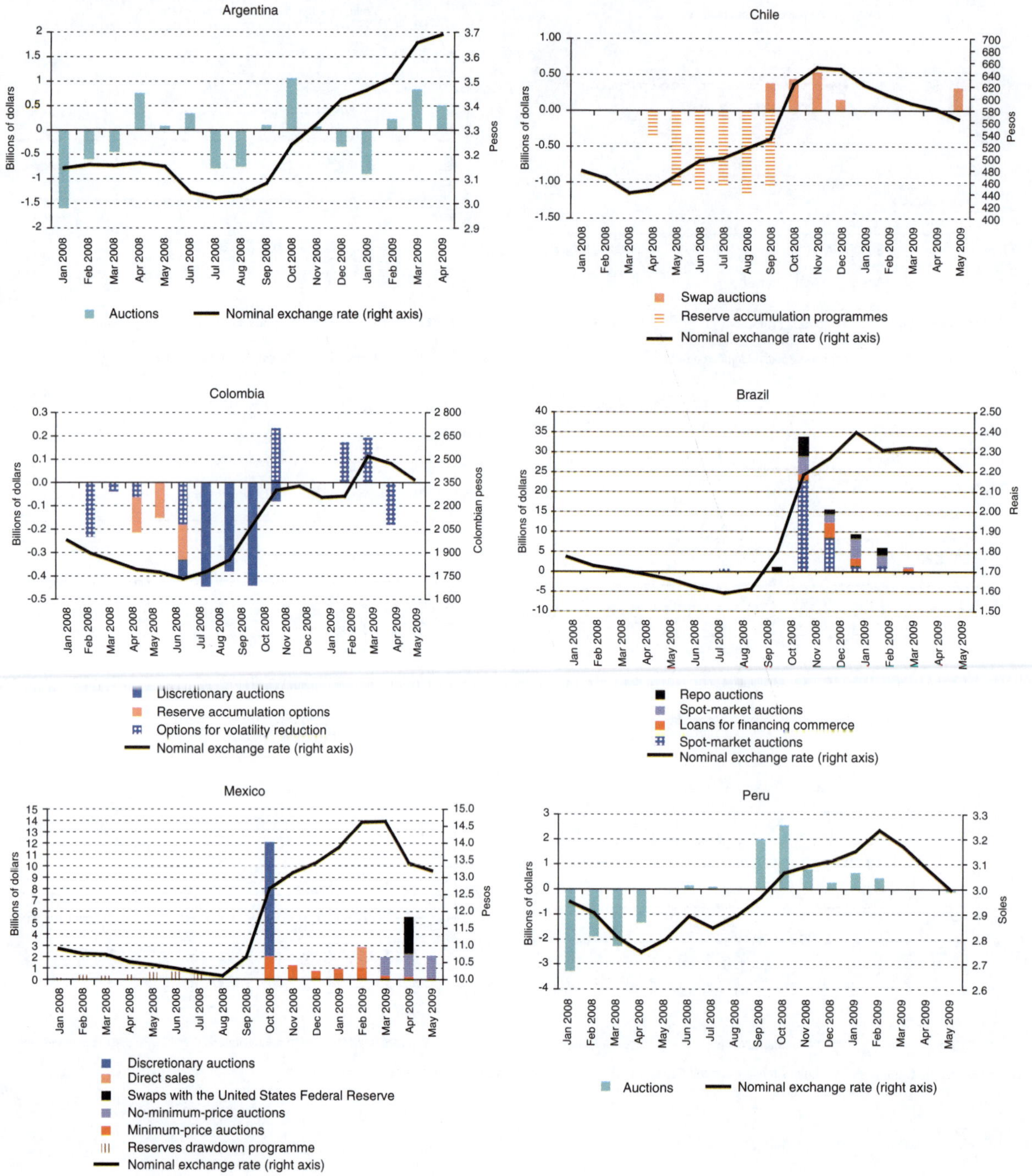

Source: Bank for International Settlements (BIS) "The global crisis and Latin America: financial impact and policy responses", *BIS Quarterly Review*, June 2009.

Financial and trade shocks led to significant depreciations in the currencies of several South American countries between August and December 2008. For example, the Brazilian real, the Mexican peso, the Chilean peso and the Colombian peso all depreciated in that period (48.8%, 32.8%, 25.6% and 21.7%, respectively), and all despite the drawdown of reserves by those countries' central banks. The types of interventions varied and included currency futures transactions as well as spot-market operations. Mexico and Peru (and to a lesser extent Colombia) conducted large spot-market auctions, whereas Brazil performed numerous swap operations in the last quarter of 2008, as did Chile (though to a smaller extent) (BIS, 2009).

Although central banks across the region cut interest rates, the currencies of the South American countries tended to rise in value in nominal terms between December 2008 and May 2009,[19] reflecting improving conditions in international financial markets. This appreciation was not sufficient to compensate for the depreciations of the previous months, however. During this period, auctions of foreign exchange gradually declined before ceasing altogether.

The Mexican peso also recorded nominal appreciation during this period. This overall trend, however, masks a sharp depreciation in the peso until mid-March 2009, due to international market volatility and uncertainty regarding the country's ability to satisfy the demand for foreign exchange. In order to boost dollar liquidity in the economy and to try to steer the depreciation of the peso, the Government of Mexico adopted a series of measures as of the fourth quarter of 2008 including the supply of dollars through auctions, the establishment of a swap mechanism with the United Sates Federal Reserve and the creation of a US$ 47-billion flexible credit line with IMF. Between March and May 2009, the combination of measures implemented (which involved substantial currency interventions), together with reduced financial volatility abroad, resulted in a 9.9% nominal appreciation of the peso.

Currency depreciations in the Central American and Caribbean countries were quite small from August to December 2008, with the exception of Jamaica, whose currency depreciated by 10%, and to a lesser extent Guatemala, where the quetzal dropped 3.1% in nominal terms. Currencies in the subregion continued to post limited depreciations in the first five months of 2009, with the exception of the two countries mentioned, whose currencies recorded steeper falls in value.[20]

3. Fiscal policy

The challenge of fiscal policy in the current economic climate lies in applying countercyclical measures in a context of lower tax revenues, while simultaneously protecting certain expenditures —education, social protection and infrastructure— which are vital for staving off an increase in poverty and laying the foundations for future growth. Although the governments of the region still have some capacity to shore up their economies through fiscal interventions, in practice, the fiscal space has narrowed considerably in the last year and varies widely from country to country depending on savings built up in good times, spending rigidities, the duration of the crisis and scope for prudent borrowing.

The crisis has placed the public finances of the Latin American economies in a complicated position. On the one hand, fiscal revenues have been substantially curtailed, owing to lower levels of activity and falling commodity prices. On the other, the fiscal stimuli countries have implemented and the measures they have taken to mitigate the distributive costs of the crisis have further eroded their fiscal balances. In addition, the fiscal downturn occurs, in many cases, amid severely constrained external borrowing conditions, and this affects the countries' ability to apply countercyclical fiscal policies.

The diversity of circumstances affecting the countries makes it particularly difficult to quantify the fiscal resources lost. Nevertheless, for analytical purposes, it is worth making a distinction between countries that have derived significant incomes from natural resources over the last few years and those which do not have access to this source of income.

Although the region is, generally speaking, much better placed than it was in past crises in terms of public finances and fiscal policy, there are matters that warrant concern about the public sector's capacity to weather the crisis successfully. Insofar as much of the improvement in the fiscal situation in recent years was due to rising commodity prices from 2002 until the first half of 2008, a deterioration in those prices represents a major risk for the fiscal space gained.

[19] The exception was Argentina, where the peso has gradually depreciated since mid-2008.

[20] Jamaica is facing a difficult fiscal and balance-of-payments situation which pushed up demand for foreign exchange in late 2008 and the first quarter of 2009.

As discussed in detail in ECLAC (2008e), in recent years the countries of the region posted structural balances that were, on average, poorer than the fiscal balances actually observed. This is particularly evident in countries that produce raw materials for export, where the gap between the structural and observed balances widened considerably in 2007 and the first half of 2008, since these countries were receiving extraordinary income that was unlikely to be sustained in the future.

The dramatic increase in fiscal revenues witnessed in 2002-2008 is closely linked to income from natural-resource extraction. Such income made up more than 30% of fiscal revenues in the Bolivarian Republic of Venezuela, Ecuador, Mexico, the Plurinational State of Bolivia and Trinidad and Tobago, and between 14% and 18% on average over the last three years in Argentina, Chile, Colombia and Peru. As recent months have shown, however, income from natural-resource extraction is significantly more volatile than revenues from other sources.

As shown in table I.3, in countries that are highly specialized in producing and exporting commodities —those in which the related fiscal revenues represent over 30% of receipts— fiscal resources will drop by 5.6 percentage points of GDP in 2009. Revenues are expected to fall by 1.7 percentage points in countries somewhat specialized in commodities. In the other countries, the drop is estimated at some 0.5% in GDP, owing to falling economic activity.

Table I.3
VARIATION IN FISCAL INCOME, 2008-2009
(Percentages of GDP)

	Variation 2008-2009	Contribution to average variation
Countries highly specialized in commodities	-5.6	-1.2
Countries somewhat specialized in commodities	-1.7	-0.3
Countries not specialized in commodities	-0.5	-0.3
Total		-1.8

Source: Economic Commission for Latin America and the Caribbean (ECLAC).

The total effect for Latin America and the Caribbean is a dip in receipts equivalent to 1.8% of GDP (simple average), which means the region would shift from an average primary surplus of 1.3% of GDP to a primary deficit of around 0.8% of GDP in 2009 (see figure I.23). This outcome will depend heavily on the extent to which the countries implement the spending increases announced to mitigate the effects of the crisis (see box I.5).

Figure I.23
LATIN AMERICA: INCOME, EXPENDITURES AND PRIMARY BALANCE OF CENTRAL GOVERNMENT [a]
(Percentages of GDP)

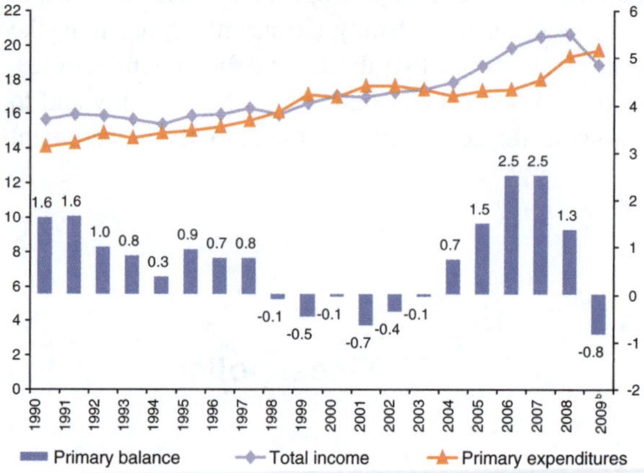

Source: Economic Commission for Latin America and the Caribbean (ECLAC).
[a] Coverage corresponds to central government, except in Ecuador and Mexico, where it refers to the non-financial public sector, and the Plurinational State of Bolivia, where it refers to general government.
[b] Projection.

The effects of the international financial crisis on fiscal income vary from country to country depending upon their tax structure, level of tax collection and other sources of current financing.21 As discussed in box I.4, the countries worst exposed to the effects of the crisis will be those with high percentages of non-tax income or revenues derived from natural resources, low tax burdens or very open markets (particularly if they export mainly to developed countries). Conversely, countries with high tax burdens and larger percentages of revenues from income tax and VAT productivity should be less exposed.

21 Jiménez and Gómez Sabaini (2009), calculated the degree of exposure of each country's fiscal income to different variables and divided the countries into three groups: high, medium and low exposure. This exercise is summarized in box I.4.

Box I.4

QUANTIFYING THE VULNERABILITY OF FISCAL REVENUE TO THE INTERNATIONAL CRISIS

Given the uncertainty created by crises and the difficulty in predicting their effects, the ways in which they are transmitted and impact the economy require careful consideration. The effect of the international crisis on tax revenues in the region differs from one country to another and will depend not only on the nature of the crisis but also on the level and structure of the tax burden and the different sources of financing employed. Be that as it may, the average impact of the crisis on fiscal income is estimated to be significant, with a drop equivalent to 1.8% of GDP projected for 2009 in relation to 2008 revenues.

The exercise presented below[a] seeks to identify the countries most likely to incur large losses of fiscal revenue, given the channels through which the current international crisis affects tax receipts in the region.

This exercise therefore quantifies the degree of exposure of fiscal revenue to several variables and classifies the countries into three groups: high, medium or low exposure. This indicator has been devised by weighting the different characteristics of the structure of tax revenue, political and institutional rigidity and the capacities of each country's tax administration.

The analysis considers the following features of the tax system: overall tax burden; importance of revenue from taxes on natural resources as a share of tax revenue; import taxes as a proportion of total taxes; value added tax (VAT) as a proportion of total revenue; VAT productivity ratio; remittances as of share of GDP; importance of social security contributions in total revenue; and income taxes collected from business as a share of total tax receipts.

LATIN AMERICA AND THE CARIBBEAN: INDEX OF EXPOSURE OF FISCAL REVENUES TO THE INTERNATIONAL CRISIS

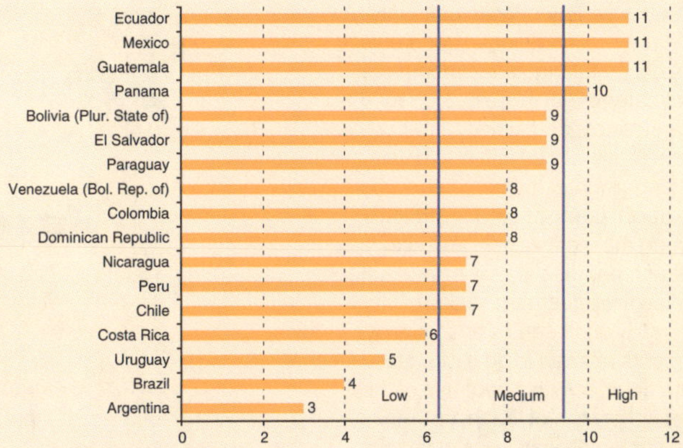

According to the findings of this exercise, Ecuador, Guatemala, Mexico and Panama are the countries with the most highly exposed fiscal revenues. These countries have at least two of the three attributes found to be the most significant in the analysis: dependence on natural-resource-based revenue (except for Guatemala and Panama); political and institutional rigidity in applying tax reforms (which translates into a very low tax burden); and a significant ratio of import taxes to tax revenue (except Mexico).

The countries in the medium-exposure group are the Bolivarian Republic of Venezuela, Chile, Colombia, the Dominican Republic, El Salvador, Nicaragua, Paraguay, Peru and the Plurinational State of Bolivia. The low-exposure group comprises Argentina, Brazil, Costa Rica and Uruguay. The figure below summarizes the findings, with countries listed from highest to lowest degree of exposure.

Nonetheless, as these results indicate the relative positions of the countries of the region, countries found to have a low exposure are in no way immune from negative impacts on their fiscal revenue; they are simply considered to be better positioned than the other countries.

In conclusion, countries with a high percentage of non-tax revenues or a high percentage of revenues from taxes on natural resources, with low tax burdens and a high degree of trade openness have a higher index of exposure of fiscal revenue to the crisis than do those with high tax burdens, a higher ratio of income tax to overall revenue and a high VAT productivity ratio.

Source: Economic Commission for Latin America and the Caribbean (ECLAC), *The Role of Tax Policy in the Context of the Global Crisis: Consequences and Prospects* (LC/L.3037), Santiago, Chile, 15 May 2009.

[a] This analysis is a revised version of a section of the document: Economic Commission for Latin America *and the Caribbean (ECLAC), The Role of Tax Policy in the Context of the Global Crisis: Consequences and Prospects* (LC/L.3037), Santiago, Chile, 15 May 2009.

The fiscal policy measures taken by the governments in the region are summarized in table I.4. On the spending side, 14 countries have announced measures to support the production sectors, generally targeting SMEs or agriculture. The same number of countries have plans for infrastructure investment and 14 have announced spending on housing. As regards taxes, eight countries have announced cuts in personal income tax, with changes in deductions, lower tax rates or increased exemptions (which have been announced as temporary in two cases), while nine have cut corporate taxes, through fresh exemptions, deductions or accelerated depreciation schemes (announced as temporary in three cases).

With regard to the impact of the measures announced, apart from the differences that may be expected between initiatives based on tax cuts and those based on public-spending hikes, in Latin America and the Caribbean

Box I.5

MEASURES TAKEN TO COUNTERACT THE CRISIS

The countries of Latin America and the Caribbean have announced and implemented a variety of policies to deal with the impact of the global economic crisis. Broadly speaking, those measures fall into two categories: those designed to restore confidence and unlock financial markets and those whose aim is to bolster weakened aggregate demand, in some cases through compensatory policies which support the most vulnerable sectors. The range of measures is very broad, not only because the effects of the crisis vary from country to country and, consequently, the instruments needed to deal with those effects also differ, but also because of the differences in terms of each country's capacity to implement initiatives of various kinds, which is determined by the availability of resources.

Initially, central banks made strenuous efforts to provide the financial systems with liquidity so that local credit markets could function normally, as well as to supply financing themselves to borrowers not covered by those markets. Nonetheless, the nature of the crisis and, in particular, the plunge in confidence, called for other kinds of measures. Although monetary and exchange-rate policies should be part of a well structured and coherent set of measures, fiscal policy is the most potent instrument in such cases.

Within fiscal policy, measures to boost spending have more potential than those based on tax cuts. The former provide a direct means of boosting demand, whereas the latter increase the private sector's disposable income and, given the prevailing level of uncertainty, a large proportion of that increase is likely to be saved rather than spent. If spending is raised by increasing direct transfers, the impact will be greater if the transfers target sectors with a higher propensity to consume. Transfers of this type are, however, harder to implement in the short term and are more demanding in institutional terms than untargeted transfers. Furthermore, when the higher spending is achieved through programmes of increased infrastructure investment, not all projects have the same impact in terms of employment and demand for locally-produced inputs; and governments do not necessarily have a list of programmes which are ready to be implemented in the short term.

LATIN AMERICA (SELECTED COUNTRIES): FISCAL COST OF ANTI-CRISIS MEASURES PLANNED FOR 2009

(Percentages of GDP)

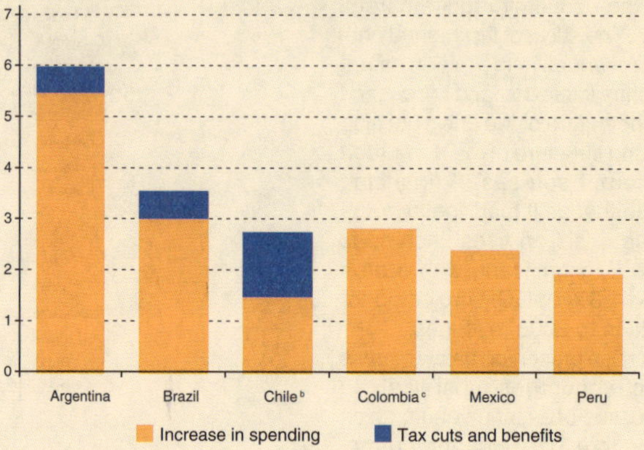

Source: Economic Commission for Latin America and the Caribbean (ECLAC).

[a] GDP 2008.

[b] The measures are to be implemented in 2009, except for the reduction in stamp duty, which continues into 2010.

[c] Includes a measure for a period after 2009.

An assessment was conducted of the fiscal cost of anti-crisis measures planned up to 2009 in six of the region's largest countries. It included all measures which have been announced and have a fiscal cost, so the estimates of the cost are not limited to a particular stimulus plan, but also include additional expenditure items. It should be noted that the calculation of costs is based on announcements and not on actual spending; this cannot be assessed until subsequently, when information becomes available on the level of implementation. Furthermore, the estimates are for 2009, so for multi-year plans the portion of costs corresponding to 2009 had to be estimated. Taking into account the steep drop in fiscal revenue, together with credit constraints, there may be doubt as to some governments' capacity to finance and execute the spending these measures call for.

The governments have announced widely varying interventions. Argentina is intervening actively, deploying fiscal measures at a cost of around 6.0% of GDP, o which over 90% is going to raise spending under the public works plan. The package of measures announced by the Government of Brazil represents some 3.6% of GDP, of which 85% is being used to increase spending and 15% is going to tax cuts or benefits. Inventions by the governments of Colombia, Chile and Mexico are estimated at some 2.4%-2.8% of GDP. In Chile 46% of the overall amount is being channelled into tax cuts and benefits, while in Colombia and Mexico the full amount is being used to increase spending. With regard to the type of measures, in Colombia the increase in fuel subsidy and transfers represents 65% of the total cost. In Chile the fiscal stimulus plan accounts for practically the full amount (93%). In Mexico, the programme to support household budgets and employment, together with the fiscal stimulus in the form of additional infrastructure spending, are the main components (around 68% of the total cost). In Peru, almost the entire array of anti-crisis measures correspond to the 2009-2010 stimulus plan.

In addition, all the countries, especially Mexico and Brazil and to a lesser extent Peru, announced measures to boost financing, such as sector-specific credit lines, soft loans and guarantee funds, whose ceiling values are shown in the table below.

	Financing ceiling *(Percentages of GDP)*
Argentina	1.5
Brazil	3.4
Chile	1.3
Colombia	0.6
Mexico	3.4
Peru	0.03

Source: Economic Commission for Latin America and the Caribbean (ECLAC), *The reactions of the Governments of the Americas to the international crisis: an overview of policy measures up to 31 May 2009* (LC/L.3025/Rev.1), Santiago, Chile, June 2009.

Table I.4

LATIN AMERICA (18 COUNTRIES): MAIN FISCAL MEASURES TAKEN TO DEAL WITH THE CRISIS

	Argentina	Bolivia (Plurinational State of)	Brazil	Chile	Colombia	Costa Rica	Dominican Republic	Ecuador	El Salvador	Guatemala	Honduras	Mexico	Nicaragua	Panama	Paraguay	Peru	Uruguay	Venezuela (Bolivarian Republic of)
Tax system																		
Corporate income tax, reductions/depreciation			X	T	X	T		X		X		T				X	T	
Personal income tax cuts	X		X	T	X					X	X	T		X				
Taxes on external trade	X		T					X				X	T					
Taxes on goods and services			T														X	X
Social contributions	X											T						
Other			X	X	X			T					X			T	X	
Public spending																		
Infrastructure investment	X	X	X	X	X	X	X	X		X	X	X	X		X	X	X	
Housing	X	X	X	T	X	X	X			X	X	X	X		X	X	X	
Support for SMEs and agricultural producers		X	X	X	X	X	X		X	X	X	X		X	X	X	X	X
Support for strategic sectors	T	X	X	X	X					X		X				X	X	
Direct transfers to households	T			T		X					X				X			
Other			X		X				X			X	X			X		

Source: Economic Commission for Latin America and the Caribbean (ECLAC).
Note: T: Temporary measures.

tax incentives and deductions, often referred to as "tax spending", are notoriously difficult to quantify and their impacts difficult to estimate.[22] The implementation of such measures bring a further element into the analysis in terms of their duration, since whether they are temporary or permanent changes the impact on the sustainability of public finances.

These limitations and difficulties aside, in practice, governments often opt, at least in the short term, for tax cuts or non-targeted subsidies, since although they offer smaller potential than spending hikes, they are easier to implement.

Lastly, although a large proportion of these measures were adopted by central governments, many of them require —or will require— human or financial resources from subnational governments, as well as coordinated actions among various levels of government. This constitutes a chink of vulnerability in fiscal policy during the crisis since, although the public accounts of subnational governments have improved in recent years, this improvement was attributable not to better tax collection by local and intermediate governments, but in large measure to growing transfers from national governments. Total transfers grew by two GDP points between 1997 and 2007, while tax receipts for subnational governments rose from 2.1% of GDP to just 2.7% in the same period.

An analysis of the income structure of subnational governments by country reveals that transfers are significant in most countries. In Argentina, Mexico and the Plurinational State of Bolivia, transfers exceed 7% of GDP and in Colombia and Ecuador they total approximately 5% of GDP. In Ecuador and Mexico transfers actually represent subnational governments' main source of financing, at 80% of total income.

Furthermore, although much has been said about the public sector's falling debt ratio in 2002-2008 as an indicator of soundness, significant differences remain between countries in this regard at the subnational level. In some countries, such as Argentina and Brazil, local government public debt is still quite high (11% and 14% of GDP, respectively) and makes up a significant proportion of non-financial public sector debt (18% in Argentina and 39% in Brazil).

22 Although the methodologies used to calculate these effects are difficult to compare, the countries of the region draw substantially on "tax expenditures", which vary from around 2% of GDP in Argentina, Brazil and Peru to over 5% of GDP in Chile, Guatemala and Mexico, which heavily eroded their tax bases. For a more detailed account of tax spending in the region, see Jiménez and Podestá (2009).

E. Outlook

Even given the still-critical state of the global economy in mid-2009, the downturn shows signs of having come to a halt and even, in some cases, gone into reverse, with an incipient improvement in a number of economic and financial indicators, even though it remains to be seen whether this trend will firm up as time goes on.

The banks' situation has improved, as indicated by changes in the level of risk perceived by the financial market for interbank lending which, after spiking sharply, has gradually returned to pre-crisis levels. This has been partly a result of financial support programmes deployed by the government of the developed countries and the outcomes of bank stress tests which have found possible losses to be of a magnitude perfectly manageable with the tools available, in addition to the announcement by several major banks that they will soon reimburse the financial assistance received during the worst moments of the crisis, which denotes a gradual return to solvency.

As to the possibility of rebuilding wealth, there has been a widespread, albeit partial, recovery of stock markets in both developed countries and emerging markets, and home prices have stopped falling in the United States.

In keeping with these indicators, consumer confidence indices show that economic agents appear to be beginning to change their perception of where the crisis is heading. Indicators of consumer and business confidence suggest that the pessimism that pervaded late 2008 is slowly being turned around. This positive development could herald the start of a gradual recovery in the second half of this year, albeit slow and not without risk.

Figure I.24

INTERBANK MARKET INTEREST RATES [a]

(TED Spread: 2007-2009)

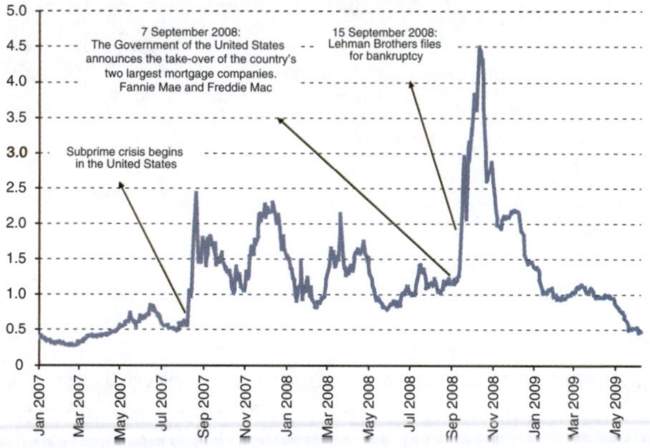

Source: Economic Commission for Latin America and the Caribbean (ECLAC), on the basis of figures from Bloomberg.

[a] The TED spread is a measure of the risk that a bank will default and corresponds to the spread between short-term interbank loans and the risk-free rate (three-month Treasury bonds).

Figure I.25

INDUSTRIALIZED COUNTRIES AND EMERGING ECONOMIES: STOCK MARKET INDICES

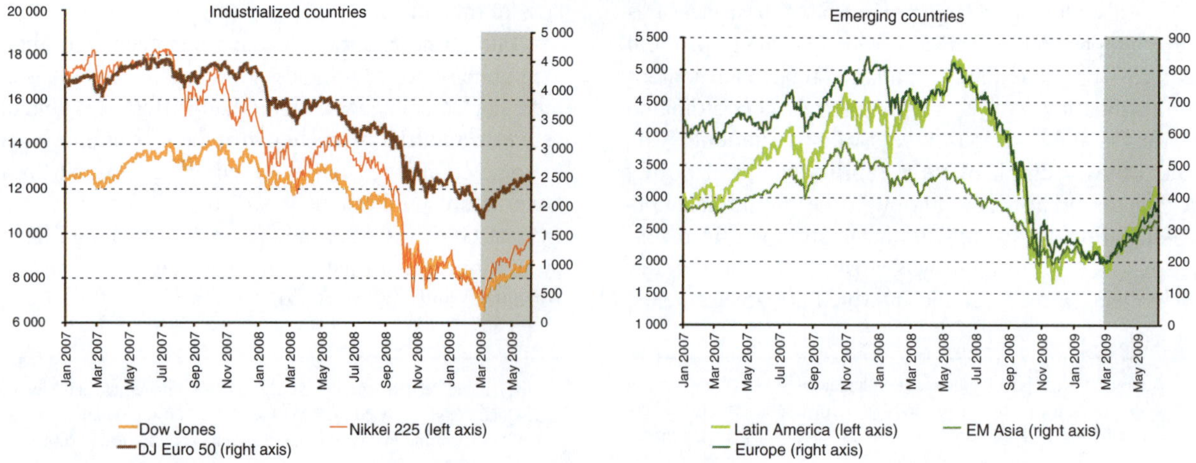

Source: Economic Commission for Latin America and the Caribbean (ECLAC), on the basis of figures from Bloomberg.

Financial markets will take time to return to business as usual and the availability of funds on the international markets will remain tight for some time. Deleveraging and slow credit growth will continue as long as banks are addressing their capitalization needs and the challenge posed by their holdings of financial assets of dubious value and outstanding delinquent loans. Moreover, the erosion of wealth (particularly non-financial wealth) has ceased but has yet to go into reverse, and this is placing a further constraint on the recovery of demand.

The slow recovery may well encounter some bumps along the road which could further delay emergence from the crisis. Close attention must be paid to the emerging economies of Eastern Europe and the Baltic nations, which have developed significant disequilibria comparable to or even worse than those seen in Latin America and the Caribbean in past crises. Some European banks are exposed enough in these countries to warrant concern that a worsening of the situation in that area could trigger contagion in Western European economies. In addition, a prolonged period of sluggish demand and economic activity at the world level could damage the asset positions of large groups of agents badly enough to strike a blow at financial systems.

It is thus difficult to predict when the crisis will end and what the path to recovery will look like. One possibility, assuming that the scenario described in the preceding paragraph does not occur, is that domestic demand will recover slowly in the developed countries on the back of a gradual return to normalcy in financial markets, the beginning of a process of recovery in the value of assets that make up the wealth of the private sector, particularly in the developed countries, and a change in the expectations of economic agents. In fact, the decline across the array of available indicators in the financial and real sectors alike is already slowing up and even showing some signs of reversing itself as uncertainty about the global economy abates, thanks to strong commitments on the part of economic authorities (particularly in developed countries but also in the developing world) to implement measures to mitigate the effects of the crisis on domestic demand.

With regard to the region, in late 2008 it was forecast that economic activity would slow in 2009, given that, as noted in the *Preliminary Overview of the Economies of Latin America and the Caribbean, 2008* (ECLAC, 2008e), the engines that had been driving growth between 2003 and mid-2008 were shutting down one by one. At that time, expectations pointed to a drop in domestic demand, in both private consumption and investment, owing to declining national income (caused, in turn, by falling raw materials prices), rising unemployment and tighter credit, all exacerbated by weakening expectations.

Figure I.26

CASE-SCHILLER HOME PRICE INDEX, 10 MAJOR CITIES

(12-month percentage variation)

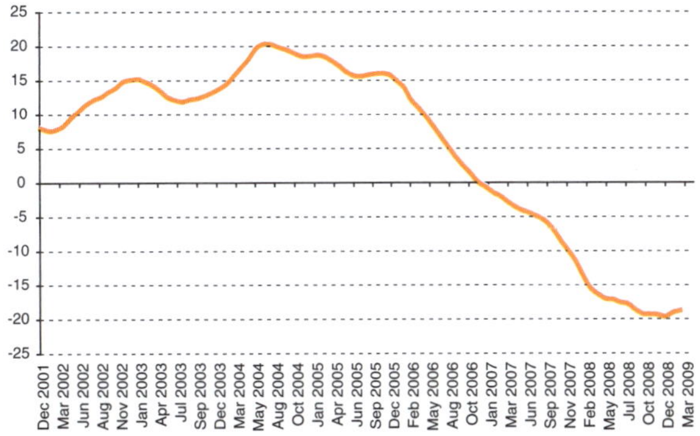

Source: Economic Commission for Latin America and the Caribbean (ECLAC), on the basis of Standard & Poor's.

Figure I.27

CONSUMER CONFIDENCE INDICES

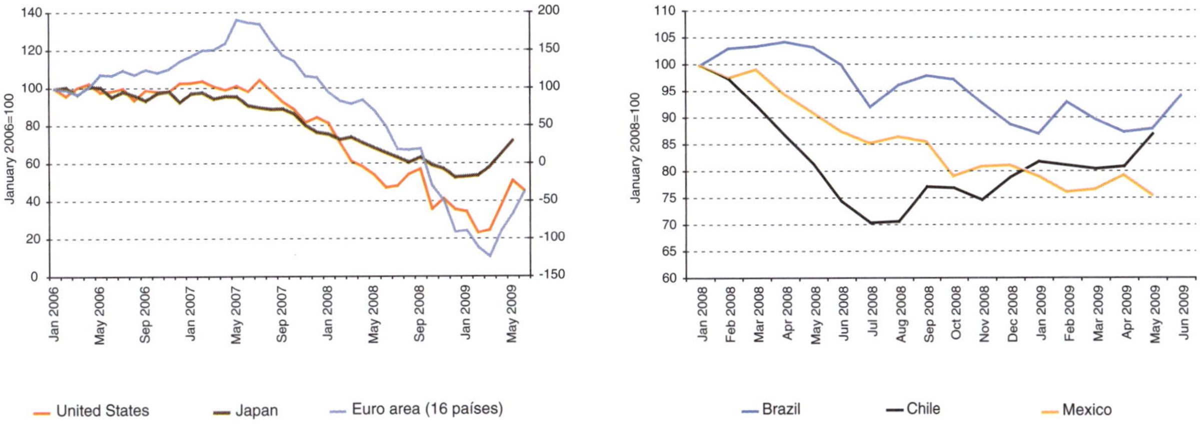

Source: Economic Commission for Latin America and the Caribbean (ECLAC), on the basis of national sources and the Statistical Office of the European Communities (EUROSTAT).

Towards mid-2009, the slowdown in international trade appeared to abate, commodity prices began to recover, access to credit eased and indicators of expectations began to improve. These developments allow for the possibility that activity levels in the region will begin to recover in the second semester: in fact, the downtrend is already showing signs of easing up in several countries. Given the extremely low starting point, this partial upturn will not be sufficient to make up for the contractions —or slowdowns— recorded in the fourth quarter of 2008 and in the first quarter of 2009. As a result, the annual rate of GDP growth will be negative for the first time in seven years. As noted earlier, the slump in economic activity will take its toll on the labour market and unemployment may be expected to rise and job quality to worsen, which will have a negative impact on poverty.

GDP in Latin America and the Caribbean is projected to contract by 1.9% in 2009, owing mainly to deteriorating activity levels in Mexico, whose GDP is expected to contract by 7%. For South America as a whole, activity will be flat (0.1%), similarly to the position in the Central American isthmus (0%), and per capita GDP will fall in many of the countries in both cases. For the Caribbean countries overall, GDP is expected to contract by 1.2%.

As noted, a gradual recovery is expected to begin in the second half of 2009 and become consolidated in 2010, when the region could return to positive growth, though at rates well below those recorded in recent years. Regional growth is projected at 3.1%, with South America (3.8%) again growing faster than Mexico (2.5%) and Central America (2.8%). Very modest growth is projected for the Caribbean (0.5%). Growth rates like these, however, are unlikely to prevent the deterioration of social indicators that will accompany the economic contraction in 2009. In fact, the growth rate projected for 2010 will barely be high enough to prevent unemployment from rising, assuming that the participation rate remains constant, but will not suffice to reverse the downturn estimated for 2009.

In order to achieve faster economic recovery that could more rapidly boost employment and thus help the region to regain the poverty reduction track it veered from in 2009, the governments would need greater capacity to tackle the impacts of the crisis through policy measures. That, however, will depend, among other things, on the volume of resources available for the purpose.

Given that the macroeconomic space for public policymaking has become tighter, all this points to the need for the international financial institutions to actively provide resources to finance countercyclical policies and measures to offset the impacts of the crisis. The region does have room to borrow sustainably, particularly from these entities, based on the behaviour observed in recent years.

Box I.6

TOWARDS A RECOVERY OF THE LATIN AMERICAN ECONOMIES

The international financial crisis has had a severe impact on the region, as evidenced by the economic activity indices observed in the fourth quarter of 2008 and the first quarter of 2009, when growth rates were close to zero or negative. Clearly, growth in Latin America was dented by the current international climate; nonetheless, as ECLAC has maintained, the region was better equipped to handle the situation than it had been on prior occasions and the question of when the recovery might begin is well worth asking.

With a view to finding some pointers in this regard, early signs of recovery were calculated using the most recent monthly data (from April and even May 2009) from six of the region's largest economies: Argentina, Brazil, Chile, Colombia, Mexico and Peru. In each country, an indicator of economic activity was taken as a reference point and a composite leading or advance indicator[a] was determined based on a set of financial and real variables. The set of variables was different in each country, but included real exports, total real imports and capital goods imports, real exchange rates, international reserves, indicators of overall and sector-specific economic activity, prices for major commodity exports, measurements of monetary liquidity, interest rates, stock markets and domestic credit, among others. In each country trend shifts were identified both for the target indicator and for each of the variables. The point at which these changes occurred was compared and those variables that changed early on were selected to feed into the composite indicator. Once the leading indicator was calculated, it was converted into a probability function to predict the likelihood of an imminent change of trend. This probability was then compared with a threshold established by referring to previous experience of business cycles in each economy. The crossing of that threshold represented a signal that the economy was about to bottom out (in the case of a contraction) or peak (in the case of an expansion) and that, consequently, a change of phase was imminent.[b]

The results of this exercise for the economies selected are shown in the figure below, in which the shaded rectangles denote periods in which economic activity was declining and the red line indicates the threshold mentioned above. The indicators for Argentina, Brazil, Chile, Colombia and Peru have all crossed the threshold, sending out a signal that the beginning of a recovery is approaching. In the case of Mexico, the threshold has yet to be reached, but significant progress has been made towards it. Based on this data, the countries of the region could be expected to enter a phase of economic recovery in the second semester of 2009.

Box I.6 (concluded)

PROBABILITY OF RECOVERY

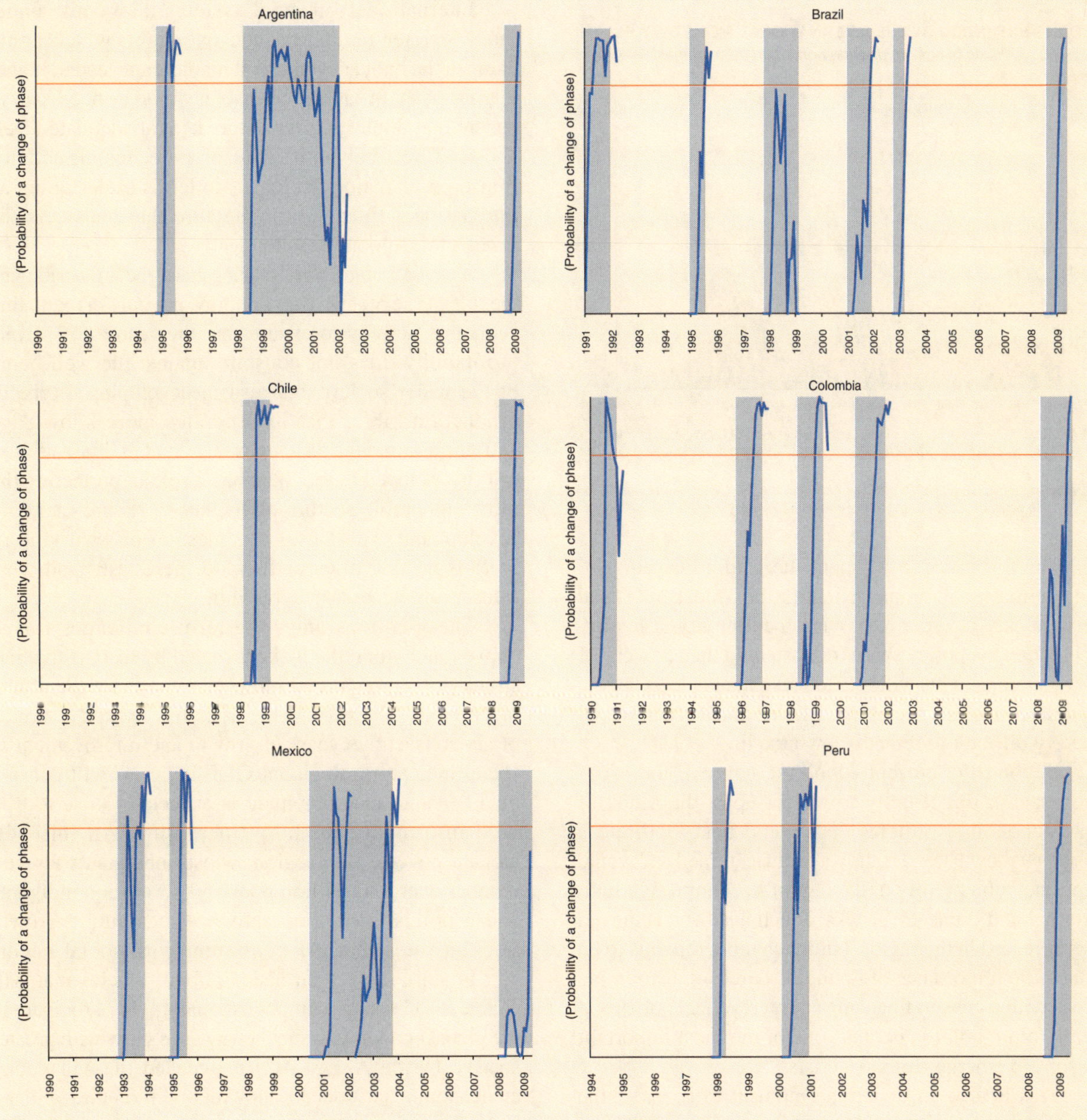

Source: Economic Commission for Latin America and the Caribbean (ECLAC).

[a] The methodology used was basically that employed by the National Bureau of Economic Research (NBER), see G. Bry and C. Boschan, *Cyclical Analysis of Time Series*, New York, 1971.

[b] For the details of these calculations, see F. Cantú, A. Acevedo and O. Bello, "Indicadores adelantados de actividad económica para algunos países de América Latina", Santiago, Chile, Economic Commission for Latin America and the Caribbean (ECLAC), 2009, unpublished.

The need for international financial institutions to play a more active role will be even greater if the recovery of the international financial system is delayed and if access to external financing continues to be precarious. In such a situation, a number of countries could have difficulty in covering their external obligations.

The manner in which countries are granted financing from international financial institutions is also very important. At the very least, conditionalities must not be procyclical, as they often were in the past. And, importantly, costs and terms of financing must fit the needs of developing countries. Much would also be gained from the institutions working together in a coordinated, consistent and complementary fashion in order to reinforce their effects.[23]

Figure I.28

LOANS EXTENDED BY THE INTERNATIONAL MONETARY FUND

(Millions of special drawing rights and percentages)

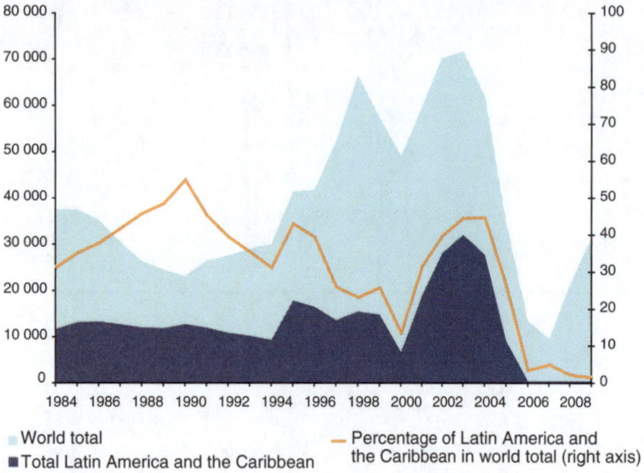

Source: Economic Commission for Latin America and the Caribbean (ECLAC), on the basis of figures from the International Monetary Fund.

The resources to augment the lending capacity of the international financial institutions must be raised very quickly in order to provide the liquidity necessary to broaden the policy space for hastening the recovery of the economies. This will help to prevent, or at least lessen, residual economic, social and political impacts that would be very difficult to remedy down the line.

Beyond the current economic context, the crisis provides an opportunity to reflect upon the kinds of macroeconomic policies that would best facilitate a sustained growth trend in the wake of the turmoil and would limit the vulnerability of the region's economies to both external and domestic shocks. Much has been achieved in this regard in the region, but much more remains to be done. The importance of saving resources in favourable times with a view to financing countercyclical policies at some future point is perhaps one of the most important lessons to emerge from this crisis.[24]

This is also an opportune moment to consider the changes on the horizon in the world economy and how the Latin American and Caribbean countries will fit into this new landscape. It is likely that developed countries will grow more slowly and, consequently, the developing world will take on a greater role in sustaining global demand. This poses new challenges in terms of competitiveness and makes export diversification —by product, but especially by destination market— imperative.

International financial systems may come under much stricter regulation and oversight, which could dampen the buoyancy of credit markets and lead to higher interest rates. In such a scenario, it would be necessary to ensure that domestic savings are kept at adequate levels and can flow freely into financing for economic activity. It also poses major challenges in terms of designing an international financial architecture that considers the needs of developing economies.[25]

A new paradigm shift is taking place and is repositioning the role of the State in the economy, not only in regulating economic activity to ensure that the search for private profitability does not conspire against the well-being of the wider society, but also in developing a type of production fabric that incorporates more knowledge and environmental efficiency and makes innovation a priority. Above all, the State has a role in protecting the most vulnerable sectors of society to ensure inclusive development. This raises the question of what kind of State is needed to carry forward these tasks and what reforms are necessary to build it.

The medium- and long-term challenges raised above touch upon the lacks revealed by a crisis that has struck the region a hard blow, albeit without the drama of previous occasions. The crisis has broken a stretch of six consecutive years of growth and improvement in social indicators. Regional GDP is projected to shrink by 1.9% and unemployment is expected to rise to 9%, with informality probably increasing. All this will worsen poverty in a region whose inhabitants already number over 180 million poor and 70 million indigents and it points to the imperative of regaining a growth track at rates that are consistent with social needs.

In sum, the region needs public policies that will enable it to become competitive enough to participate in the global economy in such a way as to grow with greater social cohesion. As ECLAC has signalled, this will require an economic and social policy mix built on three pillars: technical progress, productive employment and human capital. This strategy of production development combined with greater equity-building will, in turn, require resources to finance the necessary policies as well as a stronger State able to address these challenges successfully.

23 Some of these themes are analysed in an interesting work recently published by IDB entitled "Policy Trade-offs for Unprecedented Times: Confronting the Global Crisis in Latin America and the Caribbean" (IDB, 2009).

24 For a detailed examination of these topics, see ECLAC (2008f).

25 See Calvo (2009).

Part 2

Policies for creating quality jobs

Introduction

Economic growth in Latin America between 2003 and 2008 had a positive effect on the labour market, as the resulting rise in employment pushed down the unemployment rate and increased job quality. This contributed to a significant reduction in poverty and indigence rates during the period. This positive trend did not, however, prevent a continuation of the region's serious labour problems and their ongoing manifestations in the form of unemployment, underemployment, job insecurity and informality. In this context, the conditions of certain groups of workers are especially unfavourable, such as the least skilled and, within this group, women and young people in particular. Furthermore, the deficiencies in the region's labour markets often generate dramatically unequal income distribution and poverty situations from which many people are unable to escape —even when they are employed.

The current worldwide economic crisis also affects the region's labour markets, which means additional challenges for labour policies. All of this is playing out against a fairly volatile international backdrop, in which increased competition (as a result of more globally integrated markets) requires Latin American and Caribbean economies to have a high capacity for adjustment and adaptation.

In this context, the debate on the appropriate characteristics for labour institutions is perhaps one of the most controversial in the sphere of economic and social policy. This is largely due to the fact that the labour market is different to others —mainly because the workforce is the good being traded— and that hiring conditions are defined for a specific period of time, without a total or permanent change of ownership. Besides this, the labour market has problems of incomplete information among the economic agents involved, as the business owner does not know the worker's real performance, while the worker has no knowledge of all the labour conditions within the business. This affects the negotiation of contract terms, hampers labour mobility and restricts investment in human capital. Lastly, bargaining power between the individual worker and the firm is clearly unequal, partially due to the aforementioned information asymmetries and partially because of the need for workers to maintain a constant income (given their low capacity for saving or accessing alternative resources). All of this constitutes a further feature that renders the results of negotiation far from optimal, and calls for public-policy intervention.

Above and beyond the technical explanation based on the specific characteristics of the labour market, the reasons for appropriate regulation are also ethical ones based on the need to provide social justice. Thus it has been posited that the labour market is a social institution (Solow, 1992). As a result of social and political processes marked by conflict, legal regulations and rules based on collective bargaining have been established to complement and restrict regulations based on the market.[1]

As a result, there emerged a vast array of labour institutions covering, inter alia, the regulation of labour conditions (level and type of wage and contract, conditions

1 See an analysis of the potential advantages and risks of the three forms of regulation in Betcherman, Luinstra and Ogawa (2001).

for dismissal, etc.), mechanisms for their creation and control, the organization of labour market agents, the institutions that affect the availability and characteristics of the workforce (health, education and vocational training systems), information systems and labour organization in companies (Rodgers, 1993).

Labour institutions as a whole must pursue the double objective of ensuring the efficient functioning of the labour market, as well as the protection of structurally weaker actors, with the ultimate aim of contributing to the generation of high-quality employment.

As with other institutions, labour institutions are the products of history, the result of social, political, economic and cultural interactions in a given time and place. Achieving the above-mentioned objectives is therefore mainly dependent on the way in which the challenges of the economic, social, political and cultural context are responded to. In particular, labour institutions are expected to be consistent, and to have a long-term development strategy that stimulates systemic competitiveness, while taking account of the need to correct the region's structural heterogeneity by encouraging the convergence of the productive structure, so as to facilitate greater social inclusion. With this in mind, it is also vital to develop mechanisms to promote the expanded coverage of labour institutions, to include large swathes of the workforce that do not enjoy their benefits. This should go hand in hand with the development of non contributory protection systems (ECLAC, 2006), with a view to extending social protection to the entire population.

To reiterate what was stated earlier, there is intense debate about the optimum characteristics of labour institutions, both in terms of regulation generated by legislation, and the way in which this affects labour-market functioning. Broadly speaking, there are two viewpoints on the matter. According to one argument, high firing costs, hiring difficulties, fixed working hours and high labour costs prevent greater levels of investment and growth, and eventually have a negative effect on job creation. Those in this camp maintain that labour markets require increased flexibility, and that the solution would be the legal deregulation of labour markets in favour of market-based regulation. The opposing point of view is that legal regulation, as well regulation based on collective bargaining, does not have a negative impact on labour-market performance, and in fact is necessary for ensuring social justice and cohesion, not to mention increases in efficiency, real technical progress and productivity.[2]

Although there are obvious implications for both stances (specific interests of increased profitability for business owners and greater protection for workers) in the short term, the picture is not as clear from a more long-term perspective. In a genuine strategy of competitiveness, would maximum flexibility (and the associated high staff turnover and problems in generating human capital) really be best for business owners? On the other hand, in a constantly changing environment, is an employment strategy based on accumulating seniority in a stable job really the best way to protect workers and encourage upward career paths? Perhaps it is possible to find solutions that turn the short-term mutual compromises into win-win situations, taking into account the long-term implications.

This *Economic Survey* does not aim to answer these questions, but rather present the options that Latin American and Caribbean countries have available to enhance their labour institutions, so that they may become the means of generating quality employment. With this in mind, the first chapter offers a review of the debate on labour institutions and the elements thereof, as well as how the debate both influenced and was affected by the unsatisfactory performance of regional labour markets in recent decades. The second chapter examines the functioning and impact on labour markets of specific institutional aspects such as minimum wages, unions, collective bargaining and unemployment protection. The third chapter provides an analysis of advances and weaknesses in terms of active labour-market policies. One of the key tasks of labour policies is to encourage the entry into the productive labour market of groups who come up against specific obstacles in this area. The penultimate chapter therefore reviews policies and programmes to promote productive employment for women and young people, especially the least skilled among them. The final chapter presents some preliminary conclusions about these topics that are so important for the region.

---

2 As stated by Berg and Kucera (2008), such institutions become even more important in contexts of excess labour supply, as these make it essential to ensure a minimum level of protection for all workers.

Chapter I

Challenges and opportunities for labour institutions in Latin America and the Caribbean

A. Development of labour institutions in the region

Between the 1950s and 1960s, the Latin American and Caribbean region underwent a process of rapid economic growth, in which the labour markets changed dramatically. In addition, the labour supply rose quickly as a result of high birth rates and lower mortality, as well as (especially from the 1970s onwards) a surge in female participation. At the same time, levels of schooling rose following the expansion of the education system. High economic growth generated significant labour demand in modern sectors of the economy, which in turn pushed up the proportion of waged non-agricultural work in the occupational structure. The share of the agricultural sector in employment dropped sharply, while employment in secondary and tertiary activities grew. Lastly, average productivity increased, albeit with major intersectoral and intrasectoral gaps.

These transformations in the occupational structure were accompanied by the development of labour institutions similar to those in more industrialized countries. Such changes were intended to create a framework to substantially increase waged work in the industrial and tertiary sectors and to respond to the demands of emerging social sectors (Candia, 1994). Similarly to what happened in industrialized countries, legal instruments were created to regulate labour relations, both directly through State intervention and by means of collective agreements. One of the factors influencing the design of labour codes was the need to correct the structural imbalance between the various agents in the labour market by providing special protection for workers. Furthermore, public sector employment expanded dramatically, which had an impact on wage setting. At times, the public sector acted as employer of last resort (Echeverría, 1985). The experiences of Latin American countries differed from those of industrialized countries in the following ways:

(i) Regulatory coverage was limited to a much smaller section of the workforce.

(ii) In many countries, relations among the main socio-economic agents (public sector, business owners and unions) were characterized by a social covenant led by a populist State. In this context, unions were highly dependent on the State and political forces, and political negotiations were given priority over labour negotiations and legislatory regulation was preferred over regulation resulting from negotiations between business owners and unions.

(iii) In some cases, socio-political instability generated a cyclical movement in which regulation arising from consensus among companies, workers and the State was replaced by authoritarian regulation that dismantled or weakened union organization (although the former was eventually re-established).

(iv) In countries with a weakened production base and exclusive socio-political systems, the prevailing collective labour relations were authoritarian and repressive, and individual labour relations were often strongly biased towards protection, although the coverage of labour institutions was smaller than in more developed countries.

As a result of the way in which the labour market grew between 1950 and 1980, there were simultaneous processes of social inclusion and exclusion (PREALC, 1991, p. 2). While a growing proportion of the economically active population became involved in buoyant activities, a considerable percentage of those who left the agricultural sector and migrated to large towns —as a result of interweaving push and pull processes— were able to find work only in low-productivity and low-income activities. At the same time, labour institutions —which had been designed by adapting institutions from other socio-economic contexts to specific local situations covered only a small percentage of the labour force. Large swathes of the population (their proportion depending on the country) were excluded from these processes and benefited only indirectly from some of the progress (social policies, trickle-down income opportunities) or else experienced economic displacement and social marginalization.

As a result, although open unemployment remained generally low (PREALC, 1982, pp. 99-100), analysts highlighted serious labour problems that were reflected in the (visible and invisible) underemployment that characterized large sections of the employed among farm workers and informal urban workers. In this regard, the predominant interpretations attributed the ultimate causes of these problems to non-labour markets.[1]

Some interpretations, such as those based on the Harris-Todaro model, assigned an important role to labour-market regulation, specifically in explaining the large size of the informal urban sector. According to this interpretation, the benefits provided by law or collective bargaining to formal workers were hugely attractive to the rural workforce, but made labour costs more expensive, which then limited labour demand. A large number of migrants from rural to urban areas were therefore forced to work in informal employment while waiting for an opportunity to join the formal sector. However, in the 1970s and much of the 1980s many analysts thought that labour markets in Latin America functioned reasonably well (Squire, 1979; Gregory, 1986).

During the crisis of the 1980s, labour integration factors weakened even further both in the labour market itself (with productive employment creation at a low ebb) and at the institutional level. Within the labour market, on the one hand, the need to generate employment remained high (as the participation rate continued to rise) while, on the other hand, the capacity of the formal sector to create productive employment decreased (with most new jobs being concentrated in the informal sector). Agriculture, which had temporarily been a refuge, continued to see its share in employment fall, while the expansion of the secondary sector faltered and the pace of growth increased in the tertiary sector (which has accounted for over half of employment since the 1980s). At the same time, average labour productivity fell and structural heterogeneity deepened, owing in particular to the surge in informal sector employment, which lowered this sector's average productivity.

In this context, many aspects of labour institutions (which covered only some of the population) became even less effective. In many countries, minimum wages plummeted in real terms and lost their influence as the benchmark for wage negotiations, traditional social security systems suffered financial crises and unions lost bargaining power.

---

1 "[...] one of the special features of Latin America is the persistence of the employment of a considerable proportion of the labour force at low levels of productivity [...] The productive absorption of this labour is made more difficult by the dynamic insufficiency of the economy, which is incapable of reducing this proportion despite the high rates of accumulation and growth of the modern sectors, this being explained, in turn, by the nature of technological change and the distribution and appropriation of wealth" (Tokman, 1982, p. 129). From another perspective, Balassa and others (1986, p. 71) also detected labour problems. However, they gave another explanation: the high expectations surrounding the creation of new jobs through the import substitution strategy for Latin American development were not fulfilled. The industries established were relatively capital-intensive and therefore unable to absorb all the workers left unemployed in the agricultural sector, who were thus disadvantaged by this strategy.

The main aim of the liberalizing structural reforms driven through from the 1980s was to lay the foundations for high and sustained economic growth; employment was not considered a key variable. However, the proposed reforms were expected to have a major positive effect on labour markets, by eliminating a series of distortions that were acting against job creation.[2] The main rationales for the reforms included the following:

(i) Anti-export bias: it was suggested that import substitution strategies (characterized by, among others, tariff protectionism, currency overvaluation and a fiscal policy that discouraged exports) had shaped a production structure that did not match the region's factor endowment (underutilizing the labour factor).

(ii) Urban bias: to promote industrialization, agricultural activities (which tend to be labour-intensive) had allegedly been relegated to the role of providing foreign exchange and cheap industrial inputs and food (through price, credit, fiscal and tariff policies, and so forth), and this would have hindered their development.

(iii) Bias in favour of intensive use of capital: to promote the modernization of productive activities, the relative prices of capital had been lowered by means of machinery and equipment import facilities, as well as input subsidies and credit mechanisms.

(iv) Bias against labour demand: distortions such as non-wage labour costs, unionization, the large size of the public sector and minimum wages had made the labour factor more expensive.

As a result, the proposed reforms were to stimulate job creation in three ways: increased economic growth would boost labour demand; reorientation of investment would reflect the region's comparative advantages (thus favouring more labour-intensive sectors); and corrections in the relative prices of capital and labour would promote a move towards more labour-intensive technologies. However, with the exception of the labour plan in Chile in 1979 and, to a lesser extent, the reform in Panama in 1986, labour reforms were not a priority on structural reform agendas prior to the 1990s.[3]

This could also have been influenced by the fact that other reforms (relating to trade, finance or privatizations) were expected to have a far greater impact on economic growth and therefore on employment. In addition, since strong resistance could be anticipated to deregulatory labour reforms, it may have been thought not worthwhile to invest political capital in them.[4] A contributing factor in this decision may have been the above-mentioned perception that, despite their distortions, the region's labour markets functioned reasonably well. As a result, public policies in the labour sector of many countries concentrated their efforts more on active labour market policies rather than labour reforms, in an attempt to improve the efficiency of mediation, training and micro-enterprise development instruments (interventions that are clearly less antagonistic than labour reforms) (Weller, 2004).

However, although economic growth picked up somewhat in the early 1990s, labour indicators were clearly unsatisfactory, as indicated by high open unemployment, fresh still maintaining a very relative expansion of the informal sector and decreases in job security. Consequently, optimistic view of market functioning it was suggested that labour reforms had been a key omission from the agenda and new labour institutions were needed. This went on to be explicitly included in the proposals for second-generation reforms, this time with strong emphasis on making labour markets more flexible and giving less emphasis to other labour policy objectives (Burki & Perry, 1997; IDB, 1997).[5]

The rationale for this proposal was based on historically decontextualized theoretical considerations about the cost (monetary and non-monetary) of regulations, which would have a negative impact on the level and characteristics of hiring, the unemployment rate and the efficiency of labour-market adjustments to labour-demand and supply shocks. Accordingly, it tended to be assumed that labour markets functioned the some way as other markets and therefore the preference was for the most far-reaching labour deregulation possible.[6]

More recently, however, the limited results of the main reforms of this type (typified by low formal job creation and more precarious employment conditions) have caused the international debate to adopt greater degree of caution with respect to radical deregulation measures (Freeman, 2005).[7] This situation has refocused the debate around the areas and objectives that have conventionally been prioritized by labour policy, such as improving labour conditions, offsetting asymmetries among market agents,

2 See Weller (2000, pp. 23-27).

3 This is reflected in a key document on the proposed reforms (Williamson, 1990). Out of the 10 reforms from the Washington Consensus, labour reform is mentioned only in the proposal on deregulation (in a quotation from another document that mentions one labour aspect to reform —the high cost of dismissal— in conjunction with six other policy areas). At that time, labour reform was clearly not a priority on the agenda for market-oriented structural reforms.

4 It is noteworthy that some of the most far-reaching reforms were implemented in regimes with varying limitations on the exercise of democratic and union rights, such as that in Chile in the 1970s and 1980s and subsequently in Peru.

5 According to the interpretation of Williamson (2003), this was an uncompleted task left over from first-generation reforms.

6 "The challenge of labour policy is not very different to the challenge of trade policy up to a few years ago, i.e. to reduce distortions and increase competitiveness" (Cox Edwards, 1997, p. 91).

7 This process was accompanied by a reorientation of the vision of certain international financial agencies.

social labour protection and promoting equitable access to employment.

The current international economic crisis, which affects the region's countries to varying degrees, has begun to have a negative impact on the labour market and living conditions of the population (ECLAC/ILO, 2009). In this context, the role of labour institutions becomes even more significant, as they should help to avoid inequitable adjustments associated with any economic and social losses. More specifically, policies intended to avoid unemployment and sustain the income of those who lose their jobs not only contribute to reducing the negative impact of these episodes on family income but also lessen the secondary effects on other labour-market indicators (such as average wages and their distribution) and help to stabilize domestic demand (thereby limiting the severity of the crisis and supporting the subsequent recovery of growth). This function is particularly important, given the fact that evidence suggests that employment-output elasticity increases during a recession (see box I.1).

Box I.1

ECONOMIC CYCLE AND EMPLOYMENT

Navarro (2009) obtained traditional functions of labour demand using dynamic panel estimations from 15 Latin American countries for the period 1980-2007 and a subset of six countries for the period 1985-2008.[a] First, aggregate employment is found to contract during recessions and the signs of employment-output elasticity and employment-wage elasticity are consistent with the theory and the international empirical evidence available. In particular, the employment-output elasticity for the subset of six countries is between 0.32 and 0.34, whereas the employment-wage elasticity varies between -0.11 and -0.12; for the group of 15 countries the values drop to 0.27 and nearly -0.05, respectively. Furthermore, there seems to be a greater negative impact on wage employment creation, which appears to point to informal employment having a countercyclical role.

Second, the responses of job creation to variations in wages and in the level of activity seem to be asymmetrical depending on the phase of the cycle. In particular, employment-output elasticity increases in recessions, while the employment-wage elasticity decreases. In the case of wage employment, the employment-output elasticity increases from 0.3 in periods of stability or growth to 0.75 in the recessionary phase of the cycle. In contrast, the employment-wage elasticity drops from -0.22 to -0.03 under the same sets of circumstances. From this, it may be inferred that the reduction of labour costs is ineffective in increasing labour demand in the recessionary phase of the cycle, whereas policies that target aggregate demand and the level of domestic activity appear to have a greater impact on employment in times of crisis.

The author puts forward two arguments to account for these findings. On the one hand, a "macro" argument suggests that, in recessions, labour demand from companies is limited by the demand for their products and that wage decreases are not enough to encourage job creation. The "expectations" factor is important in this scenario, such that, even with hiring subsidies, firms will be less willing to increase hiring unless they expect demand for their products to rise in the near future. On the other hand, the "micro" argument is based on two of the rules of derived demand of Hicks and Marshall (Hammermesh, 1993): (i) if a negative demand shock results in lay-offs, the share of labour costs in the total costs of companies is expected to fall, and companies become less sensitive to wage changes; (ii) if the price elasticity of demand falls, companies have less incentive to reduce prices, which results in lower employment-wage elasticity.[b]

Source: Lucas Navarro, "Dinámica del empleo y crisis en América Latina: resultados de estimaciones de panel", document presented at the workshop on labour- market institutions' present challenges, Santiago, Chile, Economic Commission for Latin America and the Caribbean (ECLAC), 14 and 15 April 2009, unpublished.

[a] The small size of the sample is a potential source of bias in the estimations. To mitigate this problem, a technique of instrumental variables developed by Hahn, Hausman and Kuersteiner (2007) is used.

[b] According to much of the literature, the price elasticity of demand is procyclical. See Edmond and Veldkamp (2008), among others.

B. Aims of labour institutions

The ultimate aim of labour institutions is to generate quality employment. In order to achieve this, institutions must fulfil a twofold objective: ensure effective functioning of the labour market (namely an optimum allocation of resources) and guarantee the protection and strengthening of the weakest in a market with structural inequalities among actors. An appropriately designed labour policy thus stimulates economic growth, competitiveness, employment and social cohesion. It should therefore be designed with due consideration for the need to:

(i) Contribute to improved labour conditions (creating working conditions that comply with the standards of security and decent work, helping to offset power asymmetries among workers and employers during wage negotiations, promoting equitable access to the labour market and to the benefits of labour and social protection institutions and enforcing labour laws, among other things).

(ii) Promote institutions and policies to tackle the effects of variable economic activity on the labour market.

(iii) Help to create the conditions for employment and wage growth, in the framework of a development strategy.

The world's various models of the regulation of labour relations differ in the emphasis they place on achieving labour-policy objectives. For instance, European Mediterranean countries have labour legislation that prioritizes job stability, but few resources are channelled into labour-market policies. For their part, workers in France, Germany and Sweden have job security and a high level of labour and social protection. In contrast, the United Kingdom and the United States have more flexible labour regulations and spend fewer fiscal resources on protection policies (Tokman, 2008a).

Lastly, some European countries have attempted to respond to demands for increased flexibility without neglecting job security, by orienting their regulatory system towards a system known as flexicurity. Denmark, Belgium, the Netherlands, Finland and Ireland, for example, have labour legislation that does not seek to protect jobs through regulations but that involves a high level of public spending in pursuit of labour market policies that are both passive (income protection for the jobless) and active (especially training) to help safeguard workers' standards of living. Another striking feature of these countries' experiences is the intensive social dialogue that has facilitated the introduction and management of the system.

As in European countries, in the Latin American and Caribbean labour-policy objectives are promoted in a variety of ways. Tokman (2008a) identifies the following four groups of Latin American countries by the stringency of their labour legislation (HL for highly stringent legislation and LL for low) and the relative significance of their spending on social and labour protection (HP for high protection and LP for low protection):

(i) LL-HP: includes Argentina, Chile, Costa Rica and Uruguay, which have less strict labour legislation and high spending, in relative terms, on labour protection.

(ii) HL-LP: includes Mexico, Panama and the Andean countries. They have more stringent legislation that provides greater job security (through the high cost of redundancies), but they allocate limited resources to worker protection.

(iii) HL-HP: includes the Bolivarian Republic of Venezuela and Brazil.

(iv) LL-LP: includes countries of Central America, the Dominican Republic and the Plurinational State of Bolivia.

There are also major differences between Latin American and European countries that have a relatively high level of social and labour protection: Latin American countries mainly use labour legislation (especially in terms of redundancy compensation) as practically the only way of ensuring job security, whereas European countries use passive and active policies based on income and employment security.

Institutions in the Caribbean have different historical roots to those in Latin America, as they are closer to systems in the United Kingdom and the United States. More specifically, labour relations are more largely based on market regulation, although considerable efforts are also made in terms of active labour-market policies (see box I.2).

The conclusion is that the starting point for an analysis aimed at enhancing labour institutions varies greatly among the region's countries. Reflections on the most appropriate regulatory systems to promote progress in achieving labour-policy objectives should consider the historical development process of each country's system of labour institutions. The adaptation of labour institutions, as agreed upon by the various economic and social actors, seems to be the only way forward for achieving sustainable institutions in keeping with a long-term development strategy and in which each institutional component is related in a coordinated way.

The following sections provide a general overview of recent trends and the current status in the most relevant policy areas: first, aspects of social and labour protection; second, active and passive labour-market policies; and lastly, aspects of the functioning of the labour market in terms of employment protection and means of promoting a higher level of employment. Where appropriate, the results of specific experiences and of studies on labour-market reform are discussed. The chapter closes with an analysis of the structural limitations and challenges faced by countries wishing to achieve greater integration with the world economy, along with social equity and protection.

Box I.2
LABOUR INSTITUTIONS IN ENGLISH-SPEAKING CARIBBEAN COUNTRIES

Generally speaking, the labour markets of English-speaking Caribbean countries are considered more flexible than those of Latin American countries. Working hours or time-related and functional flexibility are the main forms of labour-market flexibility. There are selected forms of payment flexibility, especially in large unionized firms (particularly profit-sharing and performance-based pay). Numerical flexibility is more restricted by labour legislation, although there is a growing trend towards the use of contract labour (both domestic and migrant labour). Both Barbados and Jamaica have established institutions to promote greater use of incentive pay based on productivity or performance. Some measure of flexibility has been introduced via collective bargaining agreements as labour laws have not changed in any fundamental way over the past decade.

In the Caribbean, the social protection system for laid off workers is not fully developed. Although there are redundancy compensation schemes for those who fulfil the relevant requirements, a high percentage of the labour force working in basic activities receives no financial support during spells of unemployment. Barbados has unemployment insurance, but only people who meet certain conditions can benefit from it. Jobless workers have to resort to special social assistance programmes while unemployed. Informal labour and remittances from abroad also help to relieve the loss of income resulting from unemployment. In Jamaica, there are plans to introduce a formal assistance system for the unemployed.

There is widespread agreement among stakeholders in the labour market that active labour-market policies (especially the provision of training and information on the labour market) are key areas. Caribbean countries have implemented many such policies, particularly in terms of training programmes and State-run employment services. Most of these countries have a range of public and private agencies that provide training to employed and unemployed people. Some countries have special programmes for young people, such as the Youth Training and Employment Partnership Programme (YTEPP) in Trinidad and Tobago. As for public employment services, they tend to be underused as job information usually passes through informal channels such as word of mouth and social networks.

Although labour-market participants have made efforts to engage in social dialogue, few concrete measures have been introduced in this area by the subregion's countries (except Barbados and, to a lesser extent, Jamaica).

Source: Andrew S. Downes, "Flexible labour markets, workers' protection and active labour-market policies in the Caribbean", *Macroeconomía del desarrollo series*, Nº 86 (LC/L.3063-P), Santiago, Chile, Economic Commission for Latin America and the Caribbean (ECLAC), 2009. United Nations Publication, Sales No.: E.09.II.G.59.

C. Labour protection

Labour protection includes a gamut of public measures implemented to support individuals, families and communities in dealing with various risks, and to offset labour-market exclusions and asymmetries (with emphasis on the poorest and most vulnerable members of society).

One of the most important elements is unemployment protection, which is implemented to fulfil objectives of equity and efficiency. First, unemployment protection schemes that reach low-income households serve to smooth the effects of joblessness on family income and reduce the adverse effects on the welfare of those households, thereby helping to prevent more households from falling into poverty. Second, inasmuch as the income protection system for the unemployed represents a financial support that facilitates job-seeking, it will contribute to matching the characteristics of supply and demand (Acemoglu and Shimer, 1999) and will promote efficiency. It can thus reduce the income losses resulting from changes in employment following redundancy.

However, it is often argued in developed countries that these protection schemes generate dependency on the part of beneficiaries by discouraging them from actively seeking work. Following on from this, some developed countries that have very generous programmes have incorporated means of checking job-seeking efforts and have strengthened the active policies associated with unemployment benefits. Within this set-up, job centres have taken on an increasingly important role, improving the coordination between unemployment insurance, and the training aimed at increasing the employability and rehiring of the unemployed.

Unlike in developed countries, in Latin America and the Caribbean the scope and coverage of unemployment insurance has always been limited. As will be discussed in chapter II, even in the few countries that have such schemes (Argentina, Barbados, Bolivarian Republic of Venezuela, Brazil, Chile, Ecuador and Uruguay), the rates of coverage for the unemployed population are low. This is mainly due to widespread precarious employment conditions, a low level of affiliation and a high degree of employment instability.

Given the lack of contributory unemployment protection programmes or their limited scope, many of the region's countries have implemented non-contributory cash transfer schemes. Although there is considerable ongoing debate on the repercussions of this type of programme on the labour market (in terms of labour participation, formalization and wages), this study does not look at them in any detail since such measures are intended to increase the income of low-income households rather than to deal with unemployment.[8]

As mentioned previously, one of the purposes of labour institutions is to address the structural inequality among actors in the market. As a consequence, other aspects of social and labour protection that usually receive special attention have to do with compensation for labour-market asymmetries. These tend to be analysed from three perspectives that will be discussed in detail in the following chapters. First, there is the establishment of a level playing field, through the promotion of options that lead to a balanced negotiation of labour conditions. The tools used in developed countries and in Latin America and the Caribbean include promoting unions, establishing rules for collective bargaining and employment supervision aimed at promoting compliance with labour rules and laws. Second, with a view to tackling unequal bargaining conditions and promoting a minimum standard of living for the least skilled workers, minimum wages have been set. Third, various population groups (particularly women and young people) tend to be at a disadvantage in the labour market or find it difficult to access the formal sector of it. They are therefore excluded from formal labour protection mechanisms, experience higher unemployment and generally work in low-productivity employment. These final aspects are addressed in chapter IV.

D. Active labour-market policies

Active labour-market policies are those designed to avoid job losses or to expedite the transition between unemployment and employment. These schemes operate on three different levels: (i) on the quality and type of labour supply, through workforce training programmes; (ii) on demand, through direct or indirect job creation or support to microenterprises, and (iii) through intermediation between the two parties in the employment relationship (mainly carried out by job centres).

As noted earlier, the line between active and passive policies has become increasingly blurred, as the latter kind (especially unemployment insurance) are increasingly associated with active schemes to support the return to work —for reasons of both efficiency and equity.

In terms of efficiency, (re)training programmes can offset, at least partially, the loss in skills related to periods of unemployment by accumulating human capital, be it general or specific to a given activity. This will reduce the amount of income lost through the period of unemployment and will also boost the productivity of companies that subsequently hire workers who benefited from the scheme, thereby increasing overall efficiency. As pointed out by Bertranou and Paz (2007), active policies aimed at improving job prospects help to equal out the skills and opportunities of workers, and are therefore positive from the point of view of equity. Indeed, these measures are increasingly incorporating more equity considerations and seeking participation by groups of excluded workers.

As stated above, in recent decades the region's countries have implemented active labour-market policies owing to the dramatic transformation and restructuring of the labour market in the wake of international economic liberalization and technological change. In order to lesser the negative impacts of these changes on economic activity and unemployment, the region's countries began to implement a series of policies that would operate on the three aforementioned levels.

A major shift that occurred both developed countries and the region in the 1990s was the switch from universal policies to programmes targeting the most vulnerable social groups, including the long-term unemployed, young people and women (especially those with a low level of formal education).

The broad variety of active policies implemented in the region form the subject of a considerable body of literature, which analyses their effects and outcomes in terms of labour-market indicators with rather diverse findings (see chapter III).

[8] See a description and assessment of these programmes in their entirety in the ILO/IPEC study (2007); a review of debates on conditional transfer programmes in Ribas, Soares and Hirata (2008), Villatoro (2007, 2008) and Cecchini and others (2009); and an analysis of the possibility of implementing a level of basic non-contributory social protection in the region in ECLAC (2006) and Bertranou and others (2007a).

E. Labour policy dilemmas in promoting employment

One of the proposals to emerge from the debate on labour institutions stresses the fact that, to promote employment, it is vital to make it easier for firms to reorganize their workforce in response to changes in market conditions. In accordance with this vision, high flexibility implies having few restrictions and low costs for hiring and firing, as well as for defining employment conditions (external flexibility). Flexibility also implies having little difficulty in adapting production processes by reassigning tasks and work conditions (internal flexibility) (Velásquez Pinto, 2009a). However, these proposals are highly controversial and the evidence is not conclusively in their favour, as shown below and in the following sections.

There are arguments for and against greater labour-market flexibility. Arguments in favour include the fact that the resulting labour turnover would increase productivity thanks to the dissemination of knowledge and an improved allocation of the labour factor. It is argued that facilitating and encouraging job changes stimulates upward mobility, greater productivity, higher wages and better allocation of resources once workers have gained some experience in a given job.

It is also argued that high exit costs can reduce the number of recruitments, as companies take into account the costs associated with future redundancies. The high cost of redundancies could generate a hiring bias towards more highly skilled workers, as these tend to receive more specific training from companies, which obviously means they are less likely to be made redundant (irrespective of the existing regulatory framework). As a result, increased flexibility would stimulate job creation, boost economic growth and also partially curb the bias in recruitment (to the benefit of lower skilled workers).

Arguments against flexibility include the fact that flexible schemes increase occupational instability, especially during periods of unemployment (thereby negatively affecting the welfare of workers). This worsens households' financial stability (ILO, 2004) and is particularly difficult for low-income families, due to their greater vulnerability to social risks. Furthermore, frequent job turnover may have an adverse effect on individuals' social integration and impair their employment opportunities, as it narrows the possibilities of accumulating knowledge and skills. Indeed, unemployed workers often obtain jobs of a lower quality (in terms of responsibilities, duration and wages) than the position they had previously.[9]

This loss of income and decline in job quality following a period of unemployment also reflects the erosion of human capital caused by bouts of joblessness and the scarring effect they can have if employers use previous stability as a proxy for the supposed productivity of workers. Besides this, the experience of being unemployed and looking for a job has a negative effect on individuals' attitude and motivation.

Labour instability makes it difficult to acquire specific skills at the company level. For instance, an employer who assumes that a worker will not stay in a job for long will probably not invest in his/her training. In contrast, a context of longer-term contracts appears to be more conducive to the deployment of training policies, career development schemes and other strategies aimed at increasing productivity (Auer, Berg and Coulibaly, 2005; Chacaltana and García, 2001).

Last but not least, it is important not to disregard the bargaining-power inequalities that characterize the labour market, especially for small and medium-sized enterprises (SMEs), and the disadvantaged position of the least skilled workers (with precarious employment conditions, often in the most informal sectors of the economy). In this context of inequality, the potential benefits of any increased labour flexibility would not reach these segments of the workforce, and inequality would only deepen.

In brief, although strong competitive pressure and continual technological change are forcing the region's economies to increase their capacity for adjustment, any progress in this direction must consider the asymmetries of the region's labour markets, which could be deepened by an ill-informed adoption of flexibility measures. The State undoubtedly has an important role to play, particularly in promoting a social dialogue that can help generate consensus-based reforms that provide for mechanisms to protect workers and encourage upward labour mobility in the new labour context, while also promoting the expansion of labour institutions' coverage to include the large swathes of the workforce that are excluded from their benefits.

Finally, there is a need for a more balanced view of how ductile the region's labour markets actually are. In practice, it has recently became more common to see a variety of contractual arrangements that have considerably boosted the capacity to reassign workforce and productive resources, thereby making the productive base more flexible.

---

9 See, among others, Nickell, Jones and Quintini (2000) and Bucheli and Furtado (2002).

F. Changes in labour rules in Latin America and the Caribbean over the past 20 years

As mentioned at the beginning of this chapter, as part of structural reforms, many of the region's countries reformed labour legislation substantially, especially during the 1990s. Most of the reforms were aimed at bringing greater flexibility to specific aspects of the labour market. The most significant measures included the following: (i) a broader range of contract types, adding a range of fixed-term contracts to the traditional ones of indeterminate duration; (ii) facilitation of subcontracting; (iii) reduction of dismissal costs through various mechanisms such as a broadening of the definition of "dismissal for just cause" and the introduction of unemployment protection systems based on individual accounts; (iv) reduction of other labour costs; and (v) greater internal flexibility introduced through the more flexible working hours and the de-indexing of wages (ECLAC, 2008b).

Nevertheless, there was no single set of measures in the region and the speed and extent of changes varied among the countries. Argentina and Peru were the main reformers in the 1990s, while Brazil, Colombia, Ecuador and Panama also introduced flexibility measures.[10] In contrast, countries such as the Bolivarian Republic of Venezuela, the Dominican Republic, Guatemala, Mexico and Nicaragua made few changes or, in the case of Chile, partially reversed some liberalizing measures implemented during the previous decade (Vega Ruiz, 2005).

All of this took place in a context of notable changes in the occupational structure, partly during the 1980s but mainly in the 1990s. The changes resulted in a relatively larger informal sector (with an increase in the number of microenterprises and unskilled own-account workers) and increased the extent of employment precariousness waged work not registered with social security. Both processes contributed to reduce de facto coverage of formal labour institutions.

The region's experiences in terms of union organization were also highly varied, as some countries such as Brazil, Chile, Colombia and Costa Rica made legislative changes to strengthen unions, while the opposite occurred in Argentina and Peru.

All these patterns occurred in the context of a long process of weakening of collective labour relations and levels of unionization. The contributing factors to this can be divided into three groups: (i) changes in productive processes and the occupational structure, such as a relative increase in the number of SMEs —which makes union organization more difficult; increased proportion of certain professional and technical occupations that operate different criteria with respect to traditional union membership; the reduction of industrial and public-sector employment (where unionization is usually more extensive), and technological change that has reduced the need for large masses of workers carrying out similar tasks; (ii) union action restricted by crackdowns on union activities or legal reforms aimed at restricting their scope for action; and (iii) the conduct of unions themselves, which have directed their demands at the State rather than business owners, combined with the loss of legitimacy of some unions because of the lack of transparency that sometimes characterizes their practices (Weller, 2000).

In the present decade, on the other hand, new flexibility measures have been limited to certain sectors (SMEs and export agriculture). What has been more significant is the reversal of the labour deregulation of the 1990s and the rise in worker protection measures. Countries that have experienced these processes are Argentina, Chile and Peru, where the most far-reaching reforms had been implemented previously (Goldin, 2008; Velásquez, 2009b; Toyama, Rosas and Tostes, 2009). One important change that has strengthened protection during this decade has been a restriction on the subcontracting of staff and services, and increased regulation of their conditions, in countries such as Chile, Colombia, Costa Rica, Panama, Peru and Uruguay.

---

10 Chile had implemented a far-reaching deregulatory reform in the 1980s.

G. Some evidence of the effects of labour rules

A wide range of studies assesses the effects of changes to labour regulations. Generally speaking, the studies compare various labour indicators before and after the reforms or use a "control group" to compare its performance with that of the "treatment groups" directly affected by the changes. The results of these studies have been extremely varied, and there tends to be no conclusive evidence regarding the impact of reforms on labour indicators.

Much of this research focuses on the effects that the change in grounds for dismissal has on worker turnover. Kugler (2000) analysed the repercussions of reducing firing costs in Colombia in 1990 and concluded that it had contributed to an increase in aggregate employment and a decrease in employment duration in the formal sector in relation to the informal sector.

Paes de Barros and Leite Corseuil (1999) analysed the effects that increased firing costs introduced in Brazil in 1988 had on job turnover, using two estimation strategies. In the first, the average duration of employment spells was assessed before and after the reform, comparing those made redundant (the treatment group) and informal workers or those who resigned (the control group). The other strategy used a binary indicator for the effects of the reform on employment duration. The results supported the hypothesis that increasing firing costs tends to reduce job separation rates and therefore increase the average duration of periods in employment. The authors did, however, point out that the major changes in the macroeconomic context in the late 1980s and early 1990s made it difficult to isolate the direct effects of labour reforms in the analysis. Similarly, the findings of Gonzaga (2003) indicate that higher firing costs in 1998 and 2001 contributed to a fall in worker turnover in Brazil.

Saavedra and Torero (2000) concluded that the labour flexibility policy implemented since 1992 in Peru contributed to an increase in turnover. In particular, they concluded that in the post-reform period the average duration of employment spells decreased among both formal workers (directly affected by the reforms) and informal workers (with a larger fall among the former).

As for the results in Argentina, Galiani and Hopenhayn (2000) indicated that, in the second half of the 1990s job instability increased independently of the duration of spells of employment. However, this did not occur in the longer periods of employment, especially those of over one year. There was therefore no clear evidence to support the hypothesis that the reforms lessened the stability of jobs directly affected by them. Nevertheless, in a subsequent study, Hopenhayn (2001) found a significant effect on jobs lasting up to three months, which coincides with the maximum length of the probationary period established in 1995.

Beccaria and Maurizio (2001) concluded that the increase in worker turnover in the 1990s was due mainly to the rise in the proportion of waged jobs not registered with social security and the increased instability of this type of job, with both phenomena linked to reduced labour-market buoyancy and the steady increase in unemployment throughout the decade. Their analysis suggests, on the other hand, that there was no increase in the rate of separation for jobs covered by social security, which implies that the direct effects of labour flexibility reforms were nil.

Haltiwanger, Scarpetto and Schweiger (2008) estimated employment creation and destruction flows for 16 countries, five of which were in Latin America. For this purpose, the reference point used was the United States labour market, since it was considered competitive and only lightly regulated. They concluded that gross job flows (creation plus destruction) ranged between 25% and 30%, depending on the size of companies in each country. Furthermore, gross job flows were smaller in the countries studied than in the United States, especially in the case of Latin American and European countries. However, the authors maintained that the differences were due to firms entering and exiting the market, rather than employment dynamics in existing firms.

Another set of studies analysed the repercussions of labour reforms on the level of employment and its composition. As in the previous case, the findings on the effects of regulation on aggregate employment and unemployment are ambiguous. This is because higher firing costs may bring down the exit rates from a given occupation, but could also reduce entry flows. It is argued, for example, that higher firing costs discouraged new firms from entering the market and existing firms from creating jobs. Accordingly, the net results of regulation on aggregate employment and unemployment are unclear and must be calculated empirically in each case.

According to Kugler (2000), lower firing costs in Colombia led to a decrease in the unemployment rate. This was attributed partly to the fact that hiring rates rose by more than firing rates, and partly to a reallocation of employment in favour of the formal sector, which has greater stability and therefore smaller exit flows.

Lastly, in terms of the composition of employment, Montenegro and Pagés (2004) concluded that higher firing costs in Chile had shifted employment away from young people, women and unskilled workers, in favour of male, adult, more highly skilled waged workers.

In summary, the evidence available does not yield a clear conclusion on the effects of regulations on job creation. Furthermore, what emerges from the discussion is that maximum flexibility is not the optimum level from the social perspective, and the evidence also casts doubt on whether there can be an optimum level valid for all countries. At the same time, it is worth assessing the extent to which increased worker mobility, linked to lower hiring and firing costs, contributes to a more efficient use of resources and results in higher growth rates and greater job creation in a given country. Conversely, a rise in worker turnaround may generate negative effects not only on workers' welfare but also on the overall efficiency of the economy. Lastly, one of the requirements for achieving a virtuous circle is the existence of a social and labour protection system that covers all individuals, so as to mitigate the effects of increased uncertainty and volatility on workers' income. Otherwise, labour-market asymmetries may deepen and the benefits may not reach the most vulnerable groups.

H. Social dialogue and the search for agreement

The analysis of the two labour-policy dilemmas described above indicates that, if Latin American and Caribbean countries are to make progress in building agreements among the stakeholders involved, they must engage in an ongoing social dialogue. However, the countries do not generally have a long tradition of social dialogue, agreement-seeking, compromise or joint decision-making by employers and workers. This has resulted in greater difficulties when it comes to improving labour institutions, as well as a lack of sustainability over time of reforms that are implemented.

There is often a lack of consensus about labour regulation even at the stage of diagnosis, when stakeholders cannot agree on how to interpret the current situation, which makes it extremely difficult to move forward with the necessary reforms. This is very evident when it comes to describing labour institutions as either flexible or rigid, because there are so many variables involved, and each side is likely to make selective use of research data (ECLAC, 2008b).

The lack of consensus at the diagnostic stage is the first barrier that must be overcome if progress is to be made in reaching agreements aimed at enhancing labour regulations and the protection system. In this sense, an integrated system of labour studies and information would be very valuable for analysing the performance of labour markets, as it would serve as a basis for building consensus around a diagnosis. It is also essential for parties to acknowledge each other as legitimate interlocutors.

Given the countries' histories, reaching agreements will clearly be a long and complex process. All the available means must be used to make gradual progress in this direction, creating mutual trust among those involved. This progress should be part of wider processes to build social cohesion (ECLAC, 2007). Indeed, cooperation and communication are key instruments for generating inclusive institutions that are perceived as fair and therefore sustainable.

I. Limitations and challenges

As discussed, the strategy based on labour-market flexibility did not lead to large-scale generation of productive employment and a major productivity gains. This indicates the need for a more balanced and integrated approach to adapting labour institutions to new technological, economic and social conditions, as well as the importance of social dialogue as a means of enhancing each country's labour regulations.

Nonetheless, there is a series of obstacles to implementing this type of process:

(i) Given the level of achievement of the aims of labour institutions in many countries, experience indicates that the priority is to extend protection schemes (Goldin, 2008).[11] In this regard, it is vital to tackle head on the scarcity of resources, which is a structural problem resulting from low taxation in the region. As pointed out by Berg and Salerno (2008), however, many countries that currently have unemployment insurance with broad coverage began to develop this when their per capita income was similar to or even lower than that of many Latin American countries today. The experiences of some Latin American and Caribbean countries are an interesting starting point for the debate on models that can be matched to the regional reality.

(ii) The region's countries have vast informal sectors that represent a very significant proportion of the labour market (although the share varies among countries). Workers in the informal sector are not covered by labour regulations, protection systems or active labour-market policies. De facto flexibility is therefore very high. And since unemployment insurance is not universal in its coverage, these workers readily take informal jobs, thereby feeding back into the growth of this sector. As pointed out by ECLAC (2008b), in this case the indicators of labour-market integration problems are underemployment, stagnating productivity and the lack of social and labour protection, rather than unemployment. Having said that, informality is a heterogeneous phenomenon and there are different options for moving towards formalization (Tokman, 2008a).

(iii) There is a lack of active social dialogue among parties, in both the design and ongoing adjustment of labour institutions. As stated, despite exceptions, the labour history of many of the region's countries has been highly antagonistic with limited collective bargaining and agreement-seeking. One key requirement in this regard is to increase representativity, autonomy and the democratic structures within unions. Furthermore, in order to be effective and equitable, labour institutions need to establish minimum levels, given that large sectors of workers do not have the level of organization or bargaining ability required. Institutions also need to define whether to extend the range of issues raised in collective bargaining while reducing the level of detail of legal regulations.

(iv) Compliance with labour regulations is low and flexibility reforms implemented in the region failed to increase it. What is more, the gap between the rules and their enforcement makes it difficult to achieve consensus, as actors use one or the other to support their arguments.

(v) The prevailing vision is a short-term one. The region's countries should adopt a long-term competitiveness strategy based on innovation and the accumulation of human capital (ECLAC, 2008a). In the current context of globalization, economic growth and the welfare of the population depend on the production of goods and services with a high level of knowledge and technological innovation. Constant innovation and adjustment processes require highly skilled workers, which make training and education (not only formal education but also lifelong learning) essential. However, there has been little debate in the countries about the long-term strategy for socio-economic development. At the same time, discussions on labour institution reform have broken away from a wider debate about that strategy. Occasionally, this has facilitated the use of labour reforms as a means of increasing profitability in the short term. These components should be considered mutually complementary to promote systemic competitiveness and the inclusion of the entire population.

It should be borne in mind, however, that there are major differences among the region's countries, with their varying levels of urbanization, wage structures and labour formality. These structural aspects affect the options available in each case, such that the countries of Latin America and the Caribbean must find their own path to integrating the various components of labour institutions, in an effective and equitable way, in keeping with their social, economic, political and cultural reality.

[11] Stating that labour markets are fundamentally flexible is not to deny the heterogeneity among the region's countries or the need and possibility to negotiate specific flexibility measures to eliminate certain bottlenecks in the labour market.

Chapter II

Labour institutions and the labour market

A. Introduction

The dual objective of the institutional framework for labour is to contribute to the effective functioning of the labour market and to protect workers, taking into account the inequalities in this market's mode of operation. Although these are common objectives, there is no single model of labour institutions that can meet them. Rather, labour institutions are the result of specific historical processes in each country. In addition, there is considerable controversy, from a theoretical viewpoint, about whether labour institutions reduce economic efficiency and social well-being, have no effect, or as Freeman (2009) asserts, strengthen them. The following sections review this debate, as well as the experiences of the region's countries with respect to some labour institutions, describing their present features as well as the principal changes they have undergone in recent years and evaluating their effects on the functioning of the region's labour markets.

B. Minimum wage

1. Characteristics and recent trends of minimum wages in the region[1]

The purpose of minimum wage policies is to reduce the incidence of low wages and protect the purchasing power of the most vulnerable workers. The basis of these policies lies in the power and information asymmetries that disproportionately disadvantage these workers, particularly when the supply of unskilled workers is large. Under

1 This section is largely based on Marinakis (2008).

these circumstances, wage setting in the absence of State intervention translates into low incomes that may even fall below the standards considered socially acceptable in terms of subsistence conditions.

The minimum wage is a labour market institution that exists in most countries. Many of them have ratified International Labour Organization (ILO) Conventions 26 (1928) and 131 (1970) on minimum wage fixing setting or have established mechanisms to implement them.

However, beyond the fact that the minimum wage is widely used, there is considerable diversity in objectives, setting mechanisms and forms of interaction with collective bargaining. In fact, in several countries where collective bargaining is weak, the minimum wage has come to play an important role in wage setting.

In some countries, such as Argentina, Brazil, Chile, Peru and Uruguay, a single minimum wage is set nationwide, while in others, such as Costa Rica, Guatemala, Honduras and Paraguay, minimum wages are set by occupation. There are also different approaches to fixing the minimum wage. In Mexico, for example, three levels are applied differentially based on the development level of the regions. In Uruguay, in addition to a national minimum wage, wage councils set specific minimum wages by economic sector. In recent years, the problems associated with complex systems based on occupation have prompted some countries to simplify them by grouping different minimum wages in categories.[2]

After sharp declines in the 1980s brought on by high inflation and stabilization policies implemented to contain aggregate demand and production costs, real minimum wages held steady in the 1990s. A calculation based on the median values of the annual rates of change in real minimum wages in the region points to a 35.7% drop between 1980 and 1990 and a much smaller decline of 1.7% in the 1990s.[3] In the 2000s, several countries initiated minimum wage recovery policies which, against a backdrop of downward-trending inflation, translated into a real increase of 10.9% between 2000 and 2007. However, when inflation spiked in 2008, the real value of minimum wages slipped back again, by 0.7%.

One of the main objectives of minimum wages is to establish a wage floor that enables workers to meet their basic needs and avoid falling into poverty.[4] To evaluate the extent to which minimum wages fulfil this objective, it is useful to compare minimum wage rates to the poverty line in each country.

Marinakis (2008) notes a very wide range of situations in the 2005-2006 period:[5] at the low end of the range are the Plurinational State of Bolivia, the Dominican Republic, Guatemala, Honduras, Mexico and Uruguay, where minimum wages are close to the income level at the poverty line, and at the high end of the scale are Argentina, Chile, Costa Rica, Panama and Paraguay, where minimum wages are equivalent to roughly double poverty line income (see figure II.1). In any event, none of the countries have minimum wages high enough for a single worker to pull a four-person family out of poverty.

Figure II.1

LATIN AMERICA (17 COUNTRIES): POVERTY LINES PER PERSON COVERED BY THE MINIMUM WAGE

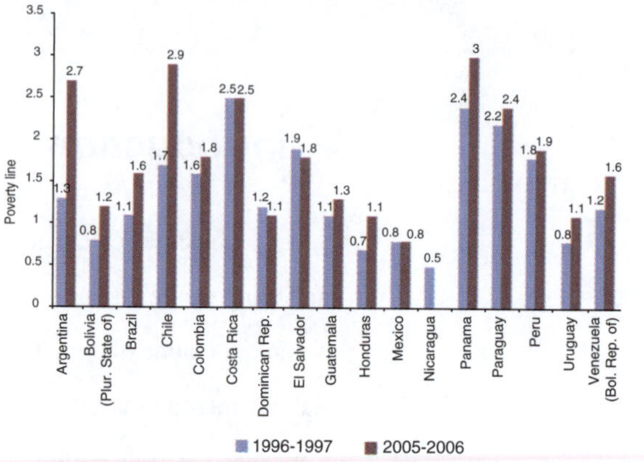

Source: A. Marinakis, *Evolución de los salarios en América Latina, 1995-2006*, Santiago, Chile, International Labour Organization (ILO), 2008.

In addition, minimum wage levels should be analysed in the context of the specific economic conditions, so the second comparison indicator is per capita GDP in each country. Here, too, there are considerable disparities between the countries. In 2006 Mexico's minimum wage represented 17% of per capita GDP and Uruguay's represented 23%, the lowest rates in the region, while Paraguay's rate was the highest at 164% of per capita GDP.[6]

A third indicator, which reflects consistency between the minimum wage and labour market indicators, is the ratio between the country's minimum and average wages. The evaluation criterion is that the minimum wage should represent the low end of the wage scale. When the minimum is very low, it will not influence the wage setting process. However, when the minimum is very high, a large percentage of actual wages will be equal to or even lower than it. In recent years, minimum to average wage ratios ranged from a low of 28% in Uruguay to a high of 98% in Paraguay. Minimum wage raising policies in, for example, Argentina, Brazil, Peru and Uruguay have pushed this ratio up in recent years (see figure II.2).

2 This is the case in Costa Rica, which went from 520 categories set by occupation, skill and industry in 1987 to 19 categories set by education and skill in 1997 (Gindling and Terrell, 2007a).

3 Calculation by ECLAC based on official country statistics.

4 Some countries have determined that minimum wages meet the needs of workers and also their families.

5 This evaluation uses the poverty line prepared by ECLAC.

6 As noted by Marinakis and Velasco (2006), in the latter case, the lower end of the wage scale is clearly below the minimum wage.

Figure II.2
LATIN AMERICA (12 COUNTRIES): RATIO OF MINIMUM WAGE TO AVERAGE WAGE
(Percentages)

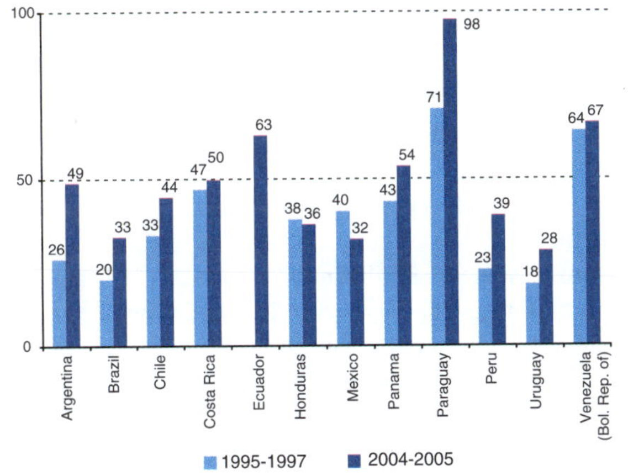

Source: A. Marinakis, *Evolución de los salarios en América Latina, 1995-2006*, Santiago, Chile, International Labour Organization (ILO), 2008.

Lastly, and in relation to the above, an indicator of the efficacy of minimum wages as a wage policy instrument is the percentage of wage-earners who earn less than the legal minimum, which reveals the rate of non-compliance with labour laws. In this connection, a significant upward adjustment in the minimum wage could result in a parallel increase in the number of workers who receive a wage lower than the legal minimum. This occurred recently in Argentina, where the percentage rose from 4% in 2000 —when, as noted earlier, the minimum wage was not operationally relevant— to 22% in 2006. This contrasts with the situation in Brazil and Chile, where minimum wage adjustments did not result in increased non-compliance with the law.

Lastly, in a large subset of countries, the non-compliance rate is higher than in the rest. This group includes Paraguay, where approximately 48% of workers earned less than the minimum wage in 2006, Ecuador, Colombia and the Bolivarian Republic of Venezuela.

2. Effects of the minimum wage on the labour market

There is a large body of literature on the effects of the minimum wage on different labour market indicators. Some of its most significant arguments and findings are presented below.

(a) The minimum wage and employment levels

From a conceptual standpoint, it is argued that when minimum wage levels and increases do not reflect productivity levels and gains, a cost is generated in the form of less employment. In addition, in this situation certain types of workers may be replaced by others —unskilled by skilled, for example— because the former are more likely to earn wages at or near the legal minimum. However, a minimum wage increase may spur productivity and strengthen domestic demand. Fields (2007, pp. 59 et seq.) concludes that the available theoretical models are ambiguous with respect to the impact of the minimum wage. Indeed, the employment effects of the minimum wage depend on the characteristics assumed by the employment demand function around the minimum wage level.

In a recent review of studies on the effects of the minimum wage on employment, Neumark and Wascher (2006) concede that the empirical evidence is mixed, but assert that most studies of highly industrialized countries, especially those considered to be the soundest methodologically, point to a negative correlation between the two variables, especially for the least skilled workers. However, the findings are very heterogeneous, principally with respect to the magnitude of the effects, and the methodological debate about the best way to analyse this relationship has yet to be resolved (Eyraud and Saget, 2008).

In any case, studies on the relationship between the minimum wage and employment levels in Latin America have yielded disparate results, with regard to both the economically active population generally and specific groups. For example, Feliciano (1998) determined that in Mexico the minimum wage adversely affects women but not men, whereas Montenegro and Pagés (2004) found the opposite in Chile: the minimum wage improves employment levels among women, compared with employment levels among adult men. Lemos (2007) discovered no significant minimum-wage effects on employment in either the public sector or the private sector in Brazil. Meanwhile, Gindling and Terrell (2007a) estimated the effect of variations in the minimum wage on total employment as low in Costa

Rica, but appreciably higher in Honduras (Gindling and Terrell, 2007a and 2007b).[7]

Moreover, because the minimum wage is generally more important for people with lower levels of education, the impact of a minimum wage increase on employment may be more significant for these groups than in aggregate terms. Sharp increases in the minimum wage in Chile in the three-year period from 1998 to 2000 were found to have adversely affected employment levels among young people, especially those with limited skills. These increases had been programmed in advance and thus did not take account of the Asian crisis that unfolded during those years (Cowan and others, 2005).[8]

Summarizing the results of studies on the effects of the minimum wage on employment in Latin America, the World Bank (2006) found that an increase in the minimum wage benefits many workers, but its negative impact (greater unemployment) is concentrated in specific groups, such as young people and women, especially those with limited skills.

Lastly, as Eyraud and Saget (2008) assert, there are a number of factors that could mitigate or even reverse the negative effect that the minimum wage may have on employment. From the supply perspective, in the wake of a minimum wage hike, business owners may see the need to change the way they organize labour for the sake of productivity. From the demand perspective, wage increases for workers with a low savings propensity can spur domestic consumption, helping to spur job creation across the economy. The outcome depends on the extent to which rises in the minimum wage are extended throughout the wage scale.

(b) The minimum wage and the informal sector

There is also a debate as to whether increases in the minimum wage affect workers in the formal sector only or whether they are also passed on to those in the informal sector. The available evidence in the region seems to indicate that the impact extends to both sectors (Gindling and Terrell, 2005; Maloney and Nuñez Mendez, 2003). In some cases, the effects even seem to be greater on the informal sector than on the formal sector.

(c) The minimum wage, poverty and inequality

The fact that most of the studies have confirmed that the elasticity of labour demand with respect to the minimum wage is significantly lower than 1 indicates that minimum wage increases could be an effective poverty-reduction tool. In poor households, the positive effects on income would far outweigh the possible negative effects on employment (Freeman, 2009). The findings of Lustig and McCleod (1997) on the ratio between the minimum wage and poverty in 22 developing countries indicate that real increases in the minimum wage can lead to lower poverty rates. The strong negative impact of minimum wage rises on employment that was observed in Honduras seems to be an exception. In any event, the differences in this area underscore the need to consider the specific characteristics of each country when determining the amount of an adjustment in the minimum wage, particularly its level relative to the factors analysed above.

Lastly, the minimum wage can have positive effects on income distribution if it benefits workers who receive lower pay, thus reducing the wage gap. Some empirical studies on less developed countries indicate that the minimum wage is effective in raising wages at the lower levels and thus reduces inequalities. In the case of Colombia, Maloney and Nuñez (2001) concluded that this was the case in both the formal and the informal sectors.

3. Role of the minimum wage in the global crisis

In the current context of the global financial crisis, it is appropriate to analyse the extent to which the minimum wage is mitigating the adverse effects of the crisis, especially among low-income workers.

In accordance with the policies to improve the purchasing power of the minimum wage that some countries in the region have implemented in recent years, thereby reviving the minimum wage as an essential instrument of wage policy, the minimum wage can help preserve the purchasing power of the lowest paid workers in these unfavourable conditions. Moreover, to the extent that this

7 The cited authors found total employment elasticity with respect to the minimum wage of -0.1 in Costa Rica and -1.0 in Honduras.

8 Between the fourth quarter of 1997 and the same period in 2000, the employment rate among Chilean adults fell from 57.5% to 55.6%, but the decline was even sharper (from 31.6% to 26.3%) among young people aged 15 to 24 years (estimate by ECLAC, based on data from Chile's National Institute of Statistics (INE)).

strategy staves off a drop in domestic consumption, it will also help diminish contractionary multiplier effects on the economy.

Protecting real wages is even more important in light of the experience of the region's countries, which seems to indicate that efforts to make up wage cuts made in times of crisis are very costly and require long periods of time. The asymmetry in wage behaviour during the different phases of the business cycle is even more pronounced for low wages, with profoundly adverse effects on distribution.

In addition, wage policy formulations should take into account the considerable heterogeneity in the relative value of the minimum wage, described above. It can be assumed that if the starting point of a policy to raise the real minimum wage were comparatively low, the policy would help support the purchasing power of poor households. However, a significant increase when the relative value of the minimum wage is higher could unleash unwanted secondary effects such as greater unemployment among specific groups and a higher non-compliance rate, which would tend to offset this favourable effect. Furthermore, during a deep crisis, the minimum wage would be a major cost factor in many companies, so under the present circumstances, many countries would be better advised to pursue a policy that protects the level of the real minimum wage, rather than one that significantly increases its purchasing power (Marinakis, 2008).

Lastly, in order to protect real wages from the negative effects of the crisis, along with efforts to buttress employment and the domestic market, social dialogue in the form of collective bargaining must be pursued within a framework of broad representation of all social actors. As noted earlier, the region has limited experience in this regard, but it would be desirable to move forward in this area, not only to moderate the effects of the economic adjustment associated with the current climate but to chart a firmer course of dialogue and consensus-building that benefits workers and employers alike.

C. Unions and collective bargaining

After having performed an important role in organizing workers and developing labour standards in the region, Latin American unionism is now facing —with obvious differences between countries— problems of lack of recognition, restrictions on the right to freedom of association and low representativeness.

Against this backdrop, the governments must follow through on their commitment to guarantee the right to freedom of association and facilitate collective bargaining, while the unions must adapt to the challenges of globalization, finding paths that accentuate its positive effects while neutralizing its negative impacts. This section analyses the state of the union movement in the region and the challenges for the future.

1. Unionism, collective bargaining and social dialogue in the region

Trade liberalization, the privatization of State-owned enterprises and the deregulation of labour markets have had a strong impact not only on the labour markets, but on the development of unionism in the region. This has been most evident in the areas of collective bargaining and the relationship between the unions and the State. Higher open unemployment rates, an increase in precarious working conditions and fewer jobs in government and manufacturing —which unions have traditionally strongly represented— have significantly weakened a union movement that is also based on the premise of a stable open-ended job (Frías, 2009).

This is in addition to the lack of union autonomy from political or government influence and internal divisions that have contributed to the fragmentation of the union movement and made it difficult to make collective demands. Furthermore, there has been a tendency towards strategies based more on confrontation than cooperation and consensus-building. In some countries reforms to labour legislation have restricted collective bargaining.

However, aside from these structural conditions, trends in unionism in the region have been very mixed in recent years, as illustrated below with some examples.

In the case of Argentina, after weakening for several years due to the aforementioned factors, the union movement has begun to recover its role in determining working conditions and to build a more direct relationship with companies through collective bargaining. As Trajtemberg (2008) indicates, Argentina's system of labour relations is based on single unionism, the centralization of collective bargaining and the mechanism of extending the coverage of agreements to all workers. Under single unionism, one union has the authority to represent all workers in a specific sector, industry or trade, upon being granted status as a legal trade union. As it is a governmental administrative agency that grants this status, the government and the unions have a close relationship. This does not preclude the presence of other unions in the same trade, but only those that have been granted legal status can represent the workers, including non-members, as a collective. In addition, they are the only ones that can collect dues through employee withholdings and establish and administer publicly funded social welfare activities, such that union relations with the State are conducted along corporativist lines.

The extension of agreements to all workers means that when specific working conditions are established for one group of workers through an industry agreement, the agreement applies obligatorily to all workers and companies within the area of representation. In other words, these negotiations benefit not only the union members but also workers who are not members of the union (Trajtemberg, 2008).

In recent years, the rate of unionization in Argentina has increased, as have the amount of collective bargaining activity and the coverage of collective labour agreements. At the same time, the rate of labour disputes in certain sectors such as education has climbed, and there are some differences between private and public negotiations. In private negotiations, strikes are shorter, which can be attributed to the existence of a greater number of institutionalized negotiation channels. Meanwhile, the public sector experiences more work stoppages, which can be attributed both to the lack of a tripartite negotiating forum (since the government plays a dual role in this case), and to the government's more limited financial capacity to meet to all union demands. Lastly, progress has been made in incorporating public services into collective bargaining, which is still only an aspiration in many countries.

In Chile, in early 2000 a number of forums were created to debate proposed labour reform legislation that would reflect the consensus of employers and workers. Among the items included in the reforms that were finally approved, which in some cases did not have the broad support of the parties, were collective bargaining and unions. With respect to collective bargaining, among other measures, the legal rights of workers who participate in collective bargaining were expanded, and provisions were approved relating to the information that workers have the right to request during collective bargaining. With respect to unions, legal protection was instituted for the establishment of unions, and the number of workers needed to form a union was lowered. Lastly, provision was made for the rehiring of workers dismissed for anti-union practices, with dismissed workers having the option to choose between being rehired and receiving a higher severance payment (Frías, 2009).

In Mexico, close relations between unions and the government date back to the end of the Mexican Revolution and were consolidated with the official incorporation of the union confederations into the Party of the Mexican Revolution (predecessor to the Institutional Revolutionary Party, or PRI) in 1938. The network of corporate relations thus formed led, in the 1960s, to quotas of popularly elected government positions for union leaders, union intervention in tripartite bodies associated with social security, union influence in the design of labour policy, the spread of collective hiring practices and of the system of contractual benefits, and clientelist relations with workers at the company level. Since the mid-1980s, scope for union activity has been shrinking owing to changes in the organization of labour and the emergence of a younger, more female working class with low wages, few skills, high turnover and no union tradition (De la Garza Toledo, 2002).

In the countries of Central America, many of which are characterized by complex labour and social conditions, there is a major shortage of institutionally recognized unions, as well as obstacles and impediments to the right to freedom of association and weaknesses in the area of collective bargaining, which is reflected in the fact that Central America leads the region and the world in the number of complaints filed with ILO (Sepúlveda Malbrán, Schapira-Felderhoff and Delpech, 2009). Accordingly, the unionization rate is very low and most workers in dependent employment lack access to collective bargaining. In many Central American countries, unionism is also stymied by the magnitude of the informal sector, which makes it hard to organize microenterprise and own-account workers.

In the Caribbean, the rate of unionization has fallen from between 30% and 40% in the 1960s to between 20% and 30% in recent years. However, unions still play an important role in key sectors of the economy such as government, ports, public infrastructure services and other services such as hotels and banks. Although it fluctuates, the rate of labour disputes has fallen compared to the past (Downes, 2009).

2. Effects of unions and collective bargaining on the performance of companies and the labour market

From a conceptual viewpoint, union involvement in wage-setting through collective bargaining is said to tend to compress income distribution and decouple pay from worker productivity.

There are many studies that attempt to evaluate this and other hypotheses on the impact of union action on labour market performance. According to one finding, there is a wage gap in favour of unionized workers, and this gap is wider at the lower end of the wage scale. In addition, a number of studies have found that collective bargaining tends to reduce wage dispersion, which should have a positive effect on income distribution (Cahuc and Zylberberg, 2004; Khan, 2003; Aidt and Tzannatos, 2002).

Popli (2006) confirmed these findings in Mexico. Fairris (2005, 2006) found a positive correlation between unionization and worker training, as a result of which unionized firms in Mexico have a higher level of productivity than their non-unionized counterparts. Conversely, Maloney and Ribeiro (1999) concluded that unionization is associated with an increase in employment, which would indicate lower productivity.

A wage gap in favour of unionized workers has also been observed in Brazil. Specifically, Menezes-Filho and others (2005) analysed panel data for a group of manufacturing firms between 1988 and 1998, a period in which union density in the country declined, and concluded that an increase in unionization tends to lower corporate profits, while boosting productivity and employment. However, this effect weakens when the unionization rate reaches 50% or higher. Unionization leads to wage gains of about 12%. The positive link between the introduction of profit-sharing arrangements and corporate performance appears to be stronger in more highly unionized companies. According to the authors, this could indicate improved communication between the two parties that promotes the effective functioning of this type of system.

Cassoni, Labadie and Fachola (2005) studied the case of Uruguay in 1988-1995, when in addition to the liberalization process, the centralized wage bargaining system was changed to a company-level system. Their findings seem to indicate that unionization translates into higher wage and employment levels and promotes investment as firms substitute capital for labour. In addition, unionization was found to have a positive effect on productivity. The authors asserted that wage increases generated by union activity induce companies to adopt more capital-intensive technologies, boosting productivity. Cassoni, Allen and Labadie (2000) concluded that the elasticity of employment with respect to output and wages falls when collective bargaining is involved, which indicates a reduction in employment flexibility.

In Argentina, too, unionization and collective bargaining have been seen to reduce wage dispersion (Trajtemberg, 2008). Meanwhile, using data from 1994-1996 in Peru, Saavedra and Torero (2005) posited that a reduction in the profitability of manufacturing companies was linked to union activity, but determined that the effect on labour productivity was not significant. By contrast, Urízar and Lée (2005) reported that the productivity of unionized coffee plantations in Guatemala fell in the period 1992-2000 compared to the productivity of other companies.

Based on the evidence described above, unionization is generally observed to have a positive effect on wages, while reducing wage dispersion and increasing instruction and training levels. However, there is also considerable heterogeneity in the findings between countries, industries and types of companies.

3. Options for strengthening worker representation and collective bargaining

Based not only on the weaknesses but also on the positive experiences in the region, the following set of actions have been identified to bolster unionism's contribution to the strengthening and improvement of an institutional framework for labour that promotes the creation of quality jobs, contributes to dialogue and brings about a sustained improvement in labour relations:[9]

[9] See Frías (2009).

(i) Expand the representativeness of unions to include the full spectrum of unprotected sectors, such as temporary, part-time and subcontracted workers.

(ii) Emphasize organizational, educational and training activities in sectors with low levels of unionization. This requires in-house training programmes or access to training through agreements with other institutions, not only to provide training to union members, but also to disseminate this knowledge to larger segments of the population.

(iii) Secure greater union commitment to company development, and thus to the challenge of increasing productivity and improving quality by contributing ideas and seeking consensus.

(iv) Recognize unions not only as agents for their members but as stakeholders in the growth of the companies and the development of the country. This calls for a process of mutual adaptation between employers and unions so they can develop joint projects and strategies, which also requires greater participation by workers through, for example, stock ownership plans.

(v) Work on strengthening unions from the inside, to make them more representative and better managed. This entails, among other measures, promoting democratic relations within unions, making management more transparent and leaders more accountable, learning about the real situation of their membership base, promoting the rotation of positions, overhauling structures and establishing internal dispute resolution mechanisms. Unions must also become gradually more autonomous from political parties to ensure that the interests of the workers prevail.

(vi) Establish agreements with civil society organizations, building strategic partnerships with other sectors.

(vii) Work towards incorporating national unions into the international union movement, which will enable the unions to learn about and gather experiences from other contexts, as well as receive greater solidarity support and training.

The foregoing suggests that in order to link the prevailing trends in the union movement with the modern institutional framework for labour in a positive way that addresses the interests of workers and employers alike, the unions must be overhauled in a way that allows them to become a key social and labour stakeholder in the development of the countries.

At the same time, employers must recognize the potential of dialogue with the union movement for achieving high levels of productivity and efficiency, and spurring growth, development and social cohesion. Lastly, governments must fulfill their international commitment to promote, respect and protect unionism and the safety of union members, as a basic condition for building fair, productive labour relations.[10]

D. Unemployment protection

1. Characteristics of unemployment protection mechanisms[11]

The existence of market failures that prevent the provision of optimal insurance against the contingency of unemployment is the argument that is typically invoked to justify implementation of a public job-loss protection policy (Velásquez Pinto, 2009a). This is why, to a greater or lesser extent, countries have implemented various types of public safety nets for unemployed workers, with differing designs and objectives. In Latin America and the Caribbean, there are at least four different mechanisms: (i) unemployment insurance; (ii) severance payment; (iii) individual savings accounts; and (iv) advance notice of dismissal.

(a) Unemployment insurance

At present, only seven countries in the region have unemployment insurance, as follows: Argentina, Barbados, the Bolivarian Republic of Venezuela, Brazil, Chile, Ecuador and Uruguay. The purpose of unemployment insurance is to provide financial support during job searches, mitigate

[10] According to the International Trade Union Confederation (ITUC, 2009), in 2008 at least 76 union members were killed worldwide as a result of their actions in defense of worker rights; 66 of them were in Latin America.

[11] This section is largely based on Velásquez Pinto (2009b).

the effects of lack of employment income and prevent situational poverty due to job loss.

These types of systems are financed with monthly contributions from participants (workers, companies or both) or with fiscal resources. In certain cases, the State covers operating deficits.

In general, the extant mechanisms follow the logic of a pay-as-you-go system and could thus be characterized as group insurance arrangements. The exception to this traditional design in the region is Chile's unemployment insurance system, which consists of individual capitalization accounts that are funded by employee and employer contributions and an unemployment solidarity fund, which operates as a distribution fund and is financed by employer contributions and a specific annual contribution by the State. If unemployed workers meet certain conditions, they have access to the fund as a backstop to their individual accounts.

Along with Chile's new unemployment insurance, the changes made to Uruguay's unemployment insurance system in 2008 were the most sweeping reforms of the decade and were introduced to improve the coverage and benefits of unemployment insurance. In Uruguay, the system is financed with general revenue and the funds that come from a single social security contribution that covers, among other things, disability, survivor, maternity and family benefits, in addition to old-age benefits. As part of these reforms, dismissed workers who have completed their employment contract or who have been totally or partially laid off have access to insurance. Workers with more than one job receive a subsidy when dismissal is found to have occurred in the higher-paying job. In addition, a system of declining benefits was created to incentivize job-seeking; the minimum amount of the benefit was doubled; the subsidy was increased by 20% for workers who are married or cohabiting, or have minor children or older children with disabilities or relatives in their care; and it was made obligatory to attend training courses during the benefit period.

In terms of scope of application, the programmes in place in the region have generally been designed to protect wage earners in the formal non-farm sector who have open-ended contracts. However, in recent years, some countries have been expanding the scope of these programmes to include other groups, such as rural or temporary workers. For example, in Argentina and Brazil coverage was extended to temporary and seasonal farm workers, and in Uruguay domestic workers are now covered. In the case of Chile, the conditions of insurance benefits have been amended to extend access to workers with fixed-term contracts. In Argentina, Brazil and Chile, the system does not extend to public-sector workers, who tend to be covered by special job security and dismissal compensation provisions.

Lastly, with respect to benefit amounts, most are determined as a percentage of average earnings received during the period leading up to dismissal (between 50% and 60%). In some cases, minimum and maximum benefit amounts are also set. Moreover, as an incentive for active job searching, a decreasing benefit schedule is usually created. An exception is Ecuador, which established a lump-sum benefit payable only if a worker remains unemployed 60 days after dismissal.

(b) Severance pay

Severance payments are monetary sums that companies must pay workers in the case of dismissals "without just cause" or "due to the needs of the company." Each country establishes the specific conditions under which a dismissal falls into one of these categories. This is the most frequently used mechanism for protecting the unemployed in the region's countries. Unlike unemployment insurance, it not only provides the unemployed worker with resources in the case of these types of dismissals, but also performs the function of discouraging dismissals, thereby promoting job protection.

Under this mechanism, the benefit is granted in the form of a lump-sum payment upon termination of employment, and the amount is based on the wage earned by the dismissed worker and the length of time in the position. The increase in the benefit according to job experience is based on the premise that the duration of unemployment increases with years of work and the acquisition of specific skills. However, some countries, including the Bolivarian Republic of Venezuela, Chile and Peru, specify a ceiling for severance pay. In all of the countries, the beneficiaries are dependently employed workers with open-ended contracts.

The purpose of severance provisions is to discourage unfair dismissals or dismissals resulting from temporary situations of falling business activity and rising employer costs. Severance pay is also intended to provide economic support in the absence of employment income after dismissal. However, severance payments have been criticized for a number of reasons. One is the potential inability of a company to pay if it is experiencing financial problems at the time of the dismissal. These problems tend to mount during the downswing in the business cycle, precisely when the unemployment risk is highest.

Another criticism is that this instrument acts as a disincentive to labour mobility, slowing global productivity growth. It is further argued that the rising costs associated with length of service discourage the dismissal of long-term workers, shifting the cost of adjustment mainly to younger workers. Lastly, there is a "moral hazard" in the sense that longstanding company employees may relax their efforts if they judge that their employer cannot afford to fire them.

In the face of these criticisms, proposals have been made on numerous occasions to eliminate this mechanism or supplement it with unemployment insurance. The assertion is that unemployment insurance would help lower severance pay. However, as Blanchard (2003) maintained, neither of the two instruments are perfect substitutes due to the intrinsic legitimacy of severance pay, its intended disincentive effect on dismissals and the limitations related to insurance, especially in the region's countries.

(c) Unemployment protection systems based on individual accounts

This instrument consists in the regular accumulation of contributions made by workers and employers that can be withdrawn by the worker upon termination of employment, often regardless of the reason for termination.

In recent years, several countries in the region have been introducing individual accounts as an alternative to severance pay. A few have already been using this instrument for some time, such as Argentina, where a system is in place in the construction sector.[12] In the case of Brazil, in addition to the regular required contributions, compensation —a percentage of the accumulated balance in the account— has been established for dismissals "without just cause." Meanwhile, Panama allows workers to make deposits in these accounts, which also serve as collateral for mortgage loans.

In Peru, the system is financed with an individual fund into which employers make semiannual contributions equivalent to 50% of wages. As in the previous case, workers are authorized to withdraw contributions in emergencies or to use them as security for a loan. In Colombia, partial withdrawals are authorized to finance education and housing expenses and to use as collateral for mortgage loans.

In the Bolivarian Republic of Venezuela, workers may choose to have employer contributions deposited into an individual account at a financial institution or to keep them with the company. In the latter case, the employer must guarantee a rate of return set by the central bank.

Lastly, as previously noted, the Chilean unemployment insurance system consists of individual accounts in conjunction with an unemployment solidarity fund. This new system directly links the two instruments as sources of financing for benefits in the event of dismissal for economic reasons. In addition, the system is tied to the severance pay mechanism, so that previous employer contributions are deducted from the severance pay upon termination of an employment contract. Use of this combined mechanism has risen sharply, with nearly 73% of private-sector wage-earners making contributions in 2007. This is explained by the fact that enrolment in the system is mandatory and automatic upon signature of an employment contract. In 2008 new reforms were implemented to increase the scope and benefits of this mechanism.

(d) Advance notice of dismissal

This mechanism requires the employer to notify the worker in advance that he or she will be dismissed, so as to give the worker time to look for a new job. In general, one or two months of advance notice is stipulated. If advance notice is not provided, the employer must add pay for the notice period to the dismissal costs. This mechanism covers formal wage earners with open-ended contracts.

2. Effects of unemployment protection policies on labour-market performance

The various instruments for protecting unemployed workers can have positive or negative effects on labour market indicators. Among their positive effects, these monetary transfers help mitigate the income loss experienced by individuals and their families as a result of unemployment and, by discouraging dismissals —in the case of severance pay— they reduce the erosion of general and specific human capital, boosting overall productivity. Conversely, these instruments are said to generate higher adjustment costs, which can reduce the ability to adapt to changing economic conditions.

The following section analyses the specific arguments made in relation to each of these instruments.

[12] The employer must make monthly contributions equal to 12% of wages during the first year and 8% thereafter, which are deposited in individual accounts in banking institutions (Velásquez Pinto, 2009b).

(a) Effects of unemployment insurance

It is argued that unemployment insurance reduces the opportunity cost of job loss and to increase in the duration of unemployment spells (moral hazard). The most salient of the arguments commonly invoked in relation to the repercussions of unemployment insurance on productivity and unemployment and employment rates are the following:

(i) Because unemployment insurance is financed with payroll contributions, it contributes to higher labour costs and lower labour demand. In addition, by increasing the reservation wage of unemployed workers, unemployment insurance raises the wage rate at which a worker will accept employment.

(ii) It has been suggested that there is a positive correlation between the level and period of unemployment benefits and the lengthening of unemployment spells as a result of lower unemployment exit rates (Narendranathan, Nicke and Stern, 1985; Meyer, 1990; Katz and Meyer, 1990; Carling, Edin and Holmlund, 1996; Bover, Arellano and Bentolila, 1996). However, the estimates for developed countries indicate that the benefit amount generally has a limited effect on the average duration of unemployment spells.[13] As for the effects of the length of the benefit period, the evidence shows that the probability of exiting unemployment increases as the insurance expiry date approaches.[14] A recent study (Fitzenberger and Wilke, 2007) indicates that the benefit period has very little effect on job search times and post-unemployment wages, but a high replacement rate leads to longer unemployment spells at the low end of the wage scale.

(iii) Other studies indicate that although there is a direct effect from unemployment insurance, longer benefit periods allow for more efficient job searches and promote better matching between the skills of wage earners and job requirements, which leads to greater job security and by extension reduces future employment-to-unemployment flows.[15]

(iv) It can also be argued that by allowing for a longer job search period, unemployment benefits save workers from having to quickly accept a job with lower pay and of poorer quality than their last position. For example, unemployment insurance can reduce the need to accept informal employment, helping to break the unemployment-to-informal employment cycle typical of the countries in the region.

(v) The longer unemployment spells resulting from unemployment insurance could adversely affect post-unemployment wages and increase the probability of another unemployment spell (scarring effect of unemployment).[16] The argument is that in a context of information asymmetry between employers and employees, the former could interpret the latter's unemployment experience as a sign of low productivity and reject an applicant as a candidate for a vacancy or hire the applicant at a lower wage. It is further argued that an unemployment spell adversely affects workers' general and specific human capital, with effects similar to those described above. These effects would become more pronounced with the duration of the unemployment spell.

(vi) A higher benefit amount could reduce employment-to-inactivity flows and create incentives for certain groups, such as women, to enter the workforce. Moreover, the existence of unemployment insurance could lead to an increase in workforce participation rates, as workers position themselves to gain access to benefits at a later time, causing both the employment rate and the unemployment rate to rise.[17]

(vii) Unemployment insurance could increase the frequency of unemployment-to-employment transition periods among those who are not eligible to receive benefits. The best way to safeguard against the risk of future unemployment is to return to work, inasmuch as the right to future protection can be obtained only through a job registered in the social security system.

(viii) A recent study on Chile (Sanhueza and Castillo, 2008) suggests that workers who have unemployment insurance are less likely to become unemployed, and

[13] For example, in the case of the United States, Meyer (1990) found that an increase of 10% in the benefit amount translated to an average increase of 1.5 weeks in the duration of the unemployment period. In the United Kingdom, the estimates are: 1.0 weeks in the study by Lancaster and Nickell (1980) and 0.5 weeks in the study by Narendranathan, Nicke and Stern (1985). See a compilation and critical review of the available empirical studies on this topic in Atkinson and Micklewright (1991).

[14] Among others, Katz and Meyer (1990) and Cebrián and others (1996).

[15] Ehrenberg and Oaxaca (1976) were the first to consider the effect of insurance on post-unemployment outcomes, particularly wages. Other treatments of this topic include studies by Belzil (2001), van Ours and Vodopivec (2006) and Tatsiramos (2006).

[16] For more information, see Arulampalam, Booth and Taylor (2000), Gregg and Wadsworth (1996), Arulampalam (2000), Gregory and Jukes (1997), Fitzenberger and Wilke (2007) and van Ours and Vodopivec (2006).

[17] Card and Riddell (1993) analysed the effects of the introduction of unemployment insurance on the unemployment rate in Canada and concluded that a significant portion of the increase in the rate could be attributed to the exit from inactivity. This incentive for workforce participation could be considered a positive effect, inasmuch as a portion of the new participants in the labour market obtained jobs, which caused the employment rate to rise. This underscores the importance of "reading" the unemployment rate in tandem with the employment rate.

the duration of unemployment spells is shorter for them than for those without access to unemployment benefits. The authors offer two possible explanations: either the Chilean system is designed effectively or there is segmentation, with the workers who have access to benefits also being those with the best chances of finding a job.

Based on the many arguments described, the real effect of unemployment insurance on labour indicators depends on the specific characteristics of each system, its design, requirements and benefits, as well as on the macroeconomic and labour-market context. It is also likely that welfare programmes and unemployment insurance produce different effects. Therefore, the challenge is to design mechanisms that perform their protective function but also establish effective incentives, help reduce possible distortions in the labour market and possess financing mechanisms that ensure their long-term sustainability.

(b) Effects of severance pay

Unintended effects similar to those mentioned above tend to be attributed to severance pay also. In addition, it is argued that severance pay could induce dismissal-seeking behaviour on the part of workers as a way to gain access to these benefits. Labour disputes about severance pay generally make up the largest portion of the caseload of labour tribunals in Latin America, which demonstrates that in many cases this benefit does not necessarily reach workers when they need it.

In an influential work, Heckman and Pagés (2003) analysed the anticipated costs associated with the termination of employment contracts —in terms of monthly wages— using information on 17 countries in Latin America and 23 member countries of the Organisation for Economic Co-operation and Development (OECD). The authors concluded, among other things, that in Latin America high adjustment costs could hinder job creation and lengthen the duration of unemployment. While acknowledging that the comparative results of their study were not very robust in econometric terms, they emphasized that the results were consistent with the findings of other studies carried out at the national level.[18] However, Berg and Kucera (2008) point out that in only two of the eight country studies presented in the work edited by Heckman and Pagés (2004) were the effects of regulations on employment and unemployment levels observed to be statistically significant. As suggested by Velásquez Pinto (2009b), this type of information may not be sufficient to draw a conclusion about the real degree of rigidity, given that the specific relationship between labour regulations and the degree of labour market flexibility in each country must be considered.

Moreover, inasmuch as these types of benefits are available to formal workers only, it is concluded that severance pay provisions reinforce segmentation and inequality. However, in general it seems wise to develop strategies that gradually expand the coverage of protection systems, which should be designed with the potential positive and negative effects of the various instruments in mind.

Lastly, it should be noted that dismissal disincentives can boost productivity by reducing turnover and allowing for more stable employment relationships with a major specific training component.

(c) Effects of individual accounts

One of the arguments in favour of individual savings accounts is that, unlike severance pay, regular contributions by the employer guarantee the availability of funds upon termination of employment, mitigating the risk of non-payment. The low cost of administering these accounts, which can be handled by the local financial system, is also mentioned.

Critics of the system argue that the funds could be used for purposes other than unemployment, either through authorization to that effect or agreements to simulate a dismissal in order to make use of the accumulated balance at a given time. The occurrence of such conduct has been confirmed in Brazil (Barros Corseuil and Foguel, 1999) as well as in Peru, where the opportunity to withdraw funds has, in practice, eroded protection for unemployed workers and turned the accounts into a de facto wage increase (Velásquez Pinto, 2009b).

However, one of the most important questions about this system concerns its actual capacity to protect the unemployed. Specifically, nothing guarantees that upon dismissal a worker will have accumulated sufficient contributions to finance long or recurring unemployment spells. This means that this instrument must be supplemented by others, as in Chile where a distribution fund is financed with employer and government contributions.

Lastly, like unemployment insurance, individual accounts are not a perfect substitute for severance pay. This is because, by converting a contingency cost into a fixed cost, this mechanism either fails to discourage dismissals or acts as only a partial disincentive, as in the case of Brazil where the employer must supplement the account balance when a worker is dismissed "without just cause."

---

18 Saavedra and Torero (2000) in the case of Peru; Mondino and Montoya (2000) in the case of Argentina and Kluger (2002) in the case of Colombia.

3. Scope of unemployment insurance mechanisms and integration with other programmes

By way of conclusion, this section offers a brief assessment of unemployment insurance mechanisms from the viewpoint of their coverage and integration with other existing programmes. The empirical evidence indicates that the situation in the region falls short in at least three areas: field of action, benefit amount and integration with other programmes.

As shown in table II.1, unemployment insurance coverage is very limited. In the past no more than 10% of the unemployed have been covered, except in the case of Uruguay, where coverage has reached 20%. Due to mandatory enrolment in the unemployment insurance programme for new employment contracts, coverage in Chile rose to 19.6% in 2007, while in Uruguay it climbed to 13.6% that year.

Table II.1

UNEMPLOYMENT INSURANCE COVERAGE

(Percentages of the total unemployed population)

Year	Argentina	Chile	Brazil	Ecuador	Uruguay
1995	5.9	...	12.0	2.3	15.8
1996	6.3	...	9.2	5.6	12.1
1997	5.1	...	8.6	6.2	11.3
1998	5.5	...	6.2	4.5	14.3
1999	6.4	...	6.0	3.1	17.0
2000	6.4	...	6.1	3.5	18.7
2001	6.5	...	7.7	4.1	16.2
2002	7.4	...	4.1	4.8	16.9
2003	5.1	2.1	4.0	2.7	9.1
2004	4.1	5.7	4.0	2.8	8.4
2005	3.2	9.7	4.3	...	10.5
2006	4.5	15.7	5.3	...	11.2
2007	4.7	19.6	5.6	...	13.6

Source: Mario Velásquez Pinto, "Seguros de desempleo y funcionamiento eficiente y equitativo de los mercados de trabajo," document presented at the workshop Challenges confronted by labour institutions, Santiago, Chile, Economic Commission for Latin America and the Caribbean (ECLAC), April 2009.

The factors associated with this sparse insurance coverage are the high percentage of informal jobs and high labour turnover —which prevents the accumulation of a minimum of contributions— driven, in many cases, by the increase in fixed-term contracts. These structural obstacles also hinder the efficacy of the other unemployment protection instruments. For example, Escobar (2009) calculates that only 6.4% of unemployed workers in Chile receive years-of-service compensation.

Another characteristic of these programmes in the region is that the benefits are low, which is directly related to the low average wages in the economies. In these circumstances, programmes must be designed either to generate an income that does not diverge greatly from the unemployed worker's previous wage —which could cause financing problems— or to contain the cost of the benefits, which would not then be enough to provide for the family's subsistence needs (Velásquez Pinto, 2009b).

Lastly, another common characteristic of unemployment insurance schemes in the region is the lack of integration with other active labour market policies. In particular, they tend to have few ties to training programmes, while the insurance beneficiaries are frequently observed to receive no job search assistance.[19]

In short, the protection of unemployed workers is one of the weakest components of labour market regulation in Latin America and the Caribbean. Very few countries have protection systems other than severance pay, and coverage and benefits are generally very low. As a result of these limitations, the region's countries often make use of emergency public-sector job creation programmes or non-contributory income transfer schemes.

Based on this overview, it may be concluded that the region must make significant progress in expanding and improving protection for unemployed workers, for both social and economic reasons. The main challenge in this area is to design protection systems that incorporate employer participation without increasing non-wage labour costs excessively. They must also have broad coverage, limit possible moral hazard and be integrated with active policies to facilitate workforce adjustment. In any event, the options that are available in this regard are closely related to the specific productive structure and productivity levels of individual countries (see box II.1).

---

19 In the current financial crisis, some countries that have unemployment insurance are using their resources to implement training programmes as a way of forestalling dismissals while improving future productivity (ECLAC/ILO, 2009).

Box II.1

FORMALIZATION, SOCIAL PROTECTION AND STRUCTURAL HETEROGENEITY

An analysis of reforms aimed at enhancing the labour market's ability to adapt to changing conditions, especially in the countries of Latin America during the 1980s and 1990s, points to the risk of an uneven impact that would damage the position of workers. In fact, the reforms that were launched focused on labour costs and regulations, relegating compensation for the loss of rights and benefits to the potential trickle-down effects that prospective growth would have on employment. The limits of that growth and its effects indicate that future attempts to regulate the labour market should balance the interests of workers and employers, for which explicit, tangible compensation mechanisms are needed.

Efforts to find impartial mechanisms to invigorate the labour market, however, inevitably come up against the structural limitations of the region's economies, which include informality and limited access to the social safety net.

Some countries have made progress in formalizing the workforce, as noted by Tokman (2008a), who proposed a strategy based on labour inspections, the simplification of procedures and the clarification of ambiguous employment relationships, among other things. These types of measures, although instrumental to the modernization of the labour markets, have limited potential in many of the region's countries in which the vast majority of workers are in the informal sector.

Increasing companies' options for adapting certain aspects of employment to their short-term needs leads to the deterioration of working conditions in the absence of effective social protection mechanisms. These mechanisms help mitigate the risks associated with fluctuations in employment and the resulting uncertainty with respect to well-being. Although formalization of the workforce is a valid option that boosts access to protection, the high proportion of unregistered businesses and the low productivity of many workers and employers limit the potential of this strategy in most of the region's countries. In many of them, universalizing social protection and decoupling it from the labour sector could be pursued as prerequisites of reforms intended to increase the capacity of companies to adjust to changing market conditions.

However, the introduction (or substantial reform) of a social safety net is a costly process, in both political and fiscal terms, and must generally be done gradually. Recent experience in some countries in the region suggests that partial progress has been made in this direction. For example, the extension of family allowances to informal workers and other groups in Uruguay is a clear step towards universal coverage of children (Arim, Cruces and Vigorito, 2009), and programmes such as *Bolsa Familia* in Brazil and *Oportunidades* in Mexico constitute progress in the same direction. In areas more directly related to labour, the expansion of non-contributory pensions in Brazil and Chile is an important step (Bertranou and others, 2007a). However, the region has seen less progress in the area of unemployment insurance, as evidenced by sparse coverage, low benefit levels with respect to wages and, above all, the exclusion of informal workers. Unemployment insurance is the key to reducing the adverse impact of transitions and promoting more efficient employment relations in the developed economies.

Due to its structural heterogeneity, the region's common objectives cannot be met with any single approach. The characteristics of the aforementioned measures —formalization and expansion of the social safety net— depend on the development of the specific labour markets of each country and, within each country, on considerations such as the urban-rural dimension. In the case of some less-developed markets, formalization is secondary in importance to the development of non-contributory mechanisms (ECLAC, 2006). Promoting education and training to support worker productivity is also essential. Specifically in the labour sector, the precariousness of working conditions suggests that more basic concerns must first be addressed, such as the "minimum threshold" of regulation of working conditions proposed by Tokman (2008a). Other countries can focus on more targeted formalization activities, especially in urban areas where the informal sector is smaller. With varying degrees of difficulty, and with proposals tailored to their needs, all of the countries in the region can make progress in expanding the social safety net.

Source: Guillermo Cruces and Andrés Ham, "La flexibilidad laboral en América Latina: las reformas pasadas y las perspectivas futuras," Santiago, Chile, Economic Commission for Latin America and the Caribbean (ECLAC), 2009, unpublished.

Chapter III

Active labour-market policies

A. Overview

Active labour-market policies are public sector interventions designed to prevent unemployment, improve employability, and underpin the demand for labour. In particular, they aim to:[1]

- Enhance worker employability by providing training programmes and promoting labour-market participation.
- Increase the demand for labour through programmes that generate direct temporary wage-earning jobs, wage or employment subsidies, or programmes to promote productive enterprise.
- Improve the workings of the labour market by providing information services and guidance in job-search and labour intermediation.

One of the advantages of active labour-market policies is that they command greater consensus among workers and employers than other approaches. The two areas in which interests tend to converge most are training programmes and employment services; but there is also agreement on programmes to create direct jobs or support microenterprise. The consensus surrounding these policies makes it a lot easier to forge strategic partnerships between the stakeholders, in order to encourage and underpin public initiatives of this type.

In the developed world, particularly among countries of the Organisation for Economic Co-operation and Development (OECD), active labour-market policies (which have a long history in many cases) have become increasingly important in view of the criticisms made of passive labour market policies in a situation of rising unemployment.

The region is currently implementing many programmes under a variety of modalities. Although these have been made more effective and efficient and fairer in recent years, the schemes implemented still show major shortcomings in these three indicators, as discussed below.

1 This follows the classification used by the International Labour Organization (ILO).

B. Active labour-market policies: strengths and weaknesses

1. Occupational training programmes

Training programmes are usually broadly accepted by all parties, given their potential for promoting productivity, job stability, upwardly mobile employment careers and wages. In particular, it is recognized that skilled labour helps enhance the region's systemic competitiveness, while knowledge acquisition is seen as an essential component of employability that facilitates labour-market participation generally and the re-engagement of the unemployed in particular.

Nonetheless, evaluations of this type of programme around the world have not always been favourable. In a review of the experiences of 49 countries Betcherman, Olivas and Dar (2004) note that several programmes achieved positive results by making it easier to find a job (although they failed to find a positive impact on wages). Nonetheless, positive results are obtained almost exclusively in developed countries and transition economies, while the benefits are marginal in many others. On-the-job training and participation by employers produced better results than classroom-based training.

The results of valuations in Latin America have also been mixed, even in different assessments of the same programme. For example, using data for 1997, an evaluation of the global supply of training provided by the National Apprenticeship Service (SENA) in Colombia (Medina and Núñez, 2001), shows that the effects on labour-market participation have been insignificant for the various beneficiary groups. The impact on earnings was also insignificant. Nonetheless, according to Sarmiento and others (2007), who use data for 2003, SENA-certified training courses increase the likelihood of being employed by 10%, and raise labour incomes by a similar amount.

The Mexican Job Training Programme for Unemployed Workers (PROBECAT) (now known as BECATE) was introduced in 1984 to cushion the adverse impact of the debt crisis on the labour market. The programme provided training for unemployed workers in short (six-month) courses, with the aim of improving their chances of rejoining the labour market and bolstering their income during the transition. Participants were paid a minimum wage during the training period, and local employment offices provided job placement services. Although training courses were initially provided in secondary schools and training centres, an on-the-job training module was introduced later to strengthen the link with the productive sector, with the employers in question being required to hire at least 70% of those trained. In 1995, a third training module was added to cover own-account workers in response to the 1994 financial crisis (Tokman, 2009).

This programme has been evaluated four times since its creation, giving positive results in two cases, insignificant in another, and variable according to personal characteristics, regions and institutions, in the last. The first evaluation was performed by the World Bank (Revenga, Riboud and Tan, 1994), and the second by the Ministry of Labour (STPS, 1995). These two evaluations show that participants spent less time job-seeking compared to non-participants and subsequently earned higher wages. Nonetheless, the results in both cases were only valid for men.

The third evaluation, also performed by the World Bank, used a different methodology (Wodon and Marinowa, 1999), but did not find significant positive results in terms of either employment or wages. On the contrary, negative effects were detected in job search in the case of men who received training in classrooms. The fourth evaluation analysed the period 1984-1998 and found positive results that were differentiated by individual characteristics, regions, modalities and institutions (Calderón-Madrid and Trejo, 2001). The wage increases for participants, in relation to non-participants, seemed to be greater for women than for men. On-the-job training is more effective than training in the classroom, and private-sector institutions achieve better results than those operated by the government.

These programmes in the region have undergone major changes in recent years, including the following: greater diversification among the suppliers of training, a larger private-sector presence, and decentralization of programmes in the public sector; a wider range of beneficiaries (employed workers with skills, youth without job experience, unemployed workers, among others), and the design of different programmes to address the specific problems being faced by the target public; certification of the skills needed by broadening the supply of training and recognizing informal learning; better matching of training with the requirements of labour demand, through participation by firms and, in some cases, labour unions; new public financing instruments for these programmes.

Special training mechanisms have been introduced or strengthened during the current crisis. Firstly, several countries (such as Argentina, Chile and Uruguay) provide incentives to train workers who are at risk of dismissal owing to the critical circumstances being endured by their firms (ECLAC/ILO, 2009). In this way, workers keep their jobs and receive training to improve their productivity for when they resume their tasks. Secondly, retraining programmes are being implemented (in Peru for example) for unemployed workers with slim chances of returning to their previous occupation.

Despite recent changes, training systems in the region still have major shortcomings. For example, their coverage is normally limited and it is generally large firms that make use of the programmes and provide greater benefits to higher-ranking staff, so their equity effect is questionable. Lastly, these systems do not usually form part of a long-term development strategy, which they would have to in order to contribute optimally to a sustained increase in systemic competitiveness (ECLAC, 2004).

The outcome of these programmes depends on a number of conditions. In particular, their success seems to require strict targeting, relatively small scale, the existence of a recognized qualification that is valued in the labour market and, above all, work in the firm. Training is ineffective for finding work in cyclical downswings when the demand for labour is weak. Nonetheless, training programmes for young people in Latin America and the Caribbean have functioned relatively well, and have had a positive effect on both employment and the income of their participants.[2] There is a consensus that preventive measures are needed to combat high levels of youth unemployment, such as access to duration of quality school education.[3]

In brief, when designing training systems, the following issues need to be borne in mind:

- There is a close link between the results of employment training and education systems and the population's general knowledge. Weaknesses in general education reduce the capacity of training programmes to improve workers' labour-market participation. It is therefore essential to promote an education of better coverage, quality, duration and equity in the region.
- Training systems need to adapt better to the different needs of the various segments of the productive system and the labour force, by diversifying the programmes supplied.
- Given the major changes that have occurred in production practices, a permanent training system needs to be set up to help workers adapt to new technologies and improve their chances of entering the labour market.
- Competency-based training needs to be strengthened. This entails transmitting not only specific knowledge, but also the capacity to adapt to new tasks and technologies in different settings. The advantage of competencies is that they can be applied in different jobs, which improves employability.

The supply of training needs to be accredited and transparent, and its results need to be evaluated using recognized and agreed-upon skill certification systems.[4]

2. Employment services

Employment services provide a link between labour supply and demand, aiming to facilitate labour-market entry, reduce unemployment and raise productivity. As noted by Mazza (2003, p. 166), they seek to increase the speed and quality with which persons looking for work are matched with vacancies and training. Their specific tasks range from assistance in job-search, through job placement, vacancy information and help in producing

2 For example, see details of the *ProJoven* programme in Peru, in Hoyle (2005) and Chacaltana (2005).

3 See chapter IV on this point.

4 In addition to the registration of institutions that provide training, Calderón (2007) calls for the creation of a personal accreditation system, such as the Mexican System of Labour Competencies operated by the Council for Standardization and Certification of Labor Competency (CONOCER), which provides the market with information not only on the training obtained by the worker, but also on the institution that provided it.

a curriculum vitae, to more complex activities such as direct or indirect training through other organizations, providing information on labour-market trends, managing unemployment insurance and other programmes, and overseeing active job-search.

The rationale for this type of policy is based on the information asymmetry that exists in the labour market and the difficulty in correctly matching labour supply and demand in a highly changeable setting. This asymmetry results in lengthy periods of job-search (and hence unemployment), compounded by under-use of labour skills and mismatches between those skills and market needs. These programmes target both the unemployed and job-seekers in general, in addition to employers.

The region has wide-ranging experience in labour intermediation services, which in recent years have gained currency as a potentially effective and low-cost instrument (Mazza, 2003). In general, these services are provided either by Ministries of Labour (such as in Argentina and Uruguay) or by public training institutes (such as the National Apprenticeship Service in Colombia and the National Training and Employment Service (SENCE) in Chile). Implementation modalities vary; in some cases, the private sector provides these services through schemes involving varying degrees of collaboration with public agencies. Several modes of cooperation have been established between the public and private sectors, thereby altering the previous exclusively public structure. Such institutions also provide services for some segments of the informal sector, whereas previously they operated only in the formal sector. In some countries (such as Mexico), employment services are also involved in dealing with international migration issues.

In some Latin American and Caribbean countries, new technologies, especially the Internet, are increasingly being used in activities of this type. In particular, online employment exchange or labour market information services are available in Chile, the Dominican Republic, Mexico, Panama and Uruguay.

Despite progress made in this area, however, a large proportion of hirings continue to be made through personal contacts, which tends to be less efficient in terms of matching supply and demand. It also further deepens labour market segmentation, since workers with the widest contact networks generally belong to the middle- and high-income brackets. Accordingly, those who make most use of these employment services tend to be those who find it hardest to enter the labour market.

Employment services also need to strengthen their use of new information and organizational technologies, supported by highly qualified staff to meet the extremely varied demand generated by the region's heterogeneous productive structures and labour forces. Services also need to be more directly integrated with other labour-market policies, both active and passive; and their coverage needs to be expanded to encompass other segments of the population, such as informal workers.

Although public employment services are comparatively inexpensive, it needs to be borne in mind that intermediation does not actually create jobs, but only brings together those who offer and those who are looking for work. Accordingly, they are far less effective when labour demand is weak. Moreover, as noted above, the presence of a large informal sector in the region, together with traditional job-search practices based on personal relationships, makes these public services less effective.

3. The creation of wage employment

Direct job creation programmes are generally introduced as an emergency measure during sharp contractions of labour demand, especially in the absence of broad-coverage unemployment protection systems. These schemes offer temporary jobs paying close to the minimum wage and generally target members of poor families (sometimes only heads of household). Low pay tends to work as a self-selection mechanism, since the programmes attract only members of low-income households. So do the tasks involved in these jobs, which tend to be labour-intensive, such as cleaning activities, construction or maintenance of physical infrastructure. Examples include the *Trabajar* programme and the *Jefes y Jefas de Hogar* programme in Argentina, emergency employment programmes in Chile, Peru and Uruguay, and the social investment funds implemented by the Plurinational State of Bolivia and Costa Rica.

The *Trabajar* programme in Argentina, which was designed to relieve poverty and targeted the unemployed, provided employment in infrastructure works of high social impact. The plan had a broader coverage than other programmes previously implemented in that country; and, according to an evaluation by Ravallion (1999), it was heavily oriented towards the poor: 80% of workers in the plan were from families belonging to the poorest 20% of the population. Jalan and Ravallion (2003) also showed that the programme increased incomes among beneficiaries in relation to the control group.

The *A trabajar urbano* programme (now called *Construyendo Perú*) was introduced in Peru in late 2001 to alleviate the cumulative effects of the Asian crisis in the late 1990s (Chacaltana, 2005). This programme was similar to *Trabajar* in Argentina, since it aimed to create temporary employment in labour-intensive public-works projects for people with low incomes, particularly heads of household and the unemployed in poor sectors. Its evaluation shows that the geographic targeting was appropriate, since it channelled 55% of expenditure into areas where the poorest 20% of the population live, and 75% to areas corresponding to the poorest 40%. Self-selection through low wages does not seem to have been very successful, because in Lima only 21% received wages below the level set by the programme, while in the rest of the country the figure was 38%. Administrative expenses were considered acceptable.

One of the weaknesses of these programmes is that they do little to help workers rejoin the labour market; as they do not generate skills or know-how valued by the market, they do not facilitate subsequent labour market re-entry for the unemployed. In practice, they merely generate temporary incomes for low-income households. Moreover —and this relates to the previous point— even when the emergency is over, it is often difficult to close down programmes of this kind because many of the beneficiaries will have few employment alternatives even in more favourable economic conditions. Another frequent criticism points to the unequal distribution of funding owing to political factors or because of differing management capacities among participating institutions (ECLAC, 2008a). They also do not seem to increase the employability of beneficiaries in the long run, and they could have a negative impact if participation in the programme is stigmatized by society.

An important component of these programmes should therefore be to develop exit strategies for the beneficiaries. Depending on individual characteristics and setting, measures should be taken to promote entry into the main labour market and avoid fostering beneficiary dependency on this type of programme.

It is also suggested that the temporary programme be made permanent, but with countercyclical flexibility —expanding in recessionary phases and contracting in upswings. This criterion is applied in Chile, where programmes were made permanent and seasonally adjustable, and were divided into direct and indirect programmes (Tokman, 2009).

An alternative to direct programmes to strengthen labour demand consists of indirect job-creation programmes that provide economic incentives for private firms to hire workers or retain those who would otherwise have been laid off. These policies consist of a subsidy that lowers non-wage labour costs or covers part of the wage. Argentina and Chile introduced this type of mechanism in the *Proempleo* programmes. Countries including Argentina, Brazil, Mexico and Panama have recently applied schemes of this sort in the context of "first job" programmes, more to overcome the structural barriers faced by young first-time job-seekers than to facilitate employment during an economic downturn.[5]

Some doubts have arisen about the efficiency of these instruments, owing to their potential "dead-weight" effects (hiring workers who would have been hired anyway) and the displacement of existing workers by subsidized hirings. A key point here is the close relation between the programme and the economic cycle: at the peak of the cycle the "dead-weight" effect could prevail, while in the trough the programme could become less efficient through the substitution effect, or else simply become ineffectual because firms see no need for further hiring, with its attendant costs, and will not take up the incentives (ECLAC, 2008b).

Nonetheless, even in those circumstances, indirect job-creation programmes seem to be effective in boosting the demand for the groups that find it hardest to obtain a job. For example, Bravo (2004) states that the programme implemented in Chile has achieved better results than direct employment programmes, and at a lower cost. Employment subsidies are more effective when combined with other programmes, such as training and assisted job-search. It is therefore essential to design these programmes correctly to strengthen their positive effects.

---

[5] See chapter IV.

4. Programmes to support self-employment and microenterprise

Given the shortfall of wage employment creation, many of the region's countries have introduced programmes to promote independent work, either in the form of own account work or through the creation of microenterprises. Incentives for microenterprises and small businesses have normally aimed at developing a favourable environment for such businesses, and implementing specific productive development policies for this type of enterprise.

Policies of the first type include those designed to reduce production and transaction costs, particularly registration, tax and labour costs. A number of procedural simplifications have been made to reduce registration costs, including a one-stop facility for business services. Other slightly more complex strategies, such as those in Honduras (*Honduras Compite*), aim to simplify not only procedures, but also the mechanisms that affect enterprise competitiveness. Lastly, there are schemes that combine a reduction in red tape with simplified tax payment systems, such as the integrated tax and contributions system for microenterprises and small businesses (SIMPLES) in Brazil.

In relation to tax costs for small business units, some countries offer exemptions from certain taxes (for example, from value-added tax in the case of craft workers in Colombia and Ecuador). Other countries operate simplified arrangements, such as the *monotributo* regime, in which the payment of some or all tax liabilities is replaced with a flat charge. These schemes are employed in Argentina, Brazil, Paraguay and Uruguay (Gonzáles, 2006). A third scheme consists of labour regimes that are differentiated by firm size, which have been introduced in some of the region's countries, such as Peru, Colombia and Chile (Chacaltana, 2009).

Experience shows that schemes to reduce production and transaction costs are needed to encourage microenterprises and small businesses to join the formal sector; but clearly they are insufficient to promote business expansion and thus generate more quality jobs in this segment. This requires a battery of instruments linked to the productive development of the establishments in question.

As shown in table III.1, the region has a wide variety of programmes designed to promote the development of smaller firms. The countries of the region have developed various instruments in three broad areas: access to domestic and international markets; access to credit; and promotion of competitiveness.[6]

Table III.1
LATIN AMERICA: PRODUCTIVE SUPPORT PROGRAMMES FOR MICROENTERPRISE AND SMALL BUSINESSES

Areas of intervention	Programmes	Countries (partial listing)
Market access	Programmes to support commercial activity in general Government procurement programmes favouring microenterprises and small businesses Export support programmes for microenterprises and small businesses	Argentina, Bolivarian Republic of Venezuela, Brazil, Chile, Colombia, Mexico, Peru, Plurinational State of Bolivia
Access to credit	Development bank Microfinance Reduction of direct risk and identification of payment capacity Credit guarantee	Argentina, Chile, Peru, Plurinational State of Bolivia
Promotion of competitiveness	Business development services Access to technology	Brazil, Chile, Peru

Source: Economic Commission for Latin America and the Caribbean (ECLAC), on the basis of J. Chacaltana, "Magnitud y heterogeneidad: políticas de fomento del empleo juvenil y las microempresas", document prepared for the workshop Challenges confronted by labour institutions, Santiago, Chile, Economic Commission for Latin America and the Caribbean (ECLAC), April 2009, unpublished.

While these programmes are generally designed to develop firms that already exist, there are also programmes to help workers set themselves up independently, in self-employment as or microentrepreneurs. Measures to promote independent work require a comprehensive approach that facilitates access to capital, knowledge, technology and markets, to create a sustainable business. A comprehensive approach is also needed to train independent workers, combining "skills acquisition and upgrading

6 For further information on this point, see Chacaltana (2009).

with practising production and income-generation activities within broader and multi-component training for entrepreneurship development, such as through establishing and managing cooperatives and producers' associations and access to finance, technology and markets." (ILO, 2007b). An increasingly important component is training in new technologies. Programmes to support independent start-up include those targeting young people and women, which are analysed in chapter IV.

In general, is unclear whether programmes to support the creation and promotion of microenterprise should be considered as part of the battery of measures to combat unemployment or as productive development policies; and this has caused confusion regarding responsibilities and institutional overlap, among other things. It would be best for these programmes to be directed by institutions responsible for productive development, which would coordinate the various aspects of the programmes (credit, technical assistance, training, and others) with the corresponding specialist organizations, while labour-sector institutions would provide information to stakeholders and handle beneficiary selection processes. They could also play an employment advisory role in programmes to promote enterprise creation.

C. Final remarks

The mixed results obtained from active labour-market policies suggest that the success of such policies depends crucially on their design, scope and targeting, and also on the specific characteristics of the economic and labour-market setting.[7] In Latin America and the Caribbean, this means taking account of the very heterogeneous productive structure and labour force. Policies should also be evaluated in terms of the contribution they make to a long-term development strategy based on innovation, diversification of the productive structure and social cohesion (ECLAC, 2008b).

The efficiency of a public employment system depends largely on its capacity to facilitate access to a wide range of services, offered by a variety of public and private institutions, to an extremely heterogeneous labour force with very diverse needs. This means that active labour-market policies —given the historical lack of funding for the public agencies involved— must have the necessary resources and form a coherent and integrated system of initiatives that exploit potential synergies and are mutually complementary.

Greater integration produces better results than independent schemes. For example, training should be preceded by labour-market orientation for the participants and should conclude with periods of internship in firms and affiliation to a labour exchange service. Support for a business undertaking should also be provided as part of a broader programme encompassing business plan formulation support to obtain financing, assistance in managing the business, and monitoring for a period after the firm has been created.

The programme itself also need to be coherent and coordinated. Coordination between the public and private sectors in labour market intermediation services would reduce costs and increase efficiency, for example. Programmes to encourage independent work should incorporate the various components needed for the business prospect. Work-training programmes should contain a theoretical component in the classroom and another practical component in firms, as a fundamental requirement for improving the chances of obtaining a job and a better income. The possibility of providing financial support to low-income participants, along with medical assistance, child-care services and flexible hours also needs to be considered; and advisory services are required for job-search and the formulation of a personal career plan.

The diversity of demand for active labour-market policy services that reflect heterogeneity of the productive structure and labour force, in a context of resource scarcity, require a high degree of targeting to improve the efficiency, effectiveness and equity of the initiatives in question. Decentralization and participation by local governments can improve the governance of employment programmes by targeting local needs, thereby making them more effective and efficient. Nonetheless, decentralization mechanisms also require high levels of coordination and supervision by the Government.

[7] On this point see Farné (2009) and Weller (2009).

Another way to address a heterogeneous demand for active labour-market policy services is to engage non-profit institutions, universities and private firms in intermediation, training and support for microenterprises and small businesses, in order to reach groups that have hitherto been neglected and thus expand coverage, taking account of specific needs and improving services.

There is also growing recognition of the importance of studies and diagnostics of labour market conditions and trends for decision-making; and several countries have responded to this need by setting up labour-market observatories. These mechanisms need to be strengthened to be able in order to exploit information from all available sources for processing and dissemination, including intermediation facilities (public and private services, communications media, Internet and others).

Observatories can also serve as centres of documentation and analysis of the activities of public employment services, generating additional information on labour supply and demand, while monitoring and evaluating programmes in this area. In fact, active labour-market policies require a permanent information system to be able to make changes when needed, prevent inappropriate use of funds and learn from the experience. In this regard, evaluations of impact and the cost-benefit ratio are highly valuable instruments that should be incorporated at the programme-design stage.

Social stakeholders have an important role to play in designing and monitoring labour-market policies, which requires intensive and continuous dialogue. Stakeholder participation and consensus on the policies implemented greatly help to increase the positive impacts of these programmes, improving their governance, avoiding abuses and generating policies that are sustainable in the long term.

Institutional governance should make programmes more flexible, to be able to adapt easily to changes in setting —such as a change in economic circumstances— or when problems are detected in their design or implementation. The empirical evidence shows that the impacts of active labour-market policies are highly dependent on the phase of the business cycle. For example, direct job-creation programmes are appropriate in crisis periods as a way to provide monetary support in the absence of other social protection policies. Once the emergency has passed, however, the programme should be progressively wound down by generating incentives for their beneficiaries to join other programmes offering better productive engagement. Nonetheless, the difficulty in making this transition stems from the shortage of employment opportunities that exist even after the crisis, particularly for certain groups of workers; so, rather than completely closing these programmes down, it might be more feasible to vary their scale in line with the trend of labour-market indicators.

In the case of subsidies for hiring in the private sector, the best time to activate such policies seems to be the start of economic recovery, since in a recession firms will not hire new workers even if they are subsidized, while in the subsequent upswing there is the risk of dead-weight losses. The incentive for hiring precisely at the start of recovery would help to shorten the time-lag that tends to exists between an upturn in production and new job creation. The risk of subsidizing the hiring of workers who would have found jobs anyway can be controlled by reducing the amount of the subsidy as the recovery consolidates.

Lastly, active labour-market policies fail to reach a major segment of the population; and it is the task of social policy to compensate for this using the specific instruments available to it. Specifically, programmes such as *Oportunidades* (previously *Progresa*) in Mexico, *Bolsa Família* in Brazil, *Familias por la inclusión social* in Argentina and *Chile Solidario* could play an important role in this respect, since they provide transfers that are conditional on the fulfilment of certain obligations, such as children's attendance at school and health centres (with the additional aim of reducing poverty in the future) or active job-search by parents. The advantage of these programmes at times of crisis is that they provide a rapid response to the lack of employment, and they also show a political willingness to address emergency situations among the worst affected groups.

Chapter IV

Labour-market integration policies for young people and women

A. Introduction

The vast literature analysing the status of young people and women in the labour market highlights the disadvantages they face and the contribution they make to the productive process and economic growth. The studies confirm that both of these population groups find it especially hard to enter the labour market; and, when they succeed in doing so, they face disadvantageous employment conditions. In particular, these groups are more vulnerable to unemployment, precarious jobs, unpaid work, horizontal and vertical segmentation and wage discrimination.[1]

These problems of labour-market integration involve three types of heterogeneity and inequality. Firstly, the structural productive heterogeneity of the region is reflected in a segmented and exclusive labour market. Secondly, this heterogeneity and the unequal opportunities that stem from it affect the various segments of the working-age population in different ways, posing special obstacles for young people and women in finding quality jobs. Many of those obstacles stem from factors external to the labour market. Moreover, both young people and women are heterogeneous groups themselves, with major disparities in terms of human, social and cultural capital that clearly differentiate employment opportunities (Weller, 2007).

In the case of young people, early dropout or expulsion from school, a mismatch between education and training and the characteristics of labour demand, major inequities between young people and their highly precarious position in the labour market integration, among other factors, have economic and social consequences that call for specific public policies to address these problems and their causes.

Moreover it is becoming increasingly urgent to incorporate the gender perspective into all labour-market policies, because: (i) employment, particularly decent employment, is the main route to reducing poverty and increasing the material well-being and autonomy of

---

1 See Abramo and Valenzuela (2006), ILO (2007b) and ECLAC/OIJ (2008), among others.

individual people, especially women; (ii) as noted above, women face less advantageous labour-market conditions than men, involving restrictions on the supply side (difficulties in combining paid work with family responsibilities) and also in terms of demand (segregation and discrimination), and (iii) women are the sole or main income-earners in a growing number of families.

Some experiences in the region, although incipient, clearly show the existence of programmes, institutions and legislative measures that have improved women's status in the labour-market, to a greater or lesser degree. The region has made progress in recognizing the role played by women as important, and often the main, family bread-winners. Although this is a significant step in itself, it is not sufficient to achieve genuine gender mainstreaming in all of the pillars of labour-market policy. This requires addressing the various dimensions of labour-market institutions, both in the regulatory framework and passive labour-market policies, and in policies to reconcile family and work (ECLAC, 2008d).

The following analysis first presents an overview of youth employment policies in Latin America; then the strengths and weaknesses of strategies implemented in the region's countries are reviewed from a gender perspective; and, lastly, a few final thoughts are offered.

B. Youth labour-market integration and employment policies

Latin America currently has over 100 million young people between 15 and 24 years of age. To differing extents in individual countries, the proportion of children in the population has diminished and that of youth or young adults —the age group facing the most serious labour-market problems— has increased.

Public policies are being challenged to improve the effectiveness, efficiency and equity of labour-market integration by young people, which requires other measures in addition to policies targeting labour-market institutions. As young people are not all in the same situation, not all policies are appropriate. Some young people only study and are interested in the quality and relevance of the education they are obtaining; some only work, and their specific concerns relate to their current and future jobs; other young people both study and work, while others are not studying, or working, or looking for work. The latter group accounts for roughly 20% of all youth in the region. Two out of every three young people in this situation are women who perform household chores, many of whom have had pregnancies during their teens (Chacaltana, 2009).

The existence of a large group of young people who neither study nor work makes for an extremely critical situation. Most of the young people concerned come from low-income families, which makes it likely that the current low-income situation of their parents will be reproduced in their children, thus reinforcing the intergenerational transmission of disadvantages.

This situation reveals a broader problem, posed by the difficulties of making the school-to-work transition. The education received by young people has major shortcomings in terms of the knowledge and skills they acquire and the information they receive for gradually moving into the world of work. Possibilities for gaining initial work experiences are few and far between, and public employment services need to enhance their role as intermediaries particularly in this segment. In the case of young people who are neither studying nor working, the responses come from domains outside the labour market, such as the education system and the implementation of programmes to reduce school dropout (Chacaltana, 2009).

Compounding this situation, most young people who have a job are working in precarious conditions on low pay and without social security, which further undermines job stability; and periods of work are frequently interspersed with spells of unemployment. This is particularly important in view of the empirical evidence that an unstable employment record in an individual's first few years in the labour market generally has a negative impact, by preventing the accumulation of experience, productivity and specific human capital. This effect is compounded by the negative implications of unemployment for a person's career and living standards. From this standpoint, the youth labour market is viewed as "chaotic" —as a milieu in which many young people driff from job to job without gaining knowledge and attitudes that will later lead to better wages and employment conditions (Maurizio, 2009a).

In contrast, some young people see a labour market with higher rates of turnover as providing opportunities for autonomy and self-realization, because they succeed in accumulating relevant experience for their personal growth and for an upwardly mobile career.[2] This benign version of a labour market with high entry and exit rates is associated with new technologies and new forms of business organization; but it is also restricted to young people with high levels of education. Another highly educated group of young people has better chances of gaining a formal job and experiencing lower exit rates. Nonetheless, for many young people, the impossibility of gaining admission to a stable and quality work environment leads to social exclusion, particularly among those who dropped out of the education system early (Jacinto, 1996; Feldman, 1996; Miranda and Salvia, 2001; Maurizio, 2009a).

There are many hypotheses to explain this instability, including, as noted above, a structural inconsistency between the nature of supply (limited by education andexperience deficits) and continuously adapting demand, problems of incomplete information among both young people and firms, labour-market distortions caused by the institutional framework of the labour market and the fact that youth employment is more sensitive to economic conditions (Weller, 2003; Tokman, 2008b). Nonetheless, account needs to be taken of the high level of heterogeneity that exists among youth cohorts, in which specific groups, differentiated by education level, sex, family of origin, area of residence, ethnic background, and special capacities, face very diverse situations in terms of their labour-market engagement (ECLAC/OIJ, 2008).

Latin American countries have implemented various types of policy to address this complex situation. This section analyses the main strategies implemented in the region with a view to identifying trends and areas for intervention. The emphasis will be placed on public policies relating to labour-market integration, labour training and promotion of youth business initiatives.[3]

1. Youth labour-market policies

The data show that a lack of job experience is a major impediment to young people's engagement in the labour market.[4] Accordingly, policies to help young people find work focus mainly on overcoming the difficulties involved in obtaining a first job.

Although employment services in the region have improved in recent years, this scheme of labour-market intermediation does not appear to be sufficient or appropriate to young people's needs. High levels of job turnover make them permanent job-seekers with few references from previous jobs. An efficient employment service that uses new technologies not only makes it easier for young people (who generally are better connected) to access relevant information, but also helps to reduce inequalities caused by the crucial importance of social capital in finding productive employment. In Peru, for example, the cost of the credentials demanded by employers (study certificate and criminal records, identity documents, and health certificates in some occupations) may be very high, particularly because such documents may be valid only for a short time. Accordingly, a service that employment agencies could usefully provide would be assistance in obtaining employment credentials.

On the demand side, a more recent instrument is first-job legislation, which provides incentives to hire young people by reducing labour costs. Such systems exist in Mexico and Chile, for example, and existed in Brazil up to 2007. Paraguay also has legislation of this type, though it has yet to be implemented, while the Dominican Republic is debating a draft law on the subject.

In Chile, the subsidy on youth hiring is applied directly to wages, whereas in Mexico the First Employment Contract Law (2007) requires the State to pay the social security contributions of the young employee. The incentives provided under this latter programme come into effect only after a minimum period of employment, to give greater stability to young people in their first job.

All of these policies are designed to help young people enter the formal sector of the economy. Similar measures need to be taken for young people whose problem is not in finding work as such, but in obtaining quality jobs, because they work in precarious and informal occupations. Measures, such as expanding social security coverage, should be considered to improve the quality of employment for these young people.

2 Albuquerque (2009) shows that job turnover among young people employed in the Brazilian formal sector has positive effects on their income, which might suggest that, for young people who succeed in entering this sector, a job generates experience that is recognized when seeking employment later. Nonetheless, this yields decreasing returns, so in the case of high turnover, the benign effect is clouded by a perception of high instability that could impair the productivity of the young people concerned.

3 The following sections are based on the conclusions of Chacaltana (2009).

4 Young first-time job-seekers generally take longer to find employment than their age-peers who already have labour-market experience; and, in any given youth cohort, women usually take longer to find a job than men (Weller, 2003).

2. Training policies

As noted in chapter III, training and education policies have a long track record in the region, involving both public and private suppliers. Nonetheless, there are various problems in youth training: access is somewhat unequal, and a large group of young people do not benefit from these programmes (Chacaltana, 2009). For those that do gain access to training, the problem is the relevance of the knowledge acquired for gaining employment and achieving job stability. Another difficulty concerns the quality of the knowledge imparted.

There are currently at least four youth-training modalities that aim to overcome these difficulties. The most common involves vocational training institutes, which aim to resolve problems of access, relevance, and lack of financing. Institutes may be public or private, or belong to universities, in which case they are generally funded through business contributions.

In the second system the firm participates directly in training activities, to ensure that the knowledge imparted really matches business needs. This is done through an instrument that is particularly suited to young people, namely training or apprenticeship contracts.[5] In Colombia, Costa Rica and Paraguay, for example, the law requires firms to hire one apprentice per given number of contracted workers, or else pay a contribution to a vocational training institution.

A third modality seeks to overcome problems of access, relevance and quality, particularly for young people whose particular difficulties in entering productive employment are due to their relatively low level of education. In terms of access, these measures target the poorest young people and work through existing educational institutions. To ensure relevance, training entities should have direct links with the productive system; and, lastly, the problem of quality is tackled by drawing up a register of service providers. The *Joven* [Youth] programmes that have been applied in several of the region's countries, based on the experience of the *Chile Joven* programme, are examples of this modality.

Lastly, a fourth, more comprehensive scheme is based on the notion that training is just one element in a broader spectrum of employability, for which reason various actors need to be involved. Examples of this modality are the *ProJovem* programme of Brazil and *Chilecalifica*. As in the *Joven* model, these are multidimensional, ranging from continuous training through to skill certification.

Although the different programmes play a major role in supporting young people's productive engagement, major problems of coverage, quality and access still remain. Specifically, there is not always a guarantee that the contents of the programmes help to reduce gender segmentation in the labour market. Lastly, the effectiveness of the various training schemes is impaired by poor quality and inequity in basic education, which disadvantage a large group of young people. The schemes are basically hampered by the fact that the young people lack the minimum basic knowledge needed to incorporate new specific knowledge for work.

3. Policies to promote youth entrepreneurship

Policies also exist to promote entrepreneurial initiatives among young people. Here it is worth noting that nearly four out of every 10 workers in the region end up working in situation that do not correspond to a direct employer-employee relationship (Chacaltana, 2009).

As noted by Llisterri and others (2006), there are two types of entrepreneur: those who start up businesses to seize an opportunity, and those who do so out of necessity or as a survival strategy. The second type is the most common among young people, since most of them start working as a wage-earners, but later become discouraged by turnover and decide to set up an activity on their own account.

In the case of young people, White and Kenyon (2004) identified two types of constraint on opportunity-driven business initiative: first, a lack of vocation for independent employment compounded by risk aversion; and second, administrative and economic constraints on setting up

5 See Barbagelata (2003).

a business and making it succeed (such as problems of access to credit, which often arise in the case of young people). Policies to promote youth business initiatives therefore need to be multi-dimensional and distinguish between young people who are thinking of setting up a firm and those that have already done so (Tueros, 2008), to implement specific policies in each case. Linares (2008) argues that entrepreneurship promotion programmes in Peru are clearly biased towards the motivation and planning stages, while only a small fraction also target the formation and follow-up phases.

Examples of these policies in the region include the Youth Entrepreneurship Success Programme (YES) of Trinidad and Tobago, the *Fondo Emprender* of Colombia and *Chile Emprende* (Camacho, 2009). While all of these are public-sector initiatives, there are also non-governmental programmes such as *Colectivo Integral de Desarrollo* in Peru, which is based on evidence showing that business and management training are more important than credit when setting up a business, since most young people start by using their own or family savings (Chacaltana, 2009).

In conclusion, the problem of youth employment is highly complex and heterogeneous, and the solution does not lie exclusively in labour-market policies, but also requires complementary actions to keep young people in the education system, for example through conditional income-transfer programmes and student grants.

Lastly, it is essential to have a macroeconomic regime that generates sufficient jobs, and quality jobs in particular. Reducing unemployment and improving precarious employment conditions will, first, lead to higher family incomes, and thus reduce the need for secondary workers in families; and, second, it will generate better quality jobs for young people.

C. Gender mainstreaming in labour-market policies

There are reasons of efficiency and equity for promoting equal opportunities and treatment between men and women. First, there is growing recognition that the female labour force is increasingly needed to undertake production processes and underpin higher rates of economic growth; and that the unpaid work performed by women is also crucial to the functioning of the economic system (ECLAC, 2008d). Accordingly, reducing and eliminating the discrimination and segregation suffered by women helps increase productivity, competitiveness and economic growth by making full use of available factors of production.

Gender equity is also a key element in strengthening social integration and building democratic societies in which citizens are empowered and citizenship is fully exercised. It is also impossible to make progress in terms of decent employment without promoting gender equality and eliminating all forms of discrimination.

Over time, the Governments of the region have ratified international conventions on this subject, thus assuming a responsibility to incorporate them into domestic legislation and enforce them. Domestic laws have also been passed in this area (Pautassi, Faur and Gerardi, 2004). The broad range of international and national laws that promote the principles of equal opportunity and non-discrimination between women and men thus serve as a starting point for effectively moving towards these objectives (Tomei, 2006). Nonetheless, the wide disparities that exist in the labour market between the two groups clearly show that a policy statement by countries, and even existing laws, are not sufficient conditions for eliminating discrimination against women in the labour market. Fully incorporating this dimension requires gender mainstreaming in all stages of policy adoption: conception, execution, evaluation and monitoring (Abramo, 2003).

Equal access to productive employment also requires consideration of issues such as reconciling work and family life, lack of access to employment networks, lack of certain qualifications, and cultural constraints, right from the design stage of the corresponding public programmes. Two of the most important aspects in this regard concern availability of free childcare services and flexible working hours in the labour market.

The following paragraphs review the various dimensions of the employment and labour-market policies implemented in Latin America from a gender perspective, assessing progress made to date and outstanding issues. To put the analysis in context, the section starts with a general overview of women's labour-market integration in the region, while also considering the dynamic of the last few years and its structural characteristics.

1. Stylized facts concerning the labour-market status of women in the region[6]

The female participation rate in the region has been rising over the last few years, although it is still very low compared to that of men. This situation reflects the high proportion of women who undertake exclusively domestic chores, revealing an unequal distribution of household tasks and family responsibilities in which women on average devote many hours to unpaid work. The greater presence of women in the labour force has not been matched by a reduction in family and social responsibilities. Women from poor families show even lower activity rates than those from non-poor households; and factors that generate this gap include lower education levels, a larger number of children, and less access to childcare services.

Female unemployment rates are persistently higher than the corresponding rates among men, largely reflecting less favourable conditions for formal employment for women. This is also reflected in the fact that a large proportion of female employment is in the informal sector. Furthermore, women tend to perform jobs at the lower end of the occupational spectrum in this sector, working on their own account, in domestic service or unpaid. Partly related to this, women's employment conditions are still often highly precarious.

Women's employment records and chances of an upwardly mobile career are worse affected by horizontal and vertical segregation than is the case among men. This prevents women workers from gaining access to certain types of job (they tend to participate most in "female" occupations), or to certain none senior posts even if they have the same levels of qualifications as men. Compounding all of this, their pay remains lower than that received by men, partly as a result of the discrimination they suffer in the labour market. This gap is usually larger, the higher their education level.

All of these factors mean that women, on average, are less protected in old age by contributory pension and retirement systems, and it is harder for them to fulfil all the requirements to be eligible for pension benefits.

2. Labour-market institutions from the gender perspective[7]

(a) Collective bargaining

Collective bargaining is a highly valuable institution for promoting equal opportunities in the labour market, although in practice it is insufficient, since it neglects to cover a large swathe of the employed female population. This is because of the high proportion of women engaged in informal activities and the fact that women are over represented in formal sectors that are explicitly excluded from collective bargaining.

Female domestic employees and rural workers, many women working in maquila plants and most home-based workers are excluded from collective bargaining by their employment contracts, antiunion practices or the bargaining process itself. Moreover, in cases where the public sector does not use this instrument, a large group of women working as teachers or in the health sector are also excluded from coverage.

Hostility to women's union organization also persists among labour unions, thereby blocking women's access to representative positions (Rodríguez, 2006); and this, together with the fact that employers are also resistant to gender-equity clauses, would help explain why such clauses are uncommon in collective bargaining processes in the region (Abramo and Rangel, 2005).

Legal changes have helped to bring about improvements on maternity and paternity protection in contractual clauses. These relate to the duration of maternity leave, the time for which expectant and breast-feeding mothers are protected from dismissal, paternity leave (establishment and duration), protection for the father against dismissal during the childbirth period, maintenance of full salary during maternity leave, length of time allowed for breast-feeding, ratification of the principle of non-discrimination and equal pay for equal work, childcare services of higher quality and for longer periods and sanctions against sexual harassment.

6 Based on Milosavljevic (2007), ECLAC (2008c), Abramo and Valenzuela (2006), Yannoulas (2005) and Rico (2003).

7 This section is largely based on Maurizio (2009b).

Progress has also been made in terms of leave and other entitlements relating to adoption and pregnancy, such as the ban on demanding a pregnancy test from prospective employees in Brazil, permission to attend prenatal check-ups, reduction in working hours, and a prohibition on tasks that could harm the mother and child.

Although improvements have been made in protecting the working woman as a mother, progress has been more limited or even non-existent on other issues, such as reconciling work and family life for women and men, working conditions, and the implementation of effective measures to promote equal opportunities. There is also less momentum on vocational training and labour organization, and there are no mechanisms for evaluating training programmes, the promotion system or performance assessment from a gender perspective.

In conclusion, while the region has made headway by introducing equal opportunity clauses into collective bargaining processes, there is still much to do to ensure that this institution actually serves as a means to eliminate discrimination based not only on gender, but also on race and ethnic origin, among other aspects.

(b) Minimum wage

The institution of the minimum wage is particularly important from the gender perspective, because it can help to close the gender wage gap, given that women on average earn lower wages than men and are over represented at levels close to the minimum wage.

Nonetheless, this possibility of a relative improvement in women's wages depends on avoiding a deterioration in their employment rate, and no substitution of female employment by men. The effectiveness of this instrument in narrowing the gender wage gap also requires the legislation to be effectively enforced, which makes mechanisms of sanction, application and control of labour legislation very important.

(c) Unemployment protection

As noted in chapter II, relatively little use has been made of passive labour-market programmes in Latin America, as shown by the limited scope and coverage of unemployment insurance and other labour protection instruments. In these circumstances, women have even less access to the corresponding benefits. More difficult access to jobs, more precarious conditions, and greater occupational instability among women all reduce their chances of fulfilling the requirements to accede to this type of protection during a spell of unemployment.

Nonetheless, the adverse conditions faced by women do not fully explain their lack of access to unemployment protection. In some countries, such as Argentina, insurance regulations play a part in restricting women's access because they exclude workers dismissed from sectors such as domestic service, private education or the public sector, where women have high participation rates.

Lastly, a further inequity occurs when women lose the right to have their employer make social security and pension system contributions on their behalf during maternity leave. This reduces their access to pension benefits and unemployment insurance.[8]

(d) Active labour-market policies

Following Abramo (2003), four different situations can be distinguished in relation to the gender perspective and women's participation in the labour-market policies applied in the region:

- Programmes that incorporate the gender dimension into their design, and hence also in the corresponding performance indicators. An example of this is the National Plan for Worker Qualification (PLANFOR) in Brazil.[9]
- Programmes targeting women exclusively, and particularly female heads of poor households. An example of this type is the training programme for women heads of household in Chile.
- Programmes in which gender is not a design concern, but measures giving priority to women are subsequently adopted in later phases of the programme, for example at the implementation stage.
- Programmes whose design completely disregards gender issues, but which for various reasons target women, who form a majority of the beneficiary group. This is seen most often in policies that make transfers to the poor, but less frequently in employment or microcredit programmes or those targeting the unemployed.

A number of experiences are described below, from which conclusions can be drawn on the gender perspective in active labour-market policies. The aim is to assess the extent to which, and how, the implementation of these programmes has helped to reduce the gender gap in access to employment, particularly to quality jobs.

(i) Vocational education and training

Women face a significantly smaller range of job possibilities than men; so training programmes need to

8 To illustrate the greater difficulties that women face in gaining access to this insurance, it should be noted that in Argentina roughly half of the unemployed population are women, yet women represent only 27% of unemployment insurance beneficiaries.

9 The design of this programme included the goal of promoting equal opportunities and ensuring access for the most vulnerable groups. For this purpose it established that participation by these groups should be at least equal to that of the economically active population.

target not only women but also policy-makers and key stakeholders, to raise their awareness of the problem experienced by women in the labour market.

Training in the gender perspective is especially important, because it can help improve women's access to skills and better quality jobs.

The region has experiences of programmes in which the gender perspective has been incorporated through various channels. These include PLANFOR (1995-2002)[10] in Brazil; FORMUJER;[11] *Chile Joven*,[12] the Women Heads of Household programme in Chile, and the Youth Training Programme Skills Development for Domestic Service, both in Argentina.

Institution-building programmes include the regional project to support the formulation of Gender-Oriented Labour-Market Policy being implemented by ECLAC and the German Agency for Technical Cooperation (GTZ), and the project to mainstream gender in policies to eradicate poverty and create employment in Latin America, implemented by ILO in six Latin American countries.[13]

Although the region has made headway with training and education programmes that incorporate the gender perspective, these efforts made are still insufficient, and broad areas of public intervention remain to be exploited. In designing these programmes it is important to consider the variety of women's situations, which diminishes the value of one-size-fits-all policies.

(ii) Business development

A growing number of women in the region are developing their own independent businesses. As noted by Valenzuela (2005), although they all share certain characteristics, such as generally being mothers in the middle stage of the life cycle, and a significant number of them are heads of household, the following distinctions can be made: (i) at the base of the pyramid are women with low educational levels, belonging to poor households, who generally undertake informal and precarious work with help from family members (often their children), operating with minimum levels of capital; (ii) an intermediate group of women with some capital and a more solid business, which has better chances of surviving through time, and (iii) at the top end of the pyramid are entrepreneurial women with access to contact networks, who direct small or medium-sized businesses and succeed in establishing themselves on a stable basis.

Independent workers, whether men or women, find it hard to stay in the market and expand their activities, because they lack access to the necessary assets, such as financing, management know-how, technology, and risk insurance, among others. Nonetheless, these constraints tend to act more heavily on activities undertaken by women (Valenzuela and Venegas, 2001).

At the same time, the job segregation women experience as wage-earners is replicated when they work independently, and they tend to congregate in activities that have low entry barriers and are therefore highly competitive, often in the services or commerce sector.

Another characteristic that self-employed women share with their wage-earning counterparts is a combination of paid and unpaid work involving family activities and care work. This constraint might be expected to be most onerous among self-employed women, particularly in the initial stages of their activities. As Valenzuela (2005) notes, this difficulty is sometimes resolved by setting up the business at home, which has certain advantages, but also drawbacks. The former include greater flexibility of working hours and less travel; the drawbacks include difficulty in separating family and work responsibilities, and lack of rest periods and adequate working conditions (Lund and Srinivas, 2000; Chant, 2007; Kantor, 2002; Lessinger, 1990; López Estrada, 2002).

Accordingly, this type of occupation in some circumstances may help to provide greater work opportunities for women and generate higher incomes that enable many of them to escape from poverty. However, the constraints involved in some types of self-employment are more burdensome for women than men.

Issues that should be included in business development programmes in order to attract more women into self-

---

10 In 2003, PLANFOR was replaced by the National Qualifications Plan, which also prioritizes access for groups that tend to be excluded on race or gender grounds.

11 The Regional Programme to Strengthen the Vocational and Technical Training of Low-Income Women (FORMUJER) arose as a regional initiative funded by the Multilateral Investment Fund of the Inter-American Development Bank (IDB), with technical coordination by the Inter-American Research and Documentation Centre on Vocational Training (CINTERFOR) of the International Labour Organization (ILO). It was aimed at strengthening gender equity by providing training for women, particularly those living in poverty. The participating countries were Argentina, Costa Rica and the Plurinational State of Bolivia. Yannoulas (2005) cites the following contributions made by the programme: (a) development of a political-educational training model that takes the gender perspective as a conceptual and strategic framework for the policy, making it possible to implement actions to target and take affirmative action in favour of deprived population groups (particularly women); (b) the design of curricular profiles by cross-referencing training with labour skills and gender, and (c) the implementation of compensatory strategies to address gender and poverty inequalities, diversifying the vocational alternatives available to women.

12 This programme included a stimulus for women's participation from the outset, by providing childcare for participating mothers, agreements with employers associations to encourage the employment of participating women, and awareness-raising workshops for officials and trainers.

13 The countries are Argentina, the Plurinational State of Bolivia, Honduras, Nicaragua, Paraguay and Peru.

employment and complement experiences to promote independent work generally, include the following:

- Property rights: women's lack of access to such rights, including intellectual property rights, means that they cannot use, build or transform or exchange their assets into productive capital with a view to generating more capital (Chant and Pedwell, 2008).
- In some situations women face difficulties in renting premises in their own name (Vera-Sanso, 2006).
- As also noted by Chant and Pedwell (2008), informal workers, particularly women, would benefit hugely if they had "empowering" capacities, ranging from negotiating skills to knowledge of their legal rights, and union skills enabling them to participate in associations to defend their rights.
- It is important to promote awareness-raising, sensitization and consensus among society regarding the new roles that women can play in the economy, including this type of activity.
- Family care services need to be built into the design of these programmes. Family responsibilities affect the workload of businesswomen and require measures to alleviate the domestic burden and promote the development of other activities.

(iii) Direct job creation programmes

Targeted employment programmes have been implemented in the region for groups facing difficulties in finding jobs, some of them oriented towards women exclusively (usually poor women). Nonetheless, even in the broader-scope programmes, a high proportion of the beneficiaries tend to be women.

Evaluating this type of programme from a gender perspective poses major challenges. First, apart from programmes targeting women exclusively, the female presence in these programmes stems from their orientation towards poor or single-parent families. But this does not mean that the gender equity objective can be considered to be fulfilled, since the design of such programmes generally does not address the constraints described above.

Second, the type of tasks to be undertaken within these programmes needs to be considered explicitly, along with the extent to which they reduce job segregation and segmentation. A major feature of these plans is that women generally end up performing the same tasks in community centres as they undertake at home, such as the provision of care and food.

Lastly the impact of programmes on a woman's future career needs to be assessed. For example, in the case of the Unemployed Male and Female Heads of Household Programme (PJJHD) in Argentina, the proportion of beneficiaries who enter a wage-earning job registered with social security is clearly biased in favour of men. Whereas men currently represent 26% of all beneficiaries, they account for almost half of those entering the labour-market by this route. This pattern is even more marked in periods of rapid economic growth, such as enjoyed by that country since 2003; and it is particularly important to analyse the employment records of those who succeed (or fail) to enter labour market after joining a programme of this sort.

(iv) Labour intermediation services

Fewer contact networks and opportunities for training and vocational education, compounded by occupational segregation, make women's job-search more difficult. This is very important in the region because a large part of job-search is based on informal contacts, many of which are developed through cumulative labour-market experience or personal contacts. As women participate less in the labour force, or do so more intermittently, they have less access to this mechanism when looking for a job.

In this regard, the supply of free intermediation services may help to reduce one of the labour-market entry barriers by helping to improve women's access to information on vacancies and the general situation of the labour market. This type of service may thus become an important tool for reducing discrimination in the labour market and contributing towards equal opportunities.

The flexibility provided when intermediation services use information and communication technologies could benefit individuals who are subject to greater time or mobility constraints, which is often the case for women.

Partnerships between the public and private sectors and non-profit organizations may also benefit women (Mazza, 2003), particularly the poorest among them. In Peru, for example, civil society organizations (NGOs, the church) could provide local services of this type in conjunction with the private sector. Local partnerships may be more efficient in adapting to the specific characteristics and problems of certain groups, such as women or young people. Mobile units that take these services into the community are particularly useful for women with childcare and other family responsibilities.

Nonetheless, one of the challenges faced by this type of service is to incorporate the gender perspective from the design stage, which involves addressing these contingencies through specialist services that deal with this specific situation. As noted by Samaniego (2002), an evaluation of this type of programme in the countries of the Organisation for Economic Co-operation and Development (OECD) seems to show that the more they are adapted to the specifics of different groups in the beneficiary population;

the more effective they are. This requires an awareness of the disadvantages and constraints these groups face and of the measures available to reduce them.[14]

Another challenge is to evaluate the performance of this type of service, for which suitable "productivity" indicators would need to be defined. Establishing adequate performance indicators is not easy and certainly cannot be based solely on the number of people who found a job (Mazza, 2003). Nonetheless, jobs obtained through the intermediation service by vulnerable groups such as women, young people and migrants, among others, could be weighted differently.

Two other features of the region's labour market are also important. One of them concerns migratory flows. In this regard, Mexico's public employment service provides information on employment opportunities outside the country, such as temporary work in Canada (in this case it also obtains visas and pays the transport cost). As women form a growing proportion of migratory flows, these services have had a direct impact on them. The other feature concerns the importance of the informal sector and female employment in it. The services provided need to be expanded to embrace these workgroups as potential beneficiaries.

D. Final remarks

In the context of a segmented and exclusive labour market that reflects the heterogeneity of the region's productive structure, opportunities for accessing quality jobs are unequally distributed. If, as claimed, one of the goals of the institutional framework in the labour market is to protect structurally disadvantaged participants, institutions are needed that address the access problems faced by specific groups.

Such groups include young people and women, who consistently display adverse labour-market indicators. These groups are also internally heterogeneous; and factors such as educational level, characteristics of the household of origin, area of residence and ethnic origin influence their chances of engaging in the labour market and result in significant differences in the labour-market variables pertaining to each group.

A review of the specific role played by labour-market institutions in integrating young people and women into the labour market shows both similarities and differences. Instruments to improve employability need to take account of the weaknesses and inequities in human, social and cultural capital among these groups. The concept of "double relevance", which is often used to analyse training programmes, should be extended to all policies. Programmes are relevant when they take account of labour demand representing quality job opportunities, on the one hand, and the profiles, expectations and needs of the target population, on the other, focusing on closing gaps in opportunities and outcomes.

This calls for activities to strengthen gender mainstreaming in employment programmes and help young people from low-income households enter the labour market, with a view to breaking the inter-generational transmission of poverty. The improvements in public employment services, programmes to promote independent employment and education and training programmes reviewed in the foregoing sections could play a major role in this regard. In the case of young people, it is also essential to strengthen the link between the education system and the world of work, which is a task to be shared by all stakeholders.

For women, measures to help reconcile family life and work, supported by the approval and enforcement of anti-discrimination laws, are crucial for overcoming the inequalities that encumber their integration into the labour market.

[14] An example of this is an ILO project undertaken in Chile, Colombia and Uruguay to reduce the difficulties faced by women in finding more and better jobs (Abramo, 2003).

Chapter V

Conclusions

Labour institutions have been the subject of an intense economic-policy debate —one characterized by a high ideological content that, particularly from the 1990s, gave rise to strong positions in favour of a series of reforms aimed at making labour markets as deregulated and flexible as possible. However, amidst low growth and uneven productivity in Latin American and Caribbean economies, the reforms did not have the expected impact on labour markets. Disappointment over the broken promises of flexibility reforms has intensified questioning about the efficiency of relatively unregulated labour markets and has resulted in proposals on labour-market regulation that have become rather more cautious in recent years (Freeman, 2005).

Although there is no consensus on the type of reform necessary, there is agreement that the region's labour institutions are not fit to face the challenges emerging from increasingly integrated markets, volatile economies and ever-changing technology. From different positions, it has been agreed that these institutions do not ensure efficient market functioning or the protection of workers as structurally weak actors. As such, labour institutions are not making a satisfactory contribution to the creation of quality employment or a development strategy based on increased systemic competitiveness and greater social inclusion. The criticisms differ in their content and nuances, depending on the stance and social interests of those behind them.

As mentioned in previous chapters, the last few decades have seen several labour institutions called to task over their lack of effectiveness and equity. Minimum wages, for example, sustained major losses in real terms, as they were often used as a means of stabilizing prices. Unionization rates dropped abruptly in many countries in the wake of changes to the production structure, anti-union policies (often associated with dictatorial governments) and the behaviour of unions themselves that has caused them to lose legitimacy. Employment-protection mechanisms have become weaker, as increasing emphasis was placed on the non-wage labour costs involved.[1] This emphasis was often intended to offset the negative impact of certain configurations of relative prices on business profitability.[2] Nonetheless, in the late 1990s and even more so in this

---

1 It should be pointed out that not all the changes implemented in that period were of the same ilk. There were also measures to improve the protection afforded to specific groups, while some countries strengthened the options for union organization.

2 Some of the region's countries have at times used the exchange rate as an anti-inflationary policy instrument, which usually triggered a process of exchange-rate appreciation that affected the profitability of the production of tradable goods.

decade, a few countries introduced policies that focused on the need to recover the minimum wage in real terms, increased unionization and stronger protection mechanisms.

The literature on the three institutions mentioned shows that their development and performance are extremely varied, which makes it impossible to formulate general recommendations and indicates that the analysis needs to be considered on a case-by-case basis, in the context of the economic and institutional specificities of each country. If we consider the case of the minimum wage, we see that there is huge regional variety in terms of its (absolute and relative) level, and that the impact of a real increase depends, among other things, on its level in relation to average wages, on average productivity, and on the needs and income sources of poor households. If the minimum wage is relatively low, then increasing it will probably have a positive impact, as it well help to boost the income of poor households without affecting employment. In contrast, the effect may be different if the minimum wage is relatively high, as any significant increase could risk reducing labour demand and pushing up levels of non-compliance.

The impact of organized labour and collective bargaining is also varied, depending on their specific characteristics. In contrast with the downward trend in unionization seen in previous decades, there are several factors now conducive to greater union organization, including the importance of social dialogue as a key to achieving sustainable reforms to labour institutions and the increased flexibility of collective bargaining as an instrument of regulation (compared with a legislation that sets down the characteristics of labour relations in detail). However, if organized labour and collective bargaining are to achieve this aim, a series of conditions must be met, including the elimination of anti-union practices and the development and strengthening of democratic, autonomous, representative and transparent structures of union organization.

In the recent past, several countries have made efforts to improve unemployment protection. Little progress has been made in this regard, however, and this has been highlighted by the current crisis. Although there have been efforts to use the instruments available to prevent a larger rise in unemployment, existing schemes are very weak, especially in terms of coverage. The region still faces the challenge of developing mechanisms that offer greater levels of protection in the context of higher rates of labour turnover resulting from globalization and far-reaching and rapid technological change. Given the high degree of labour-market informality, increasing the coverage of protection mechanisms must go hand-in-hand with the development and promotion of non-contributory social protection mechanisms (ECLAC, 2006).

Over the last few decades, the region's countries have implemented a wide range of changes to active labour-market policies. Reforms have included those related to vocational training: tailoring it to demand, targeting the needs of different population groups and improving coverage through decentralization and a broadening of the type of training-service providers.

Training can be key to improving employability, particularly for groups who find it especially difficult to enter the labour market, such as women and young people with low levels of formal skills. However, the results of assessments show that such programmes have a rather modest impact, which suggests that policies have a long way to go in terms of effectiveness, efficiency and equity. A prerequisite to significantly improving the effectiveness of training programmes is complementing them with improvements in basic and secondary education and ensuring that they provide the means for lifelong learning, which is essential if productivity, competitiveness and labour conditions are to be constantly improved.

Public employment services must offer an integrated approach for labour-market policies, as well as providing intermediation services. Besides directly carrying out certain activities (such as analysing and disseminating labour-market information, intermediation, advice and guidance), they should also forge strategic partnerships with institutions responsible for other programmes (training, self-employment promotion, emergency employment programmes, hiring subsidies, and so forth).[3] The integrated approach makes it possible to improve coordination and complementarity of the various instruments by adapting them to the needs of the actors involved. This also facilitates the implementation of a cross-cutting gender approach in active policies that is essential for reasons of efficiency and equity.

Against the backdrop of the current economic crisis, some instruments of active policy have been redesigned or reinforced, with a view to limiting the impact of the fall in aggregate demand on the labour market. Some of the main examples include funding for training as an alternative to unemployment, retraining of laid-off workers, hiring subsidies and the renewal of public emergency-employment programmes (ECLAC/ILO, 2009).

Productive heterogeneity and labour-market segmentation can give rise to major inequalities in employment status among specific groups of workers, particularly women and young people. Labour institutions should take this situation into account and develop suitable instruments for fulfilling their dual objective of ensuring labour-market efficiency and strengthening the position of workers as

---

3 Although unemployment insurance may be managed by public employment services, such schemes can also be run in other ways.

structurally weaker actors, especially those who face additional inequalities.

Whereas active policies are relatively uncontroversial, in that their potential contribution satisfies (or at least does not contradict) the interests of governments, workers and business owners, the same cannot be said of policies governing collective and individual labour relations. Here, the viewpoint that any measure favourable to the interests of one social actor must be detrimental to those of the other is still common. Only some progress has been made towards analysing measures that suit the interests of employers and workers. Generating processes of social dialogue and political consensus at various levels, in which actors recognize each other as legitimate representatives of specific interests, can be a key mechanism for making headway in this regard. Starting off by discussing less controversial topics, such as active labour-market policies, can be a useful way of building the trust that is essential if broad consensuses are to be reached subsequently on thornier issues. International experience shows that there is no one ideal form for labour institutions, but rather various systems may help the region's countries rise to the challenges they face. Ultimately, enhanced and sustainable labour institutions should result from broad social dialogue and democratic decision-making processes in each of the region's countries.

Bibliography

Abramo, L. (2003), "Notas sobre la incorporación de la dimensión de género a las políticas de empleo y erradicación de la pobreza en América Latina", *Género y mercado de trabajo. Honduras y Nicaragua*, J. Fernández Pacheco (ed.), San José, International Labour Organization (ILO).

Abramo, L. and M. Rangel (eds.) (2005), *Negociación colectiva e igualdad de género en América Latina: un análisis comparativo*, Santiago, Chile, International Labour Organization (ILO).

Abramo, L. and M. Valenzuela (2006), "Inserción laboral y brechas de equidad de género en América Latina", *Trabajo decente y equidad de género en América Latina,* L. Abramo (ed.), Santiago, Chile, International Labour Organization (ILO).

Acemoglu, Daron and Robert Shimer (1999), "Productivity gains from unemployment insurance", *NBER Working Paper Series*, vol. 7352.

Aidt, T. and Z. Tzannatos (2002), *Union and Collective Bargaining: Economic Effect in a Global Environment*, Washington, D.C., World Bank.

Albuquerque, Letícia S.G. (2009), "Mobilidade de emprego entre os jovens no Brasil" *Mercado de trabalho*, No. 38, Institute of Applied Economic Research (IPEA), febrero.

Amadeo, E. and J. Camargo (1997), "Brazil: regulation and flexibility in the labor market", *Labor Markets in Latin America. Combining Social Protection with Market Flexibility*, S. Edwards and N. Lustig (eds.), Washington, D.C., Brookings Institution Press.

Arim, Rodrigo, Guillermo Cruces and Andrea Vigorito (2009), "Programas sociales y transferencias de ingresos en Uruguay: los beneficios no contributivos y las alternativas para su extensión", *Políticas sociales series*, No. 146 (LC/L.3002-P), Santiago, Chile, Economic Commission for Latin America and the Caribbean (ECLAC). United Nations publication, Sales No. S.09.II.G.10.

Arulampalam, W. (2000), "Is unemployment really scarring? Effects on unemployment experiences and wages", *IZA Discussion Paper*, No. 189.

Arulampalam, W., A. L. Booth and M.P. Taylor (2000), "Unemployment persistence", *Oxford Economic Papers*, No. 52.

Atkinson, A. and J. Micklewright (1991), "Unemployment compensation and labor market transitions", *Journal of Economic Literature*, vol. 29.

Auer, Peter, Janine Berg and Ibrahim Coulibaly (2005), "Is a stable workforce good for productivity?", *International Labour Review*, vol. 124, No. 3.

Auer, P., U. Efendioglu and J. Leschke (2005), *Active Labour Market Policies Around the World*, Geneva, International Labour Organization (ILO).

Balassa, Bela and others (1986), *Toward Renewed Economic Growth in Latin America*, Washington, D.C., Institute for International Economics.

Barbagelata, Héctor Hugo (2003), *Formación y legislación del trabajo,* Montevideo, Inter-American Research and Documentation Centre on Vocational Training (CINTERFOR).

Beccaria, L. and F. Groisman (2008), "Informalidad y pobreza: una relación compleja", *Argentina desigual*, L. Beccaria and F. Groisman (eds.), Universidad Nacional de General Sarmiento.

Beccaria, L. and R. Maurizio (2001), "Movilidad laboral e inestabilidad de ingresos en Argentina", document presented at the fifth meeting of the Red de Economía Social, Panama City.

Belzil, C. (2001), "Unemployment insurance and subsequent job duration: job matching vs. unobserved heterogeneity", *Journal of Applied Econometrics*, vol. 16, No. 5.

Berg, Janine and David Kucera (2008), "Labour institutions in the developing world: historical and theoretical perspectives", *In Defence of Labour Market Institutions. Cultivating Justice in the Developing World,* Janine Berg and David Kucera (ed.), Palgrave-MacMillan/ International Labour Organization (ILO).

Berg, Janine and Matthew Salerno (2008), "The origins of unemployment insurance: lessons for developing countries", *In Defence of Labour Market Institutions. Cultivating Justice in the Developing World,* Janine Berg and David Kucera (ed.), Palgrave- MacMillan/ International Labour Organization (ILO).

Berg, J. and D. Contreras (2004), "Political-economic regime and the wage curve: evidence from Chile, 1957-1996", *International Review of Applied Economics*, vol. 18, No. 2, April.

Bertranou, F. and J. Paz (2007), *Políticas y programas de protección al desempleo en Argentina*, Buenos Aires, International Labour Organization (ILO).

Bertranou, Fabio and others (2007a), "Un piso de protección social en América Latina. Costos fiscales e impactos sociales", International Labour Organization (ILO), unpublished.

___ (2007b), "Un piso de protección social para Argentina: una discusión sobre sus costos fiscales e impactos sociales", International Labour Organization (ILO), unpublished.

Betcherman, Gordon, Amy Luinstra and Makoto Ogawa (2001), "Labor market regulation: international experience in promoting employment and social protection", *Social Protection Discussion Paper Series*, No. 128, Washington, D.C., World Bank.

Betcherman, G., K. Olivas and A. Dar (2004), "Impacts of active labor market programs: new evidence from evaluations with particular attention to developing and transition countries", *Social Protection Discussion Paper Series*, No. 0402, Washington, D.C., World Bank, January.

BIS (Bank for International Settlements) (2009), "The global crisis and Latin America: financial impact and policy responses", *BIS Quarterly Review,* June.

Blanchard, O. (2003), "Designing labor market institutions", document presented at the Conference on labour markets, Santiago, Chile, Central Bank of Chile, November.

Blanchflower, D. and A. Oswald (1994), *The Wage Curve*, Cambridge, MA., MIT Press.

Boone J. and J. van Ours (2004), "Effective active labour market policies", *CEPR Discussion Paper Series*, No. 4707, October.

Bover, O., M. Arellano and S. Bentolila (1996), "Unemployment duration, benefit duration and the business cycle", *Estudios económicos*, No. 57, Bank of Spain.

Bravo, D. (2004), "Evaluación de impacto Programa Pro-Empleo. Línea bonificación a la contratación y capacitación laboral", Santiago, Chile, Departament of Economics, University of Chile, August.

Bucheli, M. and C. González (2007), "An estimation of the wage curve for Uruguay", Montevideo, Universidad de la República [online] http://www.bcu.gub.uy/autoriza/peiees/jor/2007/iees03j3400807.pdf.

Bucheli, M. and M. Furtado (2002), "Impacto del desempleo sobre el salario: el caso de Uruguay", *Desarrollo económico*, No. 165.

Burki, Shahid Javed and Guillermo E. Perry (1997), *The Long March. A Reform Agenda for Latin America and the Caribbean in the Next Decade*, Washington, D.C., World Bank.

Cahuc, P. and A. Zylberberg (2004), *Labor Economics*, The MIT Press.

Calderón, Miguel (2007), "Reflexión sobre los problemas de calidad de la formación profesional. Mecanismos para hacer más transparente el mercado formativo", *Working Document*, Lima, International Labour Organization (ILO).

Calderón-Madrid, Ángel y Belem Trejo (2001), "The impact of the Mexican training program for unemployed workers on re-employment. Dynamics and on earnings" [online] http://econpapers.repec.org/cpd/2002/86_Calderon.pdf.

Calvo, Guillermo (2009), "Lender of last resort: put it on the agenda!" [online] http://www.voxeu.org/index.php?q=node/3327.

Camacho, María Claudia (2008), "Empleo para jóvenes em las Américas: estrategias y recomendaciones de política", *Boletín técnico SENAC,* vol. 34, No. 3.

Candia, José Miguel (1994), "Gestión pública y mercado de trabajo en América Latina", *Economía y trabajo*, year II, No. 4.

Card, D. and A. Kreuger (1997), *Myth and Measurement: the New Economics of the Minimum Wage*, Princeton, Princeton University Press.

Card, D. and W. Riddell (1993), "A comparative analysis of unemployment in Canada and the United States",

Small Differences That Matter: Labor Markets and Income Maintenance in Canada and the United States, National Bureau of Economic Research (NBER).

Carling, K., P. Edin and B. Holmlund (1996), "Unemployment duration, unemployment benefits and labor market programs in Sweden", *Journal of Public Economics*, No. 59.

Cassoni, A., S. Allen and G. Labadie (2000), "Unions and employment in Uruguay", *IDB Research Network Working Paper*, No. R-392.

Cassoni, A., G. Labadie and G. Fachola (2005), "The economic effects of unions in Latin America: their impact on wages and economic performance of firms in Uruguay", *What Difference Do Unions Make?*, P. Kuhn and G. Márquez (eds.), Washington, D.C., Inter-American Development Bank (IDB).

Castro Lugo, D. (2006), "Curva salarial: una aplicación para el caso de México 1993-2002", *Estudios económicos*, vol. 21.

Cebrián, I. and others (1996), "The influence of unemployment benefits on unemployment duration: evidence from Spain", *Labour*, No. 10.

Cecchini, Simone and others (2009), "Desafíos de los programas de transferencias con correspopnsabilidad. Los casos de Guatemala, Honduras y Nicaragua", *Project documents*, No. 248 (LC/W.248), Santiago, Chile, Economic Commission for Latin America and the Caribbean (ECLAC).

Chacaltana, Juan (2009), "Magnitud y heterogeneidad: políticas de fomento del empleo juvenil y las microempresas", document prepared for the workshop The labour- market institutions' present challenges, Santiago, Chile, Economic Commission for Latin America and the Caribbean (ECLAC), unpublished.

___ (2005), "Programas de empleo en el Perú: racionalidad e impacto", Lima, Center for Development and Participation Studies (CEDEP)/Consorcio de Investigación Económica y Social (CIES).

Chacaltana, Juan and Norberto García (2001), "Reforma laboral, capacitación y productividad. La experiencia peruana", *Working Document*, No. 139, Lima, ILO Regional Office for Latin America and the Caribbean.

Chant, S. (2007), "The informal sector and employment", *The Companion to Development Studies,* V. Desai and R. Potter (eds.), London, Hodder-Arnold.

Chant, S. and C. Pedwell (2008), "Las mujeres, el género y la economía informal: evaluación de los estudios de la OIT y orientaciones sobre el trabajo futuro", Geneva, International Labour Office.

Chiappe, M. (2005), "Un camino colectivo de mujeres rurales hacia el desarrollo: la Asociación de Mujeres Rurales del Uruguay-AMRU", *Participación, productividad y formación: la trayectoria de la Asociación de Mujeres Rurales del Uruguay (AMRU),* M. Chiappe (ed.), Document No. 17, Montevideo, Inter-American Research and Documentation Centre on Vocational Training (CINTERFOR).

Chile, Ministry of Labour and Social Security (2003), *El trabajo y la protección social en Chile, 2000-2002*, Santiago, Chile.

Cox Edwards, Alejandra (1997), "Comentarios a la ponencia de Gustavo Márquez", document prepared for the second technical meeting of the Círculo de Montevideo.

Cowan, Kevin and others (2005), *Un diagnóstico del desempleo en Chile*, Santiago, Chile, University of Chile.

Cruces, Guillermo and Andrés Ham (2009), "La flexibilidad laboral en América Latina: las reformas pasadas y las perspectivas futuras", Santiago, Chile, Economic Commission for Latin America and the Caribbean (ECLAC), unpublished.

Daeren, L. (2001), "Enfoque de género en la política económica-laboral. El estado del arte en América Latina y el Caribe", *Mujer y desarrollo series*, No. 29 (LC/L.1500-P/E), Santiago, Chile, Economic Commission for Latin America and the Caribbean (ECLAC). United Nations publication, Sales No. S.01.II.G.44.

Damill, M., R. Frenkel and R. Maurizio (2002), "Argentina: a decade of currency board. An analysis of growth, employment and income distribution", *Employment Paper*, No. 2002/42, Geneva, International Labour Office.

Darr, A. and Z. Tzannatos (1999), "Active labor market programs: a review of the evidence from evaluations", *Social Protection Discussion Paper,* No. 9901, Washington, D.C., World Bank, January.

De la Garza Toledo, Enrique (2002), "Libre comercio y relaciones laborales en México", document presented at the International Labor Standard Conference, Stanford, Stanford Law School, 19-21 May.

Dolton, P. and A. Vignoles (1997), "The incidence and effects of overeducation in the graduate labor market", *Economics of Education Review*, vol. 19, No. 2.

Downes, Andrew (2009), "Flexible labour markets, workers' protection and active labour market policies in the Caribbean", *Macroeconomía del desarrollo series*, No. 86 (LC/L.3063-P), Santiago, Chile, Economic Commission for Latin America and the Caribbean (ECLAC). United Nations publication, Sales No. E.09.II.G.59.

Echeverría, Rafael (1985), "Empleo público en América Latina", *Investigaciones sobre empleo*, No. 26, Santiago, Chile, Regional Employment Programme for Latin America and the Caribbean (PREALC).

ECLAC (Economic Commission for Latin America and the Caribbean) (2009a), *Foreign Direct Investment in Latin America and the Caribbean, 2008* (LC/G.2406-P), Santiago, Chile.

___ (2009b), The reactions of the Governments of the Americas to the international crisis: an overview of policy measures up to 31 May 2009 (LC/L.3025/Rev.1), Santiago, Chile, June.

___ (2008a), *Structural Change and Productivity Growth - 20 Years Later. Old problems, new opportunities* (LC/G.2367(SES.32/3)), Santiago, Chile.

___ (2008b), *Labour Markets, Worker Protection, and Lifelong Learning in a Global Economy: experiences and perspectives of Latin America and the Caribbean* (LC/L.2880), Santiago, Chile, April.

___ (2008c), *Social Panorama of Latin America, 2008* (LC/G.2402-P), Santiago, Chile, December.

___ (2008d), *Women's Contribution to Equality in Latin America and the Caribbean* (LC/L.2738(CRM.10/3)), Santiago, Chile.

___ (2008e), *Preliminary Overview of the Economies of Latin America and the Caribbean, 2008* (LC/G.2401-P), Santiago, Chile. United Nations publication, Sales No. E.08.II.G.2.

___ (2008f), *Economic Survey of Latin America and the Caribbean, 2007-2008* (LC/G.2386-P), Santiago, Chile.

___ (2007), *Soical Cohesion: Inclusion and a Sense of Belonging in Latin America and the Caribbean* (LC/G.2335), Santiago, Chile, ECLAC/Ibero-American Secretariat (SEGIB).

___ (2006), *Shaping the Future of Social Protection: Access, Financing and Solidarity* (LC/G.2294(SES.31/3)), Santiago, Chile.

___ (2004), Productive Development in Opean Economies (LC/G.2234(SES.30/3)), Santiago, Chile, June.

ECLAC/OIJ (Economic Commission for Latin America and the Caribbean/Ibero-American Youth Organization) (2008), *Juventud y cohesión social en Iberoamérica. Un modelo para armar* (LC/G.2391), Santiago, Chile.

ECLAC/ILO (Economic Commission for Latin America and the Caribbean/International Labour Organization) (2009), "Crisis and the labour market", *ECLAC/ILO Bulletin The employment situation in Latin America and the Caribbean*, No. 1, Santiago, Chile, June.

Edmond, C. and L. Veldkamp (2008), "Income dispersion and counter-cyclical markups", *NBER Working Paper*, No. 14452.

Eichengreen, Barry and K.H. O'Rourke (2009), "A tale of two depressions" [online] http://www.voxeu.org/index.php?q=node/3421.

Escobar, Luis Eduardo (2009), "El seguro de cesantía en Chile: diagnóstico y propuestas para fortalecerlo", Santiago, Chile, unpublished.

Ehrenberg, R. and R. Oaxaca (1976), "Unemployment insurance, duration of unemployment and subsequent wage gain", *American Economic Review*, vol. 66, No. 5.

Eyraud, F. and C. Saget (2008), "The revival of minimum wage setting institutions", *In Defence of Labour Market Institutions: Cultivating Justice in the Developing World*, J. Berg and D. Kucera (eds.), Palgrave MacMillan.

Fairris, D. (2006), "Union voice effects in Mexico", *British Journal of Industrial Relations*, vol. 44, No. 4.

___ (2005), "What do unions do in Mexico?", University of California Riverside [online] http://www.economics.ucr.edu/people/fairris/mexunioneffects.

Fajnzylber, P., W.F. Maloney and G.V.M. Rojas (2006), "Does formality improve micro-firm performance? Quasi-experimental evidence from the Brazilian SIMPLES program" [online] http://www.fedesarrollo.org.co/includes/scripts/open.asp?ruta=/images/dynamic/articles/521/Fajnzylber.pdf.

Fanelli, J.M. and J.P. Jiménez (2009), *Crisis, volatilidad, ciclo y política fiscal en América Latina* (LC/L.3038), Santiago, Chile, Economic Commission for Latin America and the Caribbean (ECLAC).

Farné, S. (2009), "Políticas activas del mercado de trabajo en Colombia, México y Perú", document prepared for the workshop The labour- market institutions' present challenges, Santiago, Chile, Economic Commission for Latin America and the Caribbean(ECLAC), unpublished.

Feliciano, Zadia (1998), "Does the minimum wage affect employment in Mexico?", *Eastern Economic Journal*, vol. 24, No. 2.

Feldman, S. (1996), "El trabajo de los adolescentes en Argentina. ¿Construyendo futuro o consolidando la postergación social?", *Adolescencia, pobreza, educación y trabajo*, I. Konterllnik and C. Jacinto, Buenos Aires, Losada.

Fernández Pacheco, J. (2003), "Género, pobreza y mercado de trabajo para las mujeres en Honduras", *Género y mercado de trabajo. Honduras y Nicaragua,* J. Fernández Pacheco (ed.), San José, International Labour Organization (ILO).

Fields, Gary S. (2007), "Labor market policy in developing countries: a selective review of the literature and needs for the future", *World Bank Policy Research Working Paper,* No. 4362, Washington, D.C., World Bank.

Filmus, D., A. Miranda and J. Zelarayan (2001), "En el mercado de trabajo, ¿el saber no ocupa lugar? Egresados de la Escuela Media y primer año de inserción laboral", document presented at the fifth Conference of the Association of Labor Studies Experts of Argentina (ASET), Buenos Aires.

Fitzenberger, B. and R. Wilke (2007), "New insights on unemployment duration and post unemployment earnings in Germany: censored Box-Cox quantile regression at work", *IZA Discussion Paper*, No. 2609.

Freeman, R. (2009), "Labor regulations, unions, and social protection in developing countries: market distortions or efficient institutions?", *NBER Working Paper*, No. 14789, March.

___ (2005), "Labour market institutions without blinders: the debate over flexibility and labour market performance", *NBER Working Paper*, No. 11286.

___ (1993), "Labor markets and institutions in economic development", *American Economic Review*, vol. 83, No. 2, May.

Freeman, R. and E. Lazear (1995), "An economic analysis of Works Councils", *Works Councils: Consultation, Representation, Cooperation*, Joel Rogers and Wolfgang Streeck (eds.), University of Chicago Press.

Frías, P. (2009), "Papel de los sindicatos y la negociación colectiva y su impacto en la eficiencia y la equidad del mercado de trabajo", document presented at the workshop The labour- market institutions' present challenges, Santiago, Chile, Economic Commission for Latin America and the Caribbean (ECLAC), unpublished.

Galasso, E., M. Ravallion and A. Salvia (2001), "Assisting the Transition from Workfare to Work: Argentina's Proempleo Experiment", World Bank [online] http://poverty.worldbank.org/files/11255_Martin-PROEMPLEO-Evaluation.pdf.

Galiani, S. (1999), "Wage determination in Argentina: an econometric analysis with methodology discussion", Buenos Aires, Universidad Torcuato Di Tella, unpublished.

Galiani, S. and H. Hopenhayn (2000), "Duración y riesgo de desempleo en Argentina", *Documento de trabajo FADE*, No. 18, Buenos Aires.

Gallart, María Antonia (2002), "Habilidades y competencias para el sector informal en América Latina: una revisión de literatura sobre programas y metodologías de formación", *Documento de trabajo,* No. 7, InFocus Programme on Skills, Knowledge and Employability, Geneva, International Labour Organization (ILO).

Gallart, M., M. Moreno and M. Cerruti, (1993), *Educación y empleo en el Gran Buenos Aires 1980-1991. Situación y perspectivas de investigación*, Buenos Aires, Centre for Population Studies (CENEP).

García y Santos, Rosario (2005), "A diez años de la fundación de AMRU: algunos comentarios y reflexiones sobre lecciones aprendidas y futuros desafíos", *Participación, productividad y formación: la trayectoria de la Asociación de Mujeres Rurales del Uruguay (AMRU)*, M. Chiappe (ed.), Document No. 17, Montevideo, Inter-American Research and Documentation Centre on Vocational Training (CINTERFOR).

García, Juan Manuel and Manuel Hernández (2005), *Servicios de desarrollo empresarial: ¿el por qué de su poca demanda?*, Lima, Grade.

Gindling, T. and K. Terrell (2007a), "The effects of multiple minimum wages throughout the labor market: the case of Costa Rica", *Labour Economics*, No. 12.

___ (2007b), "Minimum wages and the welfare of workers in Honduras", *IZA Discussion Paper*, No. 2892.

___ (2005), "The effect of minimum wages on actual wages in the formal and informal sectors of Costa Rica", *World Development*, vol. 33, No. 11.

Goldin, Adrián (2008), "Normas laborales y mercado de trabajo argentino; seguridad y flexibilidad", *Macroeconomía del desarrollo series*, No. 74 (LC/L.2985-P), Santiago, Chile, Economic Commission for Latin America and the Caribbean (ECLAC). United Nations publication, Sales No. S.08.II.G.91.

Gonzaga, G. (2003), "Labor turnover and labor legislation in Brazil", *Discussion Paper*, No. 475, Department of Economics, Rio de Janeiro, Catholic University of Rio de Janeiro.

Gonzáles, Darío (2006), "Regímenes especiales de tributación para pequeños contribuyentes en América Latina", Washington, D.C., Inter-American Development Bank (IDB).

Green, F., S. McIntosh and A. Vignoles (1999), "Overeducation and Skills. Clarifying the concepts", London, Centre for Economic Performance, London School of Economics and Political Science.

Gregg, P. and J. Wadsworth (1996), "Mind the gap, please? The changing nature of entry jobs in Britain", *CEP Discussion Paper*, No. 303, London, Center for Economic Performance (CEP).

Gregory, Peter (1986), *The Myth of Market Failure. Employment and the Labor Market in Mexico*, Baltimore, Johns Hopkins University Press.

Gregory, M. and R. Jukes (1997), "The effects of unemployment on subsequent earnings: A study of British men 1984-94", *The Labour Market Consequences of Technical and Structural Change*, Papers, No. 21, London, Centre for Economic Performance (CEP).

Haan, H. (2007), "Training for work in the informal economy", Geneva, International Labour Office, unpublished.

Hahn J., J. Hausman and G. Kuersteiner (2007), "Long difference instrumental variables estimation for dynamic panel models with fixed effects", *Journal of Econometrics,* No. 140.

Haltiwanger, J., S. Scarpetta and H. Schweiger (2008), "Asssessing job flows across countries: the role of industry, firm size, and regulations", *NBER Working Paper*, No. 13920.

Hammermesh, D. (1993), *Labor Demand*, Princeton, Princeton University Press.

Heckman, J. and C. Pagés (2003), "Law and employment: lessons from Latin America and the Caribbean", *NBER Working Paper*, No. 10129.

Hopenhayn, H. (2001), "Labor market policies and employment duration: the effects of labor market reform in Argentina", *IDB Research Network Working Paper*, No. R.407.

Hoyle Cox, Jenny (2005), *Investigación de programas y políticas de empleo para jóvenes. Chile-Colombia-Perú*, Regional Employment Programme for Latin America and the Caribbean (PREALC), December.

IDB (Inter-American Development Bank) (2009), "Policy Trade-offs for Unprecedented Times: Confronting the Global Crisis in Latin America and the Caribbean" [online] http://www.iadb.org/res/pub_desc.cfm?pub_id=B-635.

___ (1997), *Economic and Social Progress in Latin America, 1997 Report*, Washington, D.C.

ILO (International Labour Organization) (2009), "Update on minimum wage developments" (GB.304/ESP/3), 304th session of the Governing Body, Geneva.

___ (2007a), *Asignaciones familiares en Uruguay. Evaluación y propuestas de reformas*, Santiago, Chile, ILO Subregional Office for the Southern Cone of Latin America.

___ (2007b), "The informal economy" (GB.298/ESP/4), 298th session of the Governing Body, committee on Employment and Social Policy, Geneva [online] http://www.ilo.org/public/english/standards/relm/gb/docs/gb298/pdf/esp-4.pdf.

___ (2007c), *Trabajo decente y juventud: América Latina*, Lima.

___ (2006), *Chile: superando la crisis, mejorando el empleo. Políticas de mercado de trabajo, 2000-2005*, Santiago, Chile, International Labour Office.

___ (2004), *Economic Security for a Better World*, Geneva.

___ (2002) "Decent Work and the Informal Economy", 90th session, International Labour Conference, Geneva [online] www.ilo.org/public/english/standards/relm/ilc/ilc90/pdf/rep-vi.pdf.

ILO/IPEC (International Labour Organization/International Programme on the Elimination of Child Labour) (2007), *Trabajo infantil y los programas de transferencias en efectivo condicionadas en América Latina*, San José.

Infante, Ricardo and Osvaldo Sunkel (2009), "Chile: towards inclusive development", *CEPAL Review*, No. 97 (LC/G.2400-P), Santiago, Chile, Economic Commission for Latin America and the Caribbean (ECLAC).

ITUC (International Trade Union Confederation) (2009), "Annual survey of violation of trade union rights" [online] http://survey09.ituc-csi.org/survey.php?IDContinent=0&Lang=EN.

Jacinto, C. (1996), "Transición laboral de los jóvenes, políticas públicas y estrategias de los actores", document presented at the second National Congress on Labour Sociology, Buenos Aires, Association of Labor Studies Experts of Argentina (ASET).

Jalan, J. and M. Ravallion (2003), "Estimating the benefit incidence of an antipovery program by propensity-score matching", *Journal of Business and Economic Statistics*, vol. 21, No. 1.

___ (1999), "Income gains to the poor from workfare. Estimates for Argentina Trabajar Program", Washington, D.C., World Bank.

Jiménez, Juan Pablo and Juan Carlos Gómez Sabaini (2009), *The Role of Tax Policy in the Context of the Global Crisis: Consequences and Prospects* (LC/L.3037), Santiago, Chile, Economic Commission for Latin America and the Caribbean (ECLAC).

Jiménez, Juan Pablo and Andrea Podestá (2009), "Inversión, incentivos fiscales y gastos tributarios en América Latina", *Macroeconomía del desarrollo series,* No. 77 (LC/L.3004-P), Santiago, Chile, Economic Commission for Latin America and the Caribbean (ECLAC).

Jørgensen, Henning (2009), "Flexible labour markets, workers´ protection and 'the security of the wings': a Danish "flexicurity" solution to the unemployment and social problems in globalized economies?", *Macroeconomía del desarrollo series*, No. 76 (LC/L.2993-P), Santiago, Chile, Economic Commission for Latin America and the Caribbean (ECLAC).

Kahn, L. (2003), "Collective bargaining and the interindustry wage structure: international evidence", *Economica*, vol. 65, No. 240.

Kantor, P. (2002), "Female mobility in India: the influence of seclusion norms on economic outcomes", *International Development Planning Review*, vol. 24, No. 2.

Kaplan, D., Eduardo Piedra and Enrique Seira (2007), "Are burdensome registration procedures an important barrier on firm creation? Evidence from Mexico", Economic Research Centre, Autonomous Technological Institute of Mexico (ITAM).

Katz, L. and B. Meyer (1990), "The impact of the potential duration of unemployment benefits on the duration of unemployment", *Journal of Public Economics*, vol. 41, No. 1.

Kugler, A. (2002), "From severance pay to self-insurance: effects of severance payments savings accounts in Colombia", *Discussion Paper*, No. 3197, London, Centre for Economic Policy Research.

___ (2000), "The incidence of job security regulations on labor market flexibility and compliance in Colombia: evidence from the 1990 reform", *IDB Research Network Working Paper*, No. R.393.

Krugman, Paul (2009), "The Great Recession versus the Great Depression" [online] http://krugman.blogs.nytimes.com/2009/03/20/the-great-recession-versus-the-great-depression/.

Lanari, M. (2004), "Las políticas de empleo en los países del Mercosur, 1990-2003. Estudio analítico sobre progamas de empleo ejecutados en Argentina", document presented at the International Seminar on Employment, Unemployment and Labour Policies in MERCOSUR and the European Union, Buenos Aires.

Lancaster, T. (1990), "The econometric analysis of transition data", *Econometric Society Monographs*, No. 17, Cambridge, Cambridge University Press.

Lancaster, T. and S. Nickell (1980), "The analysis of re-employment probabilities for the unemployed", *Journal of the Royal Statistic Society*, No. 143.

Lemos, S. (2007), "Minimum wages across the public and private sectors in Brazil", *Journal of Development Studies*, vol. 43, No. 4.

___(2004), "Minimum wage policy and employment effects: evidence from Brazil", *Economia*, Fall.

Lessinger, J. (1990), "Work and modesty: the dilemma of women market traders in Madras", *Structures and Strategies*, L. Dube and R. Palriwala (eds.), New Delhi, Sage.

Linares, Dino (2008), "Emprendimiento juvenil: el caso del Colectivo Integral de Desarrollo (CID)", document presented at the International Seminar on Youth Employment Policies and Programmes in Latin America, La Paz, December.

Llisterri, J.J. and others (2006), *Is Youth Entrepreneurship a Necessity or an Opportunity. A First Exploration of Household and New Enterprise Surveys in Latin America,* Washington, D.C., May.

López Estrada, S. (2002), "Work, gender and space: women's home-based work in Tijuana, Mexico", *Journal of Developing Societies,* vol. 18, No. 2-3.

Lozano, Ricardo (2008), "Las compras estatales y las Mipymes" [online] http://www.cafamdesarrollo empresarial.com/download/las.compras.estatales.y.las.mipymes.pdf, January.

Lund, F. and S. Srinivas (2000), "Learning from experience: a gendered approach to social protection for workers in the informal economy", *Programa sobre Estrategias y Técnicas contra la Exclusión Social y la Pobreza (STEP) y el empleo informal y la mujer: mundialización y organización (WIEGO)*, Geneva, International Labour Office.

Lustig, N. and D. McCleod (1997), "Minimum wages and poverty in developing countries. Some empirical evidence", *Labor Markets in Latin America*, S. Edwards and N. Lustig (eds.), Washington, D.C., Brookings Institution.

Maloney, W. and J. Nuñez Mendez (2003), "Measuring the impact of minimum wages: evidence from Latin America", *NBER Working Paper*, No. 9800.

___(2001), "Measuring the impact of minimum wages: evidence from Latin America", *World Bank Policy Research Working Paper*, No. 2597, Washington, D.C., World Bank.

Maloney, W. and E. Ribeiro (1999), "Efficiency wage and union effects in labor demand and wage structure in Mexico. An application of quantile analysis", *World Bank Policy Research Working Paper*, No. 2131, Washington, D.C., World Bank.

Manning, A. (2003), *Monopsony in Motion: Imperfect Competition in Labor Markets*, Princeton University Press.

Marchionni, M., G. Bet and A. Navarro (2007), "Empleo, educación y entorno social de los jóvenes: una nueva fuente de información", *Documento de trabajo*, No. 61, La Plata, Centro de Estudios Distributivos Laborales y Sociales (CEDLAS).

Marinakis, A. (2008), *Evolución de los salarios en América Latina, 1995-2006*, Santiago, Chile, International Labour Organization (ILO).

Marinakis, A. and J. Velasco (2006), "Paraguay: evolución reciente y propuestas para una modernización del salario mínimo", *¿Para qué sirve el salario mínimo? Elementos para su determinación en los países del Cono Sur*, A. Marinakis and J. Velasco, Santiago, Chile, International Labour Organization (ILO).

Martin, J. and D. Grubb (2001), "What works and for whom: a review of OECD countries' experiences with active labour market policies", *Swedish Economic Policy Review*, No. 8.

Mato, Francisco (2003), "Estudio sobre las experiencias europeas con los instrumentos de evaluación de las políticas del mercado de trabajo", *Macroeconomía del desarrollo series*, No. 21 (LC/L.1846-P/E), Santiago, Chile, Economic Commission for Latin America and the Caribbean (ECLAC), January. United Nations publication, Sales No. S.03.II.G.13.

Maurizio, R. (2009a), *Inestabilidad en el mercado de trabajo. Un análisis dinámico para Argentina*, Buenos Aires, Editorial de la Universidad de La Plata, forthcoming.

___(2009b), "Enfoque de género en las políticas laborales y del mercado de trabajo en América Latina", document prepared for the workshop The labour- market institutions' present challenges, Santiago, Chile, Economic Commission for Latin America and the Caribbean (ECLAC), unpublished.

Mazza, J. (2003), "Labour intermediation services: lessons for Latin America and the Caribbean", *CEPAL Review*, No. 80 (LC/G.2204-P), Santiago, Chile, Economic Commission for Latin America and the Caribbean (ECLAC), August.

Medina, C. and J. Nuñez (2001), "The impact of public and private job training in Colombia", *IDB Research*

Network Working Paper, No. R.484, Washington, D.C., Inter-American Development Bank (IDB).

Menezes-Filho, N. and others (2005), "Unions and the economic performance of Brazilian establishments", *The Economic Effects of Unions in Latin America*, P. Kuhn and G. Márquez (coords.), Washington, D.C., Inter-American Development Bank (IDB).

Meyer, B. (1990), "Unemployment insurance and unemployment spells", *Econometrica*, No. 58.

Milosavljevic, V. (2007), "Estadísticas para la equidad de género. Magnitudes y tendencias en América Latina", *Cuadernos de la CEPAL*, No. 92 (LC/G.2321-P), Santiago, Chile, Economic Commission for Latin America and the Caribbean(ECLAC)/United Nations Development Fund for Women (UNIFEM). United Nations publication, Sales No. S.06.II.G.132.

Miranda, A. and A. Salvia (2001), "Transformaciones en las condiciones de vida de los jóvenes en los noventa. Estimación de determinantes a través de regresiones", *Cuadernos del CEPED*, No. 5, Facultad de Ciencias Económicas, Universidad de Buenos Aires.

Mondino, G. and S. Montoya (2000), "The effects of labor market regulations on employment decisions by firms: empirical evidence for Argentina", *IDB Research Network Working Paper*, No. R.391, Washington, D.C., Inter-American Development Bank (IDB).

Monteiro, Joana C. M. y Juliano J. Assunção (2006), *Outgoing the Shadows: Estimating the Impact of Bureaucracy Simplification and Tax Cut on Formality and Investment*, Rio de Janiero, Department of Economics, Catholic University of Rio de Janeiro.

Montenegro, C. and C. Pagés (2004), "Who benefits from labor market regulations? Chile, 1968-1988", Law and Employment: Lessons from Latin America and the Carribean, J. Heckman and C. Pagés (eds.), Cambridge, National Bureau of Economic Research (NBER).

Mortensen, D. (1986), "Job search and labor market analysis", *Handbook of Labor Economics*, O. Ashenfelter and D. Card (eds.), Amsterdam, North Holland.

Mortensen, D. and C. Pissarides (1999), "New developments in models of search in the labor market", *Handbook of Labor Economics*, O. Ashenfelter and D. Card (eds.), Amsterdam, North Holland.

___ (1994), "Job creation and job destruction in the theory of unemployment", *Review of Economic Studies*, vol. 61, No. 3.

Murray, U. (2006), "Gender and skills development: practical experiences and ways forward", Geneva, International Labour Office, unpublished.

Narendranathan, W., S. Nickell and J. Stern (1985), "Unemployment benefits revisited", *Economic Journal*, No. 95.

Navarro, Lucas (2009), "Dinámica del empleo y crisis en America latina: Resultados de estimaciones de panel", document presented at the workshop The labour-market institutions' present challenges, Santiago, Chile, Economic Commission for Latin America and the Caribbean (ECLAC), unpublished.

Neumark, D. and W. Wascher (2006), "Wages and employment: a review of evidence from the new minimum wage research", *NBER Working Paper*, No. 12663, November.

Nickel, S., T. Jones and G. Quintini (2000), "A picture of job insecurity facing British men", *CEP Discussion Papers*, No. 0479, London, Centre for Economic Performance (CEP).

Paes de Barros, R. and C. Leite Corseuil (1999), "Labor market regulations and the duration of employment in Brazil", *IPEA Working Paper*, No. 676.

Palomino, H. (2007), "Un nuevo indicador del Ministerio de Trabajo, Empleo y Seguridad Social. Los conflictos laborales en la Argentina 2006-2007", *Estudios series*, No. 7, Buenos Aires, Ministry of Labour, Employment and Social Security, November.

Pautassi, Laura, Eleonor Faur and Natalia Gherardi (2004), "Legislación laboral en seis países latinoamericanos. Avances y omisiones para una mayor equidad", *Mujer y desarrollo series*, No. 56 (LC/L.2140-P/E), Santiago, Chile, Economic Commission for Latin America and the Caribbean (ECLAC).

Popli, G. (2006), "The rising wage inequality in Mexico, 1984-2000: a distributional analysis", *MPRA Paper*, No. 399, University Library of Munich.

PREALC (Regional Employment Programme for Latin America and the Caribbean) (1991), *Empleo y equidad: el desafío de los 90*, Santiago, Chile.

___ (1982), *Mercado de trabajo en cifras. 1950-1980*, Santiago, Chile.

Puyo Posada, J. (2007), "Los aspectos laborales en los tratados de libre comercio con EE.UU.", Bogotá, Instituto de Ciencia Política Hernán Echevarría Olózaga.

Ravallion, M. (1999), "Appraising workfare", *The World Bank Observer*, No. 14.

Revenga, A., M. Riboud and H. Tan (1994), "The impact of Mexico's Retraining Program on Employment and Wages", *World Bank Economic Review,* No. 8.

Ribas, R., F.V. Soares and G. Hirata (2008), "The impact of CCTs. What we know and what we are not sure about", *Cash Transfers. Lesson from Africa and Latin America,* Poverty in Focus, No. 15, United Nations Development Programme (UNDP).

Rico, N. (2003), "Los sistemas de pensiones y sus deudas con la equidad de género entre las personas adultas mayores", document presented at the Regional Intergovernmental Conference on Ageing: Towards a Regional Strategy for the Implementation in Latin America and the Caribbean of the Madrid International Plan of Action on Ageing.

Rodgers, G. (1993), "Instituciones del trabajo y desarrollo económico", *Reestructuración y regulación institucional del mercado de trabajo en América Latina,* Investigación series, No. 98, Geneva, International Labour Organization (ILO).

Rodríguez, Eduardo (2006), "Igualdad de género y movimiento sindical", *Trabajo decente y equidad de género en América Latina,* L. Abramo (ed.), Santiago, Chile, International Labour Organization (ILO).

Rogerson, R., R. Shimer and R. Wright (2005), "Search-theoretic models of the labor market: a survey", *Journal of Economic Literature*, vol. XLIII.

Saavedra, J. and M. Torero (2005), "Union density changes and union effects on firm performance in Peru", *What Difference Do Unions Make?*, P. Kuhn and G. Márquez (eds.), Washington, D.C., Inter-American Development Bank (IDB).

___ (2000), "Labor market reforms and their impact on formal labor demand and job market turnover: the case of Peru", *IDB Research Network Working Paper*, No. R.394.

Samaniego, N. (2002), "Las políticas de mercado de trabajo y su evaluación en América Latina", *Macroeconomía del desarrollo series*, No. 19 (LC/L.1836-P/E), Santiago, Chile, Economic Commission for Latin America and the Caribbean (ECLAC). United Nations publication, Sales No. S.02.II.G.142.

Sanhueza, C. and J. Castillo (2008), "Seguro de desempleo y riesgo individual del desempleo: caso chileno", Santiago, Chile, unpublished.

Sarmiento, A. and others (2007), "Evaluación del impacto del SENA en el capital social", Bogotá, August, unpublished.

Schkolnik, Mariana, Consuelo Araos and Felipe Machado (2005), "Certificación de competencias como parte del sistema de protección social: la experiencia de países desarrollados y lineamientos para América Latina", *Políticas sociales series*, No. 113 (LC/L.2438-P), Santiago, Chile, Economic Commission for Latin America and the Caribbean(ECLAC). United Nations publciation, Sales No. S.05.II.G.184.

Sepúlveda Malbrán, Juan Manuel, Kirsten-María Schapira-Felderhoff and Quentin Delpech (2009), *La libertad sindical y la negociación colectiva en Centroamérica, Panamá y República Dominicana. Un panorama de su estado actual*, San José, International Labour Organization (ILO).

Sicherman, N. (1991), "Overeducation in the labor market", *Journal of Labor Economics*, vol. 9.

Silveira, S. (2005), "Introducción: desarrollo rural, género y formación para el trabajo", *Participación, productividad y formación: la trayectoria de la Asociación de Mujeres Rurales del Uruguay (AMRU)*, M. Chiappe (ed.), Document No. 17, Montevideo, Inter-American Research and Documentation Centre on Vocational Training (CINTERFOR).

Silveira, S. and A. Matosa (2003), "Género y economía informal en América Latina. Nuevos retos y respuestas posibles desde las políticas de formación para el trabajo", *Boletín Técnico Interamericano de Formación Profesional,* segunda época, Montevideo.

Solow, Robert M. (1992), *The Labour Market as Social Institution*, Blackwell.

Squire, Lyn (1981), *Employment Policy in Developing Countries. A Survey of Issues and Evidence*, New York, World Bank/Oxford University Press.

STPS (Secretariat of Labour and Social Security of Mexico) (1995), "Evaluación del programa de Becas de Capacitación para Desempleados", Mexico City.

Tatsiramos, K. (2006), "Unemployment insurance in Europe: unemployment duration and subsequent employment stability", *IZA Discussion Paper*, No. 2280.

Tokman, Víctor (2009), "El empleo en las crisis: efectos y políticas", document presented at the workshop The labour-market institutions' present challenges, Santiago, Chile, Economic Commission for Latin America and the Caribbean (ECLAC), unpublished.

___ (2008a), "Flexiguridad con informalidad: opciones y restricciones", *Macroeconomía del desarrollo series*, No. 70 (LC/L.2973-P), Santiago, Chile, Economic Commission for Latin America and the Caribbean (ECLAC).

___ (2008b), "Desempleo juvenil en América Latina: causas, consecuencias y políticas", document prepared for the United Nations Development Programme (UNDP), unpublished.

___ (1982), "Unequal development and the absorption of labour. Latin America 1950-80", *CEPAL Review*, No. 17 (E/CEPAL/G.1205), Santiago, Chile, Economic Commission for Latin America and the Caribbean (ECLAC).

Tomei, Manuela (2006), "El nexo entre discriminación e igualdad de género en el trabajo: algunas consideraciones conceptuales y de políticas", *Trabajo decente y equidad de género en América Latina*, L. Abramo (ed.), Santiago, Chile, International Labour Organization (ILO).

Toyama, Jorge (2008), "Análisis de la implementación de la propuesta de la flexibilidad laboral en el Perú", Santiago, Chile, Economic Commission for Latin America and the Caribbean (ECLAC), unpublished.

Toyama, Jorge, Victoria Rosas Chávez and Marta Tostes Vieira (2009), "Retos pendientes para implementar la flexiguridad en el Perú", *Project Documents*, No. 268 (LC/W.268), Santiago, Chile, Economic Commission for Latin America and the Caribbean (CEPAL), forthcoming.

Trajtemberg, D. (2008), "El impacto de la determinación colectiva de salarios sobre la dispersión salarial", unpublished.

Tueros, Mario (2008), "Emprendimiento juvenil", presentation at the International Seminar on Youth Employment Policies and Programmes in Latin America, La Paz, December.

___ (2005), "Los servicios de desarrollo empresarial: un paradigma en transición", document presented at the XX Latin American symposium on small and medium-sized enterprises "Desarrollo local e inserción global: el nuevo desafío de la integración", Lima, 21 September.

Universidad de Chile (2004), "Programas de empleo con apoyo fiscal: informe final, evaluación de impacto", Santiago, Chile, Faculty of Economics.

UNWTO (World Tourism Organization) (2009), *World Tourism Barometer*, June.

Urízar, C. and S. Lée (2005), "The effects of unions on productivity. Evidence from large coffee producers in Guatamala", *What Difference Do Unions Make?*, P. Kuhn and G. Márquez (eds.), Washington, D.C., Inter-American Development Bank (IDB).

Valenzuela, M. (2005), "Informality and gender in Latin America", *Working Document,* No. 60, Geneva, International Labour Organization (ILO).

___ (ed.) (2003), "Mujeres, pobreza y mercado de trabajo. Argentina y Paraguay", proyecto Incorporación de la dimensión de género en las políticas de erradicación de la pobreza y generación de empleo en América Latina, International Labour Organization (ILO).

Valenzuela, M. and S. Venegas (2001), *Mitos y realidades de la microempresa en Chile: un análisis de género,* Santiago, Chile, Centre for Women's Studies (CEM).

Van den Berg, G. (1994), "The effects of changes of the job offer arrival rate on the duration of unemployment", *Journal of Labor Economics*, vol. 12, No. 3.

Van Ours, J. and M. Vodopivec (2006), "Shortening the potential duration of unemployment benefits does not affect the quality of post-unemployment job: evidence from a natural experiment", *IZA Discussion Paper,* No. 2171.

Vega Ruiz, M. (2005), "La reforma laboral: un análisis comparado", Lima, ILO Regional Office for Latin America and the Caribbean.

Velásquez Pinto, Mario (2009a), "Flexibilidad, protección y políticas activas en Chile", *Macroeconomía del desarrollo series*, No. 78 (LC/L.3006-P), Santiago, Chile, Economic Commission for Latin America and the Caribbean (ECLAC). United Nations publication, Sales No. S.09.II.G.19.

___ (2009b), "Seguros de desempleo y funcionamiento eficiente y equitativo de los mercados de trabajo", document presented at the workshop The labour-market institutions' present challenges, Santiago, Chile, Economic Commission for Latin America and the Caribbean(CEPAL), April.

___ (2005), "Seguros de desempleo, objetivos, características y situación en América Latina", *Financiamiento del desarrollo series*, No. 133 (LC/L.1917-P/E), Santiago, Chile, Economic Commission for Latin America and the Caribbean (ECLAC). United Nations publication, Sales No. S.03.II.G.73.

Vera-Sanso, P. (2006), "Defining the neighbourhood in South India", *The Meaning of the Local: Revisiting the Urban Neighbourhood in South India,* Geert de Neve and H. Donner (eds.), London, Routledge.

Villatoro, P. (2008), "CCTs in Latin America: human capital accumulation and poverty reduction", *Cash Transfers. Lesson from Africa and Latin America,* Poverty in Focus, No. 15, United Nations Development Programme (UNDP).

___ (2007), "Las transferencias condicionadas en América Latina: luces y sombras", document presented at the International Seminar "Evolución y desafios de los programas de transferencias condicionadas", Economic Commission for Latin America and the Caribbean (ECLAC)/Institute of Applied Economic Research (IPEA).

Weller, Jürgen (2009), "Retos y respuestas: las políticas laborales y del mercado de trabajo en Costa Rica, Panamá y Uruguay", *Macroeconomía del desarrollo series*, No. 90 (LC/L.3092-P), Santiago, Chile, Economic Commission for Latin America and the Caribbean (ECLAC). United Nations publication, Sales No. S.09.II.G.76.

___ (2007), "Youth employment: characteristics, tensions and challenges", *CEPAL Review*, No. 92 (LC/G.2339-P/E), Santiago, Chile, Economic Commission for Latin America and the Caribbean (ECLAC).

___ (2006), *Los jóvenes y el empleo en América Latina. Desafíos y perspectivas ante el nuevo escenario laboral,* Bogotá, Economic Commission for Latin America and the Caribbean(ECLAC)/Mayo.

___ (comp.) (2004), *En búsqueda de efectividad, eficiencia y equidad: las políticas del mercado de trabajo y los instrumentos de su evaluación,* Santiago, Chile, Economic Commission for Latin America and the Caribbean (ECLAC)/LOM.

___ (2003), "La problemática inserción laboral de los y las jóvenes", *Macroeconomía del desarrollo series,* No. 28 (LC/L.2029-P), Santiago, Chile, Economic Commission for Latin America and the Caribbean (ECLAC).

___ (2000), *Reformas económicas, crecimiento y empleo: los mercados de trabajo en América Latina*, Santiago,

Chile, Economic Commission for Latin America and the Caribbean (ECLAC)/Fondo de Cultura Económica.

Williamson, John (2003), "Overview: an agenda for restarting growth and reform", *Restarting Growth and Reform in Latin America*, Pedro-Pablo Kuczynski and John Williamson (eds.), Washington, D.C., Institute for International Economics.

___ (1990), "What Washington means by policy reform", *Latin American Adjustment: How Much Has Happened?*, Washington, D.C., Institute for International Economics.

Wodon, Q. and M. Minowa (1999), "Training for the urban unemployed: a reevaluation of Mexico's Probecat", Washington, D.C., World Bank, unpublished.

World Bank (2007), *Las políticas de transferencia de ingresos en Uruguay: cerrando las brechas de cobertura para aumentar el bienestar*, Montevideo, Regional Office for Latin America and the Caribbean.

___ (2006), *Minimum Wages in Latin America and the Caribbean: the Impact on Employment, Inequality, and Poverty*, Washington, D.C.

Wurgaft, J. (1993), *Fondos de inversión social: América Latina,* Santiago, Chile, Regional Employment Programme for Latin America and the Caribbean (PREALC)/International Labour Organization (ILO).

Yannoulas, S. (2005), *Perspectivas de género y políticas de formación e inserción laboral en América Latina*, Buenos Aires, Red Etis.

Statistical annex

Table A-1

LATIN AMERICA AND THE CARIBBEAN: MAIN ECONOMIC INDICATORS

	2000	2001	2002	2003	2004	2005	2006	2007	2008 [a]
					Annual growth rates				
Gross domestic product [b]	4.0	0.4	-0.4	2.2	6.1	4.9	5.8	5.8	4.2
Per capita gross domestic product [b]	2.5	-1.0	-1.7	0.9	4.7	3.6	4.4	4.4	2.9
Consumer prices [c]	9.0	6.1	12.2	8.5	7.4	6.1	5.0	6.4	8.4
					Percentages				
Urban open unemployment [d]	10.4	10.2	11.0	11.0	10.3	9.1	8.6	7.9	7.4
Total gross external debt/GDP [e]	35.2	36.4	40.2	40.4	34.8	25.1	20.9	20.5	18.0 [f]
Total gross external debt/ exports of goods and services	173	181	179	171	139	101	84	84	75 [f]
					Millions of dollars				
Balance of payments [g]									
Current account balance	-48 701	-54 048	-16 188	8 580	20 889	33 921	43 817	11 301	-33 542
Merchandise trade balance	-1 301	-8 123	19 868	40 155	55 423	75 395	90 448	62 998	34 512
Exports of goods f.o.b.	363 967	348 998	352 903	384 246	473 449	569 286	677 875	763 336	883 553
Imports of goods f.o.b.	365 269	357 121	333 035	344 092	418 026	493 891	587 428	700 337	849 042
Services trade balance	-14 398	-17 006	-12 098	-10 578	-10 919	-14 799	-16 225	-21 882	-27 509
Income balance	-54 572	-55 325	-53 805	-58 916	-68 810	-79 858	-94 267	-96 454	-106 996
Net current transfers	21 570	26 405	29 846	37 915	45 194	53 183	63 861	66 639	66 450
Capital and financial balance [h]	64 428	37 870	-9 771	1 935	-8 098	22 724	16 383	111 303	68 055
Net foreign direct investment	71 520	66 111	50 261	37 197	48 680	53 766	30 173	85 384	90 484
Other capital movements	-7 092	-28 241	-60 032	-35 263	-56 778	-31 042	-13 790	25 918	-22 429
Overall balance	15 727	-16 178	-25 959	10 515	12 791	56 645	60 200	122 604	34 513
Variation in reserve assets [i]	-7 515	-43	3 539	-29 154	-21 661	-35 258	-47 263	-124 527	-38 425
Other financing	-8 212	16 222	22 420	18 639	8 870	-21 385	-12 934	1 923	3 911
Net transfer of resources [f]	975	-1 551	-41 412	-39 503	-69 202	-80 760	-97 661	12 145	-39 770
International reserves [f]	171 298	169 408	167 959	201 185	227 838	263 207	320 757	459 550	510 457
					Percentages of GDP				
Fiscal sector [j]									
Overall balance	-2.6	-3.2	-2.9	-3.0	-1.9	-1.1	-0.0	0.3	-0.4
Primary balance	-0.2	-0.8	-0.5	-0.2	0.5	1.3	2.2	2.2	1.3
Total revenue	16.4	16.4	16.5	16.6	17.0	18.0	18.9	19.4	19.6
Tax revenue [k]	12.8	12.8	12.9	13.0	13.5	14.3	14.6	15.1	15.0
Total expenditure	18.8	19.5	19.4	19.5	18.8	19.1	18.9	19.2	20.0
Capital expenditures	3.5	3.6	3.5	3.6	3.5	3.5	3.5	3.9	4.3
Central-government public debt	43.2	45.5	58.4	57.5	50.9	42.8	35.8	29.9	28.0
Public debt of the non-financial public-sector (NFPS)	47.3	49.5	64.3	61.9	55.1	47.4	39.7	32.7	30.8

Source: Economic Commission for Latin America and the Caribbean (ECLAC), on the basis of official figures.

[a] Preliminary figures.

[b] Based on official figures expressed in 2000 dollars.

[c] December-December variation.

[d] The data for Argentina and Brazil have been adjusted to allow for changes in methodology in 2003 and 2002, respectively.

[e] Estimates based on figures denominated in dollars at current prices.

[f] Does not incluye Cuba.

[g] Does not include Cuba, Guyana, Saint Kitts and Nevis, Suriname and Trinidad and Tobago.

[h] Includes errors and omissions.

[i] A minus sign (-) indicates an increase in reserve assets.

[j] Central government, except for the Plurinational State of Bolivia, where coverage corresponds to general government. Simple averages. Includes information from 19 Latin American and Caribbean countries: Argentina, Bolivarian Republic of Venezuela, Brazil, Chile, Colombia, Costa Rica, Dominican Republic, Ecuador, El Salvador, Guatemala, Haiti, Honduras, Mexico, Nicaragua, Panama, Paraguay, Peru, Plurinational State of Bolivia and Uruguay.

[k] Does not include social security contributions.

Table A-2

LATIN AMERICA AND THE CARIBBEAN: GROSS DOMESTIC PRODUCT

(Millions of current dollars)

	2000	2001	2002	2003	2004	2005	2006	2007	2008 [a]
Latin America and the Caribbean	**2 114 994**	**2 059 905**	**1 850 259**	**1 920 524**	**2 216 811**	**2 686 924**	**3 165 350**	**3 661 441**	**4 266 044**
Antigua and Barbuda	664	696	714	753	815	868	1 003	1 155	1 217
Argentina	284 346	268 831	102 042	129 596	153 129	183 196	214 267	262 451	330 196
Bahamas	5 528	5 659	5 912	5 942	6 189	6 797	7 280	7 498	7 564
Barbados	2 559	2 554	2 476	2 695	2 817	3 006	3 191	3 433	3 729
Belize	832	872	933	988	1 056	1 115	1 213	1 277	1 387
Bolivia (Plurinational State of)	8 398	8 142	7 905	8 082	8 773	9 549	11 452	13 120	16 674
Brazil	644 476	552 288	505 960	552 453	663 733	882 040	1 089 398	1 300 312	1 575 835
Chile	75 495	68 840	67 532	73 986	95 678	118 182	146 771	163 879	169 458
Colombia	94 053	92 877	93 016	91 703	113 774	144 581	162 347	207 786	242 268
Costa Rica	15 946	16 404	16 844	17 518	18 596	19 965	22 526	26 267	29 663
Cuba	30 565	31 682	33 591	35 901	38 203	42 644	52 743	58 604	62 705
Dominica	271	266	255	263	285	299	317	341	357
Dominican Republic	23 655	24 512	24 913	20 045	21 582	33 542	35 660	41 013	45 523
Ecuador	15 934	21 250	24 899	28 636	32 642	37 187	41 763	45 789	52 572
El Salvador	13 134	13 813	14 307	15 047	15 798	17 070	18 654	20 373	22 115
Grenada	430	422	437	480	469	554	564	608	644
Guatemala	17 196	18 703	20 777	21 918	23 965	27 211	30 231	34 031	38 976
Guyana	713	712	726	743	788	825	915	1 075	1 159
Haiti	3 665	3 508	3 215	2 827	3 660	4 154	4 961	6 225	7 215
Honduras	7 187	7 653	7 860	8 234	8 871	9 757	10 918	12 417	14 321
Jamaica	8 949	9 104	9 677	9 399	10 135	11 152	11 989	12 909	14 431
Mexico	636 731	681 762	711 103	700 325	758 222	844 137	945 651	1 018 221	1 080 483
Nicaragua	3 938	4 125	4 026	4 102	4 465	4 872	5 294	5 691	6 365
Panama	11 621	11 808	12 272	12 933	14 179	15 465	17 137	19 485	23 088
Paraguay	7 095	6 446	5 092	5 552	6 950	7 473	9 275	12 222	15 976
Peru	53 336	53 955	56 775	61 356	69 701	79 389	92 319	107 329	127 500
Saint Kitts and Nevis	329	343	351	362	400	439	489	512	552
Saint Vincent and the Grenadines	335	345	365	382	414	445	498	555	598
Saint Lucia	707	685	701	743	798	850	913	955	1 019
Suriname	775	665	955	1 122	1 285	1 481	1 736	1 867	2 263
Trinidad and Tobago	[illegible]	[illegible]	[illegible]	[illegible]	[illegible]	[illegible]	[illegible]	21 717	24 205
Uruguay	20 829	19 248	12 731	11 605	13 706	17 230	20 023	24 254	32 186
Venezuela (Bolivarian Republic of)	117 148	122 910	92 890	83 529	112 452	145 513	184 509	228 071	313 799

Source: Economic Commission for Latin America and the Caribbean (ECLAC), on the basis of official figures.

[a] Preliminary figures.

Table A-3
LATIN AMERICA AND THE CARIBBEAN: GROSS DOMESTIC PRODUCT
(Annual growth rates)

	2000	2001	2002	2003	2004	2005	2006	2007	2008 [a]
Latin America and the Caribbean [b]	**4.0**	**0.4**	**-0.4**	**2.2**	**6.1**	**4.9**	**5.8**	**5.8**	**4.2**
Antigua and Barbuda	1.5	2.2	2.5	5.2	7.2	4.7	12.6	10.0	2.5
Argentina	-0.8	-4.4	-10.9	8.8	9.0	9.2	8.5	8.7	7.0
Bahamas	4.3	-0.3	2.0	-2.4	3.7	5.7	4.3	0.7	-1.7
Barbados	2.3	-4.6	0.7	2.0	4.8	3.9	3.2	3.4	0.5
Belize	12.3	5.0	5.1	9.3	4.6	3.0	4.7	1.2	3.3
Bolivia (Plurinational State of)	2.5	1.7	2.5	2.7	4.2	4.4	4.8	4.6	6.1
Brazil	4.3	1.3	2.7	1.1	5.7	3.2	4.0	5.7	5.1
Chile	4.5	3.4	2.2	3.9	6.0	5.6	4.6	4.7	3.2
Colombia	2.9	2.2	2.5	4.6	4.7	5.7	6.9	7.5	2.5
Costa Rica	1.8	1.1	2.9	6.4	4.3	5.9	8.8	7.8	2.6
Cuba	5.9	3.2	1.4	3.8	5.8	11.2	12.1	7.3	4.3
Dominica	0.6	-3.6	-4.2	2.2	6.3	3.4	5.2	3.4	3.4
Dominican Republic	5.7	1.8	5.8	-0.3	1.3	9.3	10.7	8.5	5.3
Ecuador	2.8	5.3	4.2	3.6	8.0	6.0	3.9	2.5	6.5
El Salvador	2.2	1.7	2.3	2.3	1.9	3.1	4.2	4.7	2.5
Grenada	17.5	-3.9	2.1	8.4	-6.5	12.0	-1.9	3.6	2.1
Guatemala	3.6	2.3	3.9	2.5	3.2	3.3	5.4	6.3	4.0
Guyana	-0.7	1.6	1.2	-0.7	1.6	-2.0	5.1	5.3	3.1
Haiti	0.9	-1.0	-0.3	0.4	-3.5	1.8	2.3	3.4	1.3
Honduras	5.7	2.7	3.8	4.5	6.2	6.1	6.6	6.3	4.0
Jamaica	0.7	1.3	1.0	3.5	1.4	1.0	2.7	1.4	-0.6
Mexico	6.6	-0.0	0.8	1.4	4.0	3.2	4.8	3.3	1.3
Nicaragua	4.1	3.0	0.8	2.5	5.3	4.3	3.9	3.2	3.2
Panama	2.7	0.6	2.2	4.2	7.5	7.2	8.5	11.5	9.2
Paraguay	-3.3	2.1	-0.0	3.8	4.1	2.9	4.3	6.8	5.8
Peru	3.0	0.2	5.0	4.0	5.0	6.8	7.7	8.9	9.8
Saint Kitts and Nevis	4.3	2.0	1.0	0.5	7.6	5.6	5.3	4.0	9.7
Saint Vincent and the Grenadines	1.8	1.0	3.7	3.2	6.2	3.6	9.6	7.7	1.0
Saint Lucia	-0.2	-5.1	3.1	4.3	5.2	6.0	4.0	1.1	2.3
Suriname	1.9	5.7	2.7	6.8	7.2	6.3	4.5	5.3	5.2
Trinidad and Tobago	6.9	4.2	7.9	14.4	8.0	5.4	13.3	5.5	3.5
Uruguay	-1.4	-3.4	-11.0	2.2	11.8	6.6	7.0	7.6	8.9
Venezuela (Bolivarian Republic of)	3.7	3.4	-8.9	-7.8	18.3	10.3	9.9	8.9	4.8

Source: Economic Commission for Latin America and the Caribbean (ECLAC), on the basis of official figures.
[a] Preliminary figures.
[b] On the basis of figures expressed in constant 2000 dollars.

Table A-4

LATIN AMERICA AND THE CARIBBEAN: PER CAPITA GROSS DOMESTIC PRODUCT

(Annual growth rates)

	2000	2001	2002	2003	2004	2005	2006	2007	2008 [a]
Latin America and the Caribbean [b]	**2.5**	**-1.0**	**-1.7**	**0.9**	**4.7**	**3.6**	**4.4**	**4.4**	**2.9**
Antigua and Barbuda	-0.7	0.3	0.8	3.7	5.7	3.3	11.2	8.7	1.3
Argentina	-1.8	-5.4	-11.7	7.8	8.0	8.1	7.4	7.6	5.9
Bahamas	2.8	-1.6	0.7	-3.6	2.4	4.4	3.0	-0.5	-2.9
Barbados	1.8	-5.0	0.3	1.6	4.4	3.5	2.8	3.1	0.2
Belize	9.5	2.4	2.6	6.8	2.2	0.7	2.4	-0.9	1.2
Bolivia (Plurinational State of)	0.1	-0.6	0.2	0.4	1.9	2.2	2.6	2.4	4.0
Brazil	2.8	-0.2	1.2	-0.3	4.2	1.8	2.6	4.3	3.8
Chile	3.2	2.2	1.0	2.8	4.9	4.5	3.5	3.6	2.1
Colombia	1.3	0.6	0.9	3.0	3.1	4.2	5.5	6.2	1.3
Costa Rica	-0.5	-1.0	0.9	4.4	2.4	4.0	6.9	6.0	0.9
Cuba	5.6	2.9	1.2	3.6	5.6	11.1	12.0	7.3	4.3
Dominica	0.8	-3.5	-4.0	2.4	6.5	3.6	5.5	3.8	3.8
Dominican Republic	3.9	0.1	4.1	-1.8	-0.3	7.6	9.0	6.9	3.8
Ecuador	1.3	3.8	2.8	2.1	6.5	4.5	2.4	1.0	5.0
El Salvador	0.2	-0.2	0.4	0.5	0.1	1.3	2.4	2.9	0.9
Grenada	16.8	-4.8	1.1	7.2	-7.4	11.3	-2.3	3.6	2.2
Guatemala	1.2	-0.1	1.3	0.0	0.6	0.7	2.8	3.7	1.5
Guyana	-0.7	1.6	1.0	-0.9	1.4	-2.0	5.2	5.5	3.4
Haiti	-0.8	-2.7	-1.8	-1.2	-5.0	0.2	0.7	1.7	-0.4
Honduras	3.6	0.6	1.7	2.5	4.1	3.9	4.5	4.2	1.9
Jamaica	-0.1	0.6	0.2	2.8	0.7	0.4	2.1	0.9	-1.1
Mexico	5.1	-1.1	-0.1	0.6	3.2	2.3	3.7	2.2	0.2
Nicaragua	2.4	1.5	-0.6	1.2	4.0	2.9	2.5	1.8	1.9
Panama	0.8	-1.3	0.4	2.3	5.6	5.4	6.7	9.7	7.4
Paraguay	-5.3	0.0	-2.0	1.8	2.1	0.9	2.4	4.8	3.9
Peru	1.6	-1.1	3.7	2.8	3.7	5.6	6.5	7.6	8.6
Saint Kitts and Nevis	3.0	0.7	-0.3	-0.8	6.3	4.3	3.9	2.6	8.3
Saint Vincent and the Grenadines	1.3	0.4	3.2	2.6	5.6	3.1	9.0	7.1	0.5
Saint Lucia	-1.1	-6.1	2.0	3.1	4.0	4.8	2.9	-0.0	1.2
Suriname	1.0	4.8	1.9	6.1	6.5	5.6	3.8	4.7	4.6
Trinidad and Tobago	6.5	3.8	7.6	14.0	7.6	5.0	12.9	5.1	3.1
Uruguay	-1.8	-3.6	-11.0	2.2	11.9	6.6	6.8	7.3	8.6
Venezuela (Bolivarian Republic of)	1.8	1.5	-10.5	-9.4	16.2	8.4	8.0	7.1	3.1

Source: Economic Commission for Latin America and the Caribbean (ECLAC), on the basis of official figures.

[a] Preliminary figures.

[b] On the basis of figures expressed in constant 2000 dollars.

Table A-5

LATIN AMERICA AND THE CARIBBEAN: COMPONENTS OF TOTAL DEMAND [a]

(Indices 2000=100)

	2000	2001	2002	2003	2004	2005	2006	2007	2008 [b]
Total supply	**100.0**	**100.3**	**99.1**	**100.7**	**108.2**	**114.9**	**123.3**	**132.1**	**139.0**
Gross domestic product	100.0	100.4	99.9	102.1	108.3	113.7	120.2	127.2	132.6
Imports of goods and services	100.0	99.9	94.3	95.6	109.5	122.4	140.1	158.1	172.3
Total demand	**100.0**	**100.3**	**99.1**	**100.7**	**108.2**	**114.9**	**123.3**	**132.1**	**139.0**
Total consumption	100.0	101.0	100.7	102.5	107.9	113.9	120.7	128.4	134.1
Private consumption	100.0	100.9	100.2	102.1	107.9	114.3	121.6	130.0	135.6
Government consumption	100.0	101.3	102.9	104.6	107.8	112.3	116.7	121.6	127.1
Gross capital formation	100.0	98.0	90.5	88.8	99.2	105.2	119.0	132.5	148.1
Gross fixed capital formation	100.0	97.3	90.6	90.4	101.9	113.2	127.5	143.0	155.8
Domestic demand	100.0	100.3	98.5	99.6	106.0	112.1	120.4	129.3	137.0
Exports of goods and services	100.0	100.0	102.1	106.1	119.2	129.0	138.3	146.6	149.3

Source: Economic Commission for Latin America and the Caribbean (ECLAC), on the basis of official figures.

[a] On the basis of figures expressed in constant 2000 dollars. Includes information from 20 Latin American and Caribbean countries: Argentina, Bolivarian Republic of Venezuela, Brazil, Chile, Colombia, Costa Rica, Cuba, Dominican Republic, Ecuador, El Salvador, Guatemala, Haiti, Honduras, Mexico, Nicaragua, Panama, Paraguay, Peru, Plurinational State of Bolivia and Uruguay.

[b] Preliminary figures.

Table A-6

LATIN AMERICA AND THE CARIBBEAN: GROSS DOMESTIC PRODUCT BY ECONOMIC SECTOR [a]

(Indices 2000=100)

	2000	2001	2002	2003	2004	2005	2006	2007	2008 [b]
Total gross domestic product at market prices	**100.0**	**100.4**	**99.9**	**102.1**	**108.3**	**113.7**	**120.2**	**127.2**	**132.6**
Agriculture, forestry, hunting and fishing	100.0	104.0	106.7	111.6	114.1	117.0	121.8	127.6	132.1
Mining and quarrying	100.0	101.9	100.0	103.1	107.5	109.3	110.8	110.3	111.3
Manufacturing	100.0	97.8	96.4	98.5	105.8	110.0	115.2	120.9	123.6
Construction	100.0	97.2	93.5	93.6	102.0	109.0	121.0	129.4	133.4
Electricity, gas, water and sanitation services	100.0	98.8	100.5	103.8	109.8	114.1	120.3	125.1	130.8
Transport, storage and communications	100.0	102.7	103.9	107.4	115.4	123.7	132.7	143.7	153.0
Wholesale and retail trade, restaurants and hotels	100.0	98.9	96.3	98.5	106.1	112.2	120.3	128.7	134.3
Financial establishments, insurance, real estate and business services	100.0	102.4	104.0	105.9	110.6	117.0	125.1	133.8	140.6
Community, social and personal services	100.0	101.2	102.9	104.7	109.0	113.6	118.2	122.6	127.8

Source: Economic Commission for Latin America and the Caribbean (ECLAC), on the basis of official figures.

[a] On the basis of figures expressed in constant 2000 dollars. Includes information from 20 Latin American and Caribbean countries: Argentina, Bolivarian Republic of Venezuela, Brazil, Chile, Colombia, Costa Rica, Cuba, Dominican Republic, Ecuador, El Salvador, Guatemala, Haiti, Honduras, Mexico, Nicaragua, Panama, Paraguay, Peru, Plurinational State of Bolivia and Uruguay.

[b] Preliminary figures.

Table A-7

LATIN AMERICA AND THE CARIBBEAN: GROSS FIXED CAPITAL FORMATION [a]

(Percentages of GDP)

	2000	2001	2002	2003	2004	2005	2006	2007	2008 [b]
Latin America and the Caribbean	**18.5**	**18.0**	**16.8**	**16.4**	**17.4**	**18.5**	**19.7**	**20.9**	**21.8**
Argentina	16.2	14.3	10.2	12.9	15.9	17.9	19.5	20.4	20.8
Bahamas	33.8	31.2	29.8	31.1	28.5	33.6	39.3	38.9	35.1
Belize	28.7	25.6	23.1	18.1	16.4	17.2	16.7	17.4	16.6
Bolivia (Plurinational State of)	17.9	13.8	16.0	13.9	13.2	13.4	14.0	15.1	16.9
Brazil	16.8	16.6	15.4	14.5	15.0	15.0	15.7	16.9	18.3
Chile	19.8	19.9	19.8	20.2	20.9	24.5	24.0	25.7	29.8
Colombia	13.0	14.0	14.7	16.0	17.4	19.9	21.8	23.4	23.6
Costa Rica	17.8	18.0	18.7	18.8	18.0	17.7	18.0	19.7	21.5
Cuba	11.9	12.6	6.8	6.1	6.2	6.7	8.6	8.2	8.6
Dominican Republic	20.5	19.3	19.1	15.3	14.8	15.4	16.9	17.5	18.2
Ecuador	20.5	24.0	27.4	26.4	25.7	26.8	26.8	26.8	29.2
El Salvador	16.9	16.9	17.1	17.1	15.9	15.8	16.9	17.1	15.8
Guatemala	19.1	19.0	20.0	18.9	18.1	18.3	20.1	19.8	18.5
Haiti	27.3	27.3	28.0	28.8	28.9	28.8	28.8	28.6	28.7
Honduras	25.8	24.3	21.7	22.1	25.7	23.8	25.3	28.5	30.7
Mexico	21.4	20.2	19.9	19.7	20.5	21.1	22.1	22.9	23.7
Nicaragua	29.9	27.4	25.5	25.0	25.4	26.8	26.7	27.9	29.3
Panama	21.2	15.7	14.4	17.1	17.4	17.3	18.6	22.4	25.5
Paraguay	17.5	16.1	15.0	15.5	15.6	16.4	16.2	17.3	19.7
Peru	20.2	18.5	17.5	17.8	18.3	19.2	21.2	24.0	28.0
Uruguay	16.3	15.3	11.6	10.1	11.7	12.9	15.2	15.1	16.4
Venezuela (Bolivarian Republic of)	21.0	23.1	20.7	14.1	17.9	22.4	26.4	29.8	27.8

Source: Economic Commission for Latin America and the Caribbean (ECLAC), on the basis of official figures.

[a] On the basis of figures expressed in constant 2000 dollars.

[b] Preliminary figures.

Table A-8

LATIN AMERICA AND THE CARIBBEAN: FINANCING OF GROSS DOMESTIC INVESTMENT [a]

(Percentages of GDP)

	Gross domestic investment				National saving				External saving			
	2005	2006	2007	2008 [b]	2005	2006	2007	2008 [b]	2005	2006	2007	2008 [b]
Latin America and the Caribbean	**20.2**	**21.3**	**21.9**	**22.7**	**21.6**	**22.8**	**22.3**	**22.1**	**-1.4**	**-1.5**	**-0.5**	**0.7**
Argentina	20.9	23.0	24.2	25.0	23.8	26.7	27.0	27.1	-2.9	-3.6	-2.8	-2.1
Bolivia (Plurinational State of)	14.3	13.9	14.4	14.4	20.8	25.4	26.5	26.5	-6.5	-11.5	-12.1	-12.1
Brazil	16.2	16.8	17.7	18.9	17.8	18.0	17.9	17.1	-1.6	-1.3	-0.1	1.8
Chile	22.2	20.1	20.6	24.7	23.4	24.9	25.0	22.6	-1.2	-4.9	-4.4	2.0
Colombia	21.6	24.3	24.3	24.3	20.3	22.5	21.5	21.5	1.3	1.8	2.8	2.8
Costa Rica	24.3	26.4	24.6	25.6	19.4	21.9	18.3	16.5	4.9	4.5	6.3	9.0
Cuba	10.8	11.7	10.2	...	11.1	11.3	11.0	...	-0.3	0.4	-0.8	...
Dominican Republic	16.5	18.4	18.9	18.3	15.1	14.8	13.8	8.6	1.4	3.6	5.1	9.7
Ecuador	23.8	23.4	24.1	25.6	24.7	27.3	27.7	27.8	-0.9	-3.9	-3.6	-2.3
El Salvador	15.7	16.1	16.1	15.0	12.4	12.5	10.3	7.7	3.3	3.6	5.8	7.2
Guatemala	19.7	20.8	20.7	18.7	15.2	15.8	15.5	13.9	4.6	5.0	5.2	4.8
Haiti	27.4	28.9	27.7	25.7	27.6	27.1	27.9	21.6	-0.2	1.7	-0.2	4.1
Honduras	27.6	28.3	33.4	34.7	24.6	24.6	23.1	20.9	3.0	3.7	10.3	13.8
Mexico	23.9	25.7	25.4	26.0	23.3	25.2	24.6	24.5	0.5	0.5	0.8	1.5
Nicaragua	30.1	30.2	33.2	33.3	15.0	16.7	15.7	10.1	15.1	13.4	17.6	23.2
Panama	18.4	19.5	23.5	30.9	11.8	16.4	16.2	18.8	6.6	3.1	7.3	12.1
Paraguay	19.3	19.1	17.4	19.6	19.5	20.4	18.7	17.5	-0.2	-1.4	-1.3	2.2
Peru	17.9	20.0	22.9	26.6	19.3	23.1	24.1	23.3	-1.4	-3.1	-1.1	3.3
Uruguay	15.7	20.3	21.0	23.0	15.9	18.4	20.6	19.5	-0.2	2.0	0.3	3.5
Venezuela (Bolivarian Republic of)	23.0	25.3	28.0	24.5	40.5	40.0	36.7	37.0	-17.5	-14.7	-8.8	-12.5

Source: Economic Commission for Latin America and the Caribbean (ECLAC), on the basis of official figures.

[a] Based on values calculated in national currency and expressed in current dollars.

[b] Preliminary figures.

Table A-9
LATIN AMERICA AND THE CARIBBEAN: BALANCE OF PAYMENTS
(Millions of dollars)

	Exports of goods f.o.b.			Exports of services			Imports of goods f.o.b.			Imports of services		
	2006	2007	2008 [c]	2006	2007	2008 [c]	2006	2007	2008 [c]	2006	2007	2008 [c]
Latin America and the Caribbean [d]	**693 911**	**778 842**	**903 060**	**87 282**	**100 821**	**114 923**	**596 063**	**710 357**	**861 929**	**103 563**	**122 802**	**142 497**
Antigua and Barbuda	74	76	76	477	517	520	560	649	662	259	283	290
Argentina	46 546	55 980	70 021	8 023	10 376	12 090	32 588	42 525	54 557	8 523	10 828	12 979
Bahamas	694	802	997	2 436	2 599	2 543	2 727	2 956	3 129	1 611	1 580	1 353
Barbados	465	481	461	1 529	1 635	1 634	1 468	1 528	1 685	718	816	808
Belize	427	426	465	363	398	389	612	642	788	152	168	170
Bolivia (Plurinational State of)	3 875	4 458	6 448	477	499	500	2 632	3 455	4 980	827	688	700
Brazil	137 807	160 649	197 942	19 476	23 954	30 451	91 351	120 617	173 107	29 116	37 173	47 140
Chile	58 680	67 666	66 455	7 830	8 952	10 754	35 900	44 031	57 610	8 462	9 927	11 401
Colombia	25 181	30 577	38 546	3 377	3 636	4 042	24 859	31 173	37 556	5 496	6 243	7 171
Costa Rica	8 102	9 299	9 738	2 972	3 551	4 096	10 829	12 285	14 551	1 621	1 818	1 985
Cuba	3 167	3 830	...	6 667	8 192	...	9 498	10 083	...	211	292	...
Dominica	44	39	36	100	109	116	147	172	197	52	66	71
Dominican Republic	6 610	7 160	6 949	4 543	4 767	4 911	12 174	13 597	16 095	1 558	1 746	1 819
Ecuador	13 176	14 870	19 147	1 037	1 200	1 409	11 408	13 047	17 786	2 341	2 572	2 957
El Salvador	3 759	4 039	4 611	1 426	1 494	1 510	7 291	8 144	9 004	1 506	1 746	2 008
Grenada	31	41	31	130	147	146	263	328	343	99	111	111
Guatemala	6 082	6 983	7 848	1 519	1 731	1 789	10 934	12 470	13 422	1 778	2 041	2 159
Guyana	585	698	798	148	173	...	885	1 063	1 300	245	272	...
Haiti	495	522	490	194	257	343	1 548	1 618	2 107	593	674	763
Honduras	5 277	5 642	6 046	745	788	910	7 303	8 820	10 389	1 036	1 137	1 215
Jamaica	2 134	2 363	2 761	2 649	2 707	2 777	5 077	6 204	7 742	2 021	2 282	2 421
Mexico	249 925	271 875	291 343	16 221	17 489	18 040	256 058	281 949	308 603	21 957	23 794	25 119
Nicaragua	2 034	2 336	2 675	344	373	399	3 485	4 094	4 848	478	555	608
Panama	8 478	9 338	10 289	3 938	4 924	5 864	10 190	12 521	15 003	1 728	2 107	2 601
Paraguay	4 401	5 471	7 769	798	966	1 062	5 022	6 027	8 809	384	460	584
Peru	23 830	27 882	31 529	2 660	3 159	3 637	14 844	19 595	28 439	3 397	4 346	5 566
Saint Kitts and Nevis	59	58	57	173	174	173	220	242	270	102	102	112
Saint Vincent and the Grenadines	41	51	53	171	162	143	240	288	302	88	114	110
Saint Lucia	97	101	186	334	356	368	521	542	578	169	188	189
Suriname	1 174	1 359	1 722	234	245	284	1 013	1 045	1 344	264	317	411
Trinidad and Tobago	14 217	13 391	16 929	...	...	...	6 517	7 670	9 973	...	...	...
Uruguay	4 400	5 043	7 100	1 387	1 807	2 158	4 898	5 598	8 654	979	1 124	1 414
Venezuela (Bolivarian Republic of)	65 210	69 165	93 542	1 572	1 673	1 867	32 498	45 463	48 095	6 005	7 524	8 264

Table A-9 (continued)

	Trade balance			Income balance			Current transfers balance			Current account balance		
	2006	2007	2008 [c]	2006	2007	2008 [c]	2006	2007	2008 [c]	2006	2007	2008 [c]
Latin America and the Caribbean [d]	**82 017**	**47 050**	**14 060**	**-95 356**	**-97 453**	**-107 898**	**64 201**	**67 096**	**66 951**	**50 862**	**16 692**	**-26 887**
Antigua and Barbuda	-267	-340	-356	-64	-64	-51	22	24	23	-309	-379	-384
Argentina	13 458	13 003	14 574	-6 148	-5 927	-7 651	459	336	111	7 770	7 412	7 034
Bahamas	-1 208	-1 135	-941	-218	-232	-169	52	52	56	-1 374	-1 315	-1 055
Barbados	-192	-227	-398	-171	-101	-85	86	145	101	-277	-182	-382
Belize	26	14	-104	-125	-159	-156	74	93	112	-25	-52	-149
Bolivia (Plurinational State of)	892	815	1 267	-397	-489	-536	822	1 266	1 284	1 317	1 591	2 015
Brazil	36 816	26 813	8 146	-27 480	-29 291	-40 561	4 306	4 029	4 188	13 643	1 551	-28 227
Chile	22 149	22 660	8 200	-18 401	-18 595	-14 563	3 406	3 123	2 924	7 154	7 189	-3 440
Colombia	-1 797	-3 203	-2 139	-5 929	-7 865	-10 138	4 743	5 231	5 515	-2 983	-5 837	-6 761
Costa Rica	-1 376	-1 252	-2 701	4	-865	-407	349	470	433	-1 023	-1 647	-2 676
Cuba	125	1 647	...	-618	-960	...	278	-199	...	-215	488	...
Dominica	-54	-90	-115	-17	-16	-18	20	21	21	-52	-85	-112
Dominican Republic	-2 579	-3 416	-6 054	-1 853	-2 081	-1 815	3 144	3 401	3 432	-1 288	-2 096	-4 437
Ecuador	464	452	-187	-1 950	-2 047	-1 607	3 104	3 246	2 989	1 618	1 650	1 194
El Salvador	-3 612	-4 357	-4 892	-531	-576	-536	3 472	3 750	3 832	-671	-1 183	-1 596
Grenada	-200	-251	-279	-29	-34	-36	36	24	25	-193	-261	-289
Guatemala	-5 112	-5 797	-5 944	-680	-843	-929	4 268	4 854	5 010	-1 524	-1 786	-1 863
Guyana	-398	-465	-613	-69	-11	-15	216	287	329	-250	-189	-299
Haiti	-1 452	-1 513	-2 038	7	5	16	1 361	1 517	1 726	-85	10	-295
Honduras	-2 317	-3 527	-4 647	-537	-400	-350	2 450	2 652	3 021	-404	-1 275	-1 977
Jamaica	-2 316	-3 417	-4 626	-616	-662	-680	1 749	2 040	2 083	-1 183	-2 038	-3 223
Mexico	-11 869	-16 379	-24 340	-18 455	-18 368	-16 846	25 949	26 415	25 461	-4 375	-8 331	-15 725
Nicaragua	-1 585	-1 941	-2 382	-129	-135	-161	1 003	1 075	1 068	-710	-1 001	-1 475
Panama	498	-365	-1 452	-1 278	-1 311	-1 579	253	253	238	-527	-1 422	-2 792
Paraguay	-207	-50	-562	-92	-158	-151	426	373	369	128	165	-345
Peru	8 249	7 099	1 161	-7 580	-8 374	-8 144	2 185	2 494	2 803	2 854	1 220	-4 180
Saint Kitts and Nevis	[illegible]	[illegible]	[illegible]	[illegible]	[illegible]	11	[illegible]	[illegible]	[illegible]	[illegible]	-110	-131
Saint Vincent and the Grenadines	-116	-189	-216	-24	-21	-21	20	20	20	-120	-190	-217
Saint Lucia	-259	-272	-214	-56	-68	-74	12	14	14	-303	-327	-272
Suriname	130	242	252	-52	8	21	36	76	87	115	326	360
Trinidad and Tobago	8 151	6 268	7 571	-936	-964	-897	55	60	51	7 271	5 364	6 725
Uruguay	-90	128	-811	-428	-345	-454	126	136	146	-392	-80	-1 119
Venezuela (Bolivarian Republic of)	28 279	17 851	39 050	-1 092	2 565	707	-38	-415	-555	27 149	20 001	39 202

Table A-9 (concluded)

	Capital and financial balance [a]			Overall balance			Reserve assets (variation) [b]			Other financing		
	2006	2007	2008 [c]	2006	2007	2008 [c]	2006	2007	2008 [c]	2006	2007	2008 [c]
Latin America and the Caribbean [d]	**10 610**	**107 636**	**64 179**	**61 472**	**124 328**	**37 292**	**-48 554**	**-126 290**	**-41 242**	**-12 916**	**1 962**	**3 949**
Antigua and Barbuda	324	380	377	15	1	-7	-15	-1	7	0	0	0
Argentina	6 439	4 188	-10 724	14 208	11 600	-3 690	-3 529	-13 098	-9	-10 679	1 499	3 699
Bahamas	1 295	1 269	1 164	-79	-46	109	79	46	-109	0	0	0
Barbados	320	461	132	43	278	-249	-41	-278	249	0	0	0
Belize	75	75	207	50	23	58	-50	-23	-58	0	0	0
Bolivia (Plurinational State of)	121	361	359	1 439	1 952	2 374	-1 286	-1 952	-2 374	-152	0	0
Brazil	16 927	85 933	31 196	30 569	87 484	2 969	-30 569	-87 484	-2 969	0	0	0
Chile	-5 144	-10 387	9 887	2 011	-3 198	6 447	-2 011	3 198	-6 447	0	0	0
Colombia	3 005	10 550	9 399	23	4 714	2 638	-23	-4 714	-2 638	0	0	0
Costa Rica	2 053	2 795	2 328	1 031	1 148	-348	-1 031	-1 148	348	0	0	0
Cuba	...	...	...	...	...	...	...	...	...	...	...	...
Dominican Republic	1 452	2 716	4 117	164	620	-320	-314	-679	303	150	59	17
Dominica	65	84	109	13	-1	-3	-13	1	3	0	0	0
Ecuador	-1 748	-263	-246	-131	1 387	948	124	-1 497	-952	7	111	4
El Salvador	742	1 463	1 930	72	280	334	-72	-280	-334	0	0	0
Grenada	198	271	283	6	11	-6	-6	-11	6	0	0	0
Guatemala	1 776	2 002	2 195	252	216	333	-252	-216	-333	0	0	0
Guyana	293	188	306	43	-1	7	-61	-37	-45	18	39	38
Haiti	179	151	393	94	161	97	-109	-208	-171	15	47	73
Honduras	687	1 090	1 912	283	-185	-65	-282	109	42	-1	76	23
Jamaica	1 413	1 598	3 118	230	-440	-105	-230	440	105	0	0	0
Mexico	3 372	18 617	23 163	-1 003	10 286	7 438	1 003	-10 286	-7 438	0	0	0
Nicaragua	772	1 093	1 460	62	92	-14	-186	-173	-30	124	80	45
Panama	699	2 044	3 377	172	622	584	-162	-611	-579	-10	-10	-5
Paraguay	259	562	723	387	728	378	-387	-727	-378	-0	-0	0
Peru	-128	8 368	7 292	2 726	9 588	3 112	-2 753	-9 654	-3 169	27	67	57
Saint Kitts and Nevis	106	117	145	17	7	15	-17	-7	-15	0	0	0
Saint Vincent and the Grenadines	132	188	213	12	-2	-3	-12	2	3	0	0	0
Saint Lucia	317	345	269	14	19	-3	-14	-19	3	0	0	0
Suriname	-21	-148	-308	94	177	52	-94	-177	-52	0	0	0
Trinidad and Tobago	-6 152	-3 824	-4 019	1 119	1 541	2 706	-1 119	-1 541	-2 706	0	0	0
Uruguay	2 791	1 091	3 352	2 399	1 010	2 233	15	-1 005	-2 233	-2 414	-5	-0
Venezuela (Bolivarian Republic of)	-22 011	-25 743	-29 927	5 138	-5 742	9 275	-5 138	5 742	-9 275	0	0	0

Source: Economic Commission for Latin America and the Caribbean (ECLAC), on the basis of official figures from the International Monetary Fund (IMF) and national sources.
[a] Includes errors and omissions.
[b] A minus sign (-) indicates an increase in reserve assets.
[c] Preliminary figures.
[d] Does not include Cuba.

Table A-10
LATIN AMERICA AND THE CARIBBEAN: EXPORTS OF GOODS, F.O.B.
(Indices 2000=100)

	Value			Volume			Unit value		
	2006	2007	2008 [a]	2006	2007	2008 [a]	2006	2007	2008 [a]
Latin America and the Caribbean	**186.7**	**210.3**	**243.4**	**136.9**	**141.5**	**142.3**	**136.4**	**148.7**	**171.0**
Argentina	176.7	212.5	265.8	144.4	155.6	155.7	122.4	136.6	170.7
Bolivia (Plurinational State of)	310.9	357.8	517.5	176.6	180.1	242.6	176.1	198.6	213.3
Brazil	250.2	291.6	359.3	184.8	195.0	190.2	135.4	149.6	188.9
Chile	305.5	352.2	345.9	145.4	155.3	153.7	210.1	226.9	225.0
Colombia	183.0	222.2	280.1	135.7	143.3	149.3	134.8	155.1	187.6
Costa Rica	139.4	160.0	167.5	147.2	167.3	171.7	94.7	95.6	97.5
Cuba	189.0	228.6	...	96.7	98.1	...	195.5	232.9	...
Dominican Republic	115.2	124.8	121.1	103.4	103.3	94.5	111.4	120.9	128.1
Ecuador	256.5	289.5	372.7	184.8	189.6	196.9	138.8	152.7	189.3
El Salvador	126.8	136.3	155.6	118.4	121.1	134.2	107.2	112.5	115.9
Guatemala	153.5	176.3	198.1	136.6	148.0	151.2	112.4	119.1	131.1
Haiti	149.3	157.4	147.8	133.5	136.7	123.4	111.8	115.2	119.8
Honduras	157.8	168.8	180.8	167.0	170.0	165.7	94.5	99.2	109.2
Mexico	150.4	163.7	175.4	124.4	126.5	126.9	120.9	129.4	138.2
Nicaragua	231.0	265.2	303.7	225.8	249.3	264.3	102.3	106.4	114.9
Panama	145.2	159.9	176.2	137.2	145.3	152.5	105.9	110.1	115.6
Paraguay	189.0	234.9	333.6	173.4	195.9	235.8	109.0	119.9	141.5
Peru	342.6	400.9	453.3	175.5	179.5	193.1	195.2	223.4	234.7
Uruguay	184.6	211.6	297.8	163.1	171.0	185.2	113.2	123.7	160.8
Venezuela (Bolivarian Republic of)	194.5	206.3	279.0	91.0	84.7	83.6	213.7	243.6	333.8

Source: Economic Commission for Latin America and the Caribbean (ECLAC), on the basis of official figures from the International Monetary Fund (IMF) and national sources.
[a] Preliminary figures.

Table A-11
LATIN AMERICA AND THE CARIBBEAN: IMPORTS OF GOODS, F.O.B.
(Indices 2000=100)

	Value			Volume			Unit value		
	2006	2007	2008 [a]	2006	2007	2008 [a]	2006	2007	2008 [a]
Latin America and the Caribbean	**161.5**	**192.3**	**233.1**	**136.6**	**152.6**	**165.4**	**118.2**	**126.0**	**140.8**
Argentina	136.4	178.0	228.4	126.4	153.2	177.6	107.9	116.2	128.6
Bolivia (Plurinational State of)	163.5	214.6	309.3	129.8	153.5	208.7	125.9	139.8	148.2
Brazil	163.8	216.2	310.3	126.3	154.1	181.3	129.6	140.3	171.2
Chile	210.0	257.6	337.1	183.2	215.1	246.9	114.7	119.7	136.5
Colombia	224.2	281.1	338.7	191.5	225.5	249.3	117.0	124.6	135.9
Costa Rica	179.8	203.9	241.6	162.8	181.1	202.4	110.4	112.6	119.4
Cuba	198.1	210.3	...	166.1	155.8	...	119.2	135.0	...
Dominican Republic	128.4	143.5	169.8	109.4	116.4	124.1	117.4	123.3	136.9
Ecuador	304.8	348.6	475.2	241.4	258.0	311.2	126.3	135.1	152.7
El Salvador	155.0	173.2	191.5	138.1	145.5	150.4	112.3	119.0	127.3
Guatemala	196.7	224.3	241.4	156.7	165.5	157.7	125.5	135.5	153.1
Haiti	142.5	148.9	193.9	113.3	111.7	101.1	125.7	133.2	191.9
Honduras	183.1	221.2	260.5	161.2	181.9	193.0	113.6	121.6	135.0
Mexico	146.8	161.6	176.9	126.3	131.2	135.5	116.2	123.2	130.5
Nicaragua	193.5	227.3	269.1	150.1	168.0	176.0	128.9	135.3	152.9
Panama	146.0	179.3	214.9	125.3	146.6	159.7	116.5	122.3	134.6
Paraguay	175.2	210.3	307.4	153.6	175.5	233.2	114.1	119.8	131.8
Peru	201.5	266.0	386.1	157.0	187.7	225.1	128.4	141.7	171.5
Uruguay	147.9	169.1	261.4	115.8	121.3	150.0	127.8	139.4	174.3
Venezuela (Bolivarian Republic of)	192.7	269.6	285.2	166.3	223.6	213.1	115.9	120.5	133.8

Source: Economic Commission for Latin America and the Caribbean (ECLAC), on the basis of official figures from the International Monetary Fund (IMF) and national sources.
[a] Preliminary figures.

Table A-12
LATIN AMERICA AND THE CARIBBEAN: TERMS OF TRADE FOR GOODS, F.O.B./F.O.B.
(Indices 2000=100)

	2000	2001	2002	2003	2004	2005	2006	2007	2008 [a]
Latin America and the Caribbean	**100.0**	**96.3**	**96.6**	**98.6**	**103.6**	**108.7**	**115.3**	**118.0**	**121.4**
Argentina	100.0	99.3	98.7	107.2	109.2	106.9	113.4	117.5	132.7
Bolivia (Plurinational State of)	100.0	95.8	96.2	98.5	104.1	111.8	139.8	142.1	144.0
Brazil	100.0	99.6	98.4	97.0	97.9	99.2	104.4	106.6	110.4
Chile	100.0	93.3	97.2	102.8	124.9	139.8	183.2	189.5	164.9
Colombia	100.0	94.2	92.5	95.2	102.3	111.0	115.2	124.4	138.1
Costa Rica	100.0	98.4	96.9	95.5	91.9	88.3	85.8	84.9	81.7
Cuba	100.0	114.0	105.1	121.0	133.3	129.8	164.0	172.6	...
Dominican Republic	100.0	100.9	101.5	97.9	96.7	95.8	94.9	98.0	93.6
Ecuador	100.0	84.6	86.8	89.8	91.5	102.4	109.9	113.0	124.0
El Salvador	100.0	102.5	101.6	97.7	96.8	96.8	95.5	94.6	91.0
Guatemala	100.0	96.7	95.8	93.0	92.1	91.3	89.6	87.9	85.6
Haiti	100.0	101.2	100.2	98.7	96.0	92.4	88.9	86.4	62.4
Honduras	100.0	94.8	92.0	88.0	87.2	87.2	83.2	81.6	80.9
Mexico	100.0	97.4	97.9	98.8	101.6	103.6	104.1	105.1	105.9
Nicaragua	100.0	88.4	87.0	84.1	82.5	81.4	79.4	78.6	75.2
Panama	100.0	102.7	101.6	97.2	95.3	93.5	90.8	90.0	85.9
Paraguay	100.0	100.2	96.7	101.4	104.3	97.4	95.5	100.1	107.3
Peru	100.0	95.6	98.4	102.2	111.3	119.4	152.1	157.6	136.9
Uruguay	100.0	104.0	102.6	103.5	99.9	90.7	88.6	88.7	92.3
Venezuela (Bolivarian Republic of)	100.0	82.2	87.6	98.7	118.1	154.4	184.4	202.1	249.5

Source: Economic Commission for Latin America and the Caribbean (ECLAC), on the basis of official figures from the International Monetary Fund (IMF) and national sources.
[a] Preliminary figures.

Table A-13
LATIN AMERICA AND THE CARIBBEAN: NET RESOURCE TRANSFER [a]
(Millions of dollars)

	2000	2001	2002	2003	2004	2005	2006	2007	2008 [b]
Latin America and the Caribbean	**975**	**-1 551**	**-41 412**	**-39 503**	**-69 202**	**-80 760**	**-97 061**	**12 145**	**-39 770**
Antigua and Barbuda	16	48	49	85	56	136	260	316	326
Argentina	993	-16 030	-20 773	-12 535	-7 175	-3 722	-10 388	-241	-14 676
Bahamas	240	366	175	279	213	358	1 077	1 037	994
Barbados	241	241	42	131	58	-16	149	360	47
Belize	161	115	91	61	8	25	-50	-84	50
Bolivia (Plurinational State of)	182	30	-156	-226	-565	-535	-428	-128	-177
Brazil	4 077	6 778	-10 252	-14 234	-29 955	-35 633	-10 553	56 642	-9 366
Chile	-1 621	-2 022	-2 068	-4 076	-10 102	-10 220	-23 545	-28 982	-4 676
Colombia	-2 214	-323	-1 439	-2 609	-850	-1 846	-2 924	2 686	-739
Costa Rica	-714	-63	580	443	432	1 166	2 058	1 930	1 921
Dominica	31	39	36	32	23	64	49	68	91
Dominican Republic	-85	168	-881	-2 787	-2 324	-321	-251	694	2 319
Ecuador	-2 020	-817	-100	-953	-1 084	-1 580	-3 691	-2 200	-1 850
El Salvador	132	-293	-42	595	117	-69	211	887	1 394
Grenada	61	67	109	83	30	131	170	237	247
Guatemala	1 494	1 618	993	1 251	1 359	995	1 096	1 160	1 266
Guyana	48	-3	20	-6	-10	143	242	215	329
Haiti	45	129	26	5	94	-20	201	204	482
Honduras	348	322	86	94	743	177	149	766	1 584
Jamaica	517	1 168	208	-246	612	561	797	937	2 438
Mexico	6 491	11 161	8 502	4 315	-1 286	-2 674	-15 083	250	6 317
Nicaragua	624	455	607	520	616	590	768	1 039	1 344
Panama	3	202	-39	-539	-414	418	-589	723	1 792
Paraguay	-30	237	-134	168	-98	72	168	405	572
Peru	-293	391	512	-670	-1 262	-4 596	-7 681	61	-796
Saint Kitts and Nevis	32	84	95	71	43	23	74	85	135
Saint Vincent and the Grenadines	19	30	18	55	99	70	108	167	192
Saint Lucia	64	73	75	115	45	62	261	277	195
Suriname	-17	54	70	118	112	55	-72	-140	-287
Trinidad and Tobago	-732	-453	-441	-1 344	-1 309	-2 461	-7 087	-4 787	-4 917
Uruguay	672	707	-2 602	979	-137	84	-52	741	2 897
Venezuela (Bolivarian Republic of)	-7 792	-6 030	-14 783	-8 679	-17 292	-22 195	-23 103	-23 178	-29 220

Source: Economic Commission for Latin America and the Caribbean (ECLAC), on the basis of official figures from the International Monetary Fund (IMF) and national sources.
[a] The net resource transfer is calculated as total net capital income minus the income balance (net payments of profits and interest). Total net capital income is the balance on the capital and financial accounts plus errors and omissions, plus loans and the use of IMF credit plus exceptional financing. Negative figures indicate resources transferred outside the country.
[b] Preliminary figures.

Table A-14

LATIN AMERICA AND THE CARIBBEAN: NET FOREIGN DIRECT INVESTMENT [a]

(Millions of dollars)

	2000	2001	2002	2003	2004	2005	2006	2 007	2 008 [b]
Latin America and the Caribbean	**72 190**	**66 914**	**50 996**	**37 806**	**49 692**	**54 563**	**30 735**	**86 235**	**92 155**
Antigua and Barbuda	43	98	66	166	80	214	374	356	253
Argentina	9 517	2 005	2 776	878	3 449	3 954	3 099	4 969	7 502
Bahamas	250	192	209	247	443	563	706	746	700
Barbados	18	17	17	58	-16	53	...	...	...
Belize	23	61	25	-11	111	126	108	139	176
Bolivia (Plurinational State of)	734	703	674	195	63	-242	278	362	508
Brazil	30 498	24 715	14 108	9 894	8 339	12 550	-9 380	27 518	24 601
Chile	873	2 590	2 207	2 701	5 610	4 801	4 556	9 568	9 896
Colombia	2 111	2 526	1 277	783	2 873	5 590	5 558	8 136	8 406
Costa Rica	400	451	625	548	733	904	1 371	1 634	2 010
Dominican Republic	953	1 079	917	613	909	1 123	1 528	1 579	2 885
Dominica	18	17	20	31	26	33	27	53	52
Ecuador	720	1 330	1 275	872	837	493	271	193	974
El Salvador	178	289	496	123	366	398	268	1 408	719
Grenada	37	59	54	89	65	70	85	174	161
Guatemala	230	488	183	218	255	470	552	720	822
Guyana	67	56	44	26	30	77	102	110	179
Haiti	13	4	6	14	6	26	161	75	30
Honduras	375	301	269	391	553	599	669	928	875
Jamaica	394	525	407	604	542	582	797	...	...
Mexico	17 789	23 045	22 158	15 183	19 216	15 325	13 558	19 022	21 264
Nicaragua	267	150	204	201	250	241	287	382	626
Panama	624	467	99	818	1 019	918	2 498	1 907	2 402
Paraguay	98	78	12	22	32	47	167	178	311
Peru	810	1 070	2 156	1 275	1 599	2 579	3 467	5 425	4 079
Saint Kitts and Nevis	96	88	80	76	46	93	110	158	88
Saint Vincent and the Grenadines	38	21	34	55	66	40	109	110	121
Saint Lucia	54	59	52	106	77	78	234	253	105
Suriname	-148	-27	-74	-76	-37	28	-163	-247	-234
Trinidad and Tobago	654	685	684	583	973	599	513	830	1 638
Uruguay	274	291	180	401	315	811	1 495	1 139	2 049
Venezuela (Bolivarian Republic of)	4 180	3 479	-244	722	864	1 422	-2 666	-1 591	-1 041

Source: Economic Commission for Latin America and the Caribbean (ECLAC), on the basis of official figures from the International Monetary Fund (IMF) and national sources.

[a] Corresponds to direct investment in the reporting economy after deduction of outward direct investment by residents of that country. Includes reinvestment of profits.

[b] Preliminary figures.

Table A-15

LATIN AMERICA AND THE CARIBBEAN: INTERNATIONAL BOND ISSUES [a]

(Millions of dollars)

	2000	2001	2002	2003	2004	2005 [b]	2006 [c]	2007 [d]	2008 [e]	2009	
										1 Q	2 Q [f]
Latin America and the Caribbean	**40 255**	**38 503**	**20 208**	**37 906**	**36 383**	**45 054**	**44 647**	**41 176**	**18 466**	**9 123**	**13 733**
Argentina	13 468	2 711	-	100	200	540	1 896	3 256	65	...	...
Bahamas	-	-	-	-	-	-	-	-	100	...	...
Barbados	200	150	-	-	-	325	215	-	-	...	...
Belize	-	-	125	100	-	-	-	-	-	...	...
Bolivia (Plurinational State of)	-	-	-	-	108	-	-	-	-	...	...
Brazil	12 068	13 010	6 857	19 364	11 603	15 334	19 079	10 608	6 400	2 500	5 210
Chile	676	1 515	1 694	3 200	2 350	1 000	1 062	250	-	600	900
Colombia	1 622	4 329	695	1 545	1 545	2 435	3 177	3 065	1 000	1 000	2 000
Costa Rica	250	250	250	490	310	-	-	-	-	...	...
Cuba	-	-	-	-	-	-	400	200	-	...	...
Dominican Republic	-	500	-	600	-	160	675	605	-	...	...
Ecuador	-	-	-	-	-	650	-	-	-	...	...
El Salvador	50	354	1 252	349	286	375	925	-	-	...	...
Grenada	-	-	100	-	-	-	-	-	-	...	...
Guatemala	-	325	-	300	380	-	-	-	30	...	...
Jamaica	422	812	300	-	814	1 050	930	1 900	350	...	250
Mexico	9 777	11 016	6 505	7 979	13 312	11 703	9 200	10 296	5 835	3 700	4 050
Panama	350	1 100	1 030	275	770	1 530	2 076	670	686	323	323
Paraguay	-	-	-	-	-	-	-	-	-	...	...
Peru	-	-	1 000	1 250	1 305	2 675	733	1 827	-	1 000	1 000
Trinidad and Tobago	250	-	-	-	-	100	500	-	-	...	...
Uruguay	641	856	400	-	350	1 062	3 679	999	-	...	...
Venezuela (Bolivarian Republic of)	482	1 575	-	2 354	3 050	6 115	100	7 500	4 000	...	...

Source: Economic Commission for Latin America and the Caribbean (ECLAC), on the basis of figures from the International Monetary Fund (IMF), Merrill-Lynch and JP Morgan.

[a] Includes sovereign, bank and corporate bonds.

[b] Does not include US$ 584 million issued by the Andean Development Corporation (ADC) and US$ 200 million issued by the Central American Bank for Economic Integration (CABEI).

[c] Does not include US$ 250 million issued by the Andean Development Corporation (ADC), US$ 250 million issued by the Latin American Reserve Fund (FLAR) and US$ 567 million issued by the Central American Bank for Economic Integration (CABEI).

[d] Does not include US$ 539 million issued by the Andean Development Corporation (ADC).

[e] Does not include US$ 447 million issued by the Andean Development Corporation (ADC).

[f] Does not include US$ 1 billiion issued by the Andean Development Corporation (ADC).

Table A-16

LATIN AMERICA AND THE CARIBBEAN: TOTAL GROSS EXTERNAL DEBT [a]

(Millions of dollars)

	2000	2001	2002	2003	2004	2005	2006	2007	2008 [b]
Latin America and the Caribbean	**743 532**	**750 019**	**743 955**	**775 759**	**771 919**	**675 054**	**663 050**	**751 084**	**778 247**
Antigua and Barbuda	465	493	539	607	706	470	491	501	524
Argentina	155 014	166 272	156 748	164 645	171 205	113 799	108 873	124 575	128 112
Bahamas [c]	350	328	309	363	345	338	334	326	427
Barbados	951	1 135	1 163	1 241	1 222	1 353	1 501	1 572	1 530
Belize [c]	431	495	652	822	913	970	985	973	955
Bolivia (Plurinational State of)	6 740	6 861	6 945	7 709	7 562	7 666	6 278	5 386	5 913
Brazil	216 921	209 935	210 711	214 929	201 373	169 451	172 589	193 219	198 361
Chile	37 177	38 527	40 504	43 067	43 517	44 934	47 590	55 822	64 768
Colombia	36 130	39 163	37 382	38 065	39 497	38 507	40 103	44 553	46 392
Costa Rica	5 307	5 265	5 310	5 575	5 710	6 485	6 994	8 341	9 082
Cuba [c d]	10 961	10 893	10 900	11 300	5 806	5 898	7 794	8 908	9 906
Dominica	154	182	209	230	224	242	249	247	248
Dominican Republic [c]	3 679	4 176	4 536	5 987	6 380	5 847	6 296	6 556	7 220
Ecuador	13 216	14 376	16 236	16 756	17 211	17 237	17 099	17 445	16 514
El Salvador [e]	2 831	3 148	3 987	7 917	8 211	8 761	9 586	9 075	9 711
Grenada	132	176	316	352	420	447	473	491	494
Guatemala [c]	2 644	2 925	3 119	3 467	3 844	3 723	3 958	4 226	4 382
Guyana [c]	1 193	1 197	1 247	1 085	1 071	1 215	1 043	719	834
Haiti [c]	1 170	1 189	1 229	1 316	1 376	1 335	1 419	1 541	1 885
Honduras	4 711	4 757	4 922	5 242	5 912	5 093	3 879	3 028	3 321
Jamaica [c]	3 375	4 146	4 348	4 192	5 115	5 372	5 794	6 123	6 344
Mexico	148 652	144 526	140 099	140 554	139 152	130 731	117 506	141 823	150 142
Nicaragua [c]	6 660	6 374	6 363	6 596	5 391	5 348	4 527	3 385	3 512
Panama [c]	5 604	6 263	6 349	6 504	7 219	7 580	7 788	8 276	8 477
Paraguay	3 275	3 074	3 336	3 371	3 330	3 056	3 069	3 174	3 507
Peru	27 981	27 195	27 872	29 587	31 244	28 657	28 672	33 137	34 587
Saint Kitts and Nevis	162	214	265	317	317	311	306	285	296
Saint Vincent and the Grenadines	163	172	172	207	243	250	255	220	240
Saint Lucia	178	213	260	338	369	388	404	415	415
Suriname [c]	291	350	371	382	382	388	389	299	316
Trinidad and Tobago [c]	1 680	1 666	1 549	1 568	1 382	1 361	1 295	1 278	1 445
Uruguay	8 895	8 937	10 548	11 013	11 593	11 418	10 560	12 218	12 027
Venezuela (Bolivarian Republic of)	36 437	35 398	35 460	40 456	43 679	46 427	44 952	52 949	46 360

Source: Economic Commission for Latin America and the Caribbean (ECLAC), on the basis of official figures from the International Monetary Fund (IMF) and national sources.

[a] Includes debt owed to the International Monetary Fund.

[b] Preliminary figures.

[c] Refers to external public debt.

[d] From 2004 on refers only to active external debt; excludes other external debt, 60.2% of which is official debt owed to the Paris Club.

[e] Up to 2002 corresponds to public external debt.

Table A-17

LATIN AMERICA AND THE CARIBBEAN: GROSS INTERNATIONAL RESERVES

(Millions of dollars)

	2000	2001	2002	2003	2004	2005	2006	2007	2008	2009	
										I Q	II Q [a]
Latin America and the Caribbean	**171 298**	**169 408**	**167 959**	**201 185**	**227 838**	**263 207**	**320 757**	**459 550**	**510 457**	**482 382**	**478 688**
Antigua and Barbuda [b]	64	80	88	114	120	127	143	144	138	94	133 [c]
Argentina	32 478	15 318	10 420	13 820	19 299	27 262	31 167	45 711	46 198	46 933	46 026
Bahamas [b]	350	319	381	491	674	586	461	464	568	634	768 [d]
Barbados [b]	473	690	669	738	580	603	636	839	753 [e]	...	...
Belize [b]	123	112	115	85	48	71	114	109	166	168	180 [d]
Bolivia (Plurinational State of)	1 160	1 129	897	1 096	1 272	1 798	3 193	5 319	7 722	7 762	7 895 [d]
Brazil	33 011	35 866	37 823	49 296	52 935	53 799	85 839	180 334	193 783	190 388	195 264 [d]
Chile	15 110	14 400	15 351	15 851	16 016	16 963	19 429	16 910	23 162	23 382	23 448
Colombia	8 740	9 956	10 540	10 608	13 220	14 634	15 109	20 607	23 672	23 475	23 356
Costa Rica	1 318	1 384	1 502	1 839	1 922	2 313	3 115	4 114	3 799	4 167	3 971
Dominica	29	31	45	48	42	49	63	61	55	57	58 [c]
Dominican Republic	818	1 341	829	279	825	1 929	2 251	2 946	2 644	2 539	2 476 [c]
Ecuador	1 180	1 074	1 008	1 160	1 437	2 147	2 023	3 521	4 473	3 244	2 675
El Salvador	1 894	1 712	1 591	1 910	1 893	1 833	1 908	2 198	2 545	2 524	2 788
Grenada [b]	58	64	88	83	122	94	100	111	105	88	90 [c]
Guatemala	1 885	2 359	2 381	2 932	3 529	3 783	4 061	4 310	4 745	5 030	...
Guyana [b]	305	287	284	276	232	252	280	313	356	405	...
Haiti	232	191	139	112	166	187	305	494	587	602	...
Honduras	...	1 578	1 687	1 609	2 159	2 526	2 824	2 733	2 690	2 784	2 804 [c]
Jamaica	1 049	1 903	1 643	1 196	1 882	2 169	2 399	1 906	1 795	1 663	1 661
Mexico	35 585	44 814	50 674	59 028	64 198	74 110	76 330	87 211	95 302	85 636	83 173 [d]
Nicaragua	497	383	454	504	670	730	924	1 103	1 141	1 078	1 143
Panama [b]	723	1 092	1 183	1 011	631	1 211	1 335	1 935	...	...	...
Paraguay	714	662	603	853	1 191	1 292	1 594	2 240	2 737	2 834	2 870 [d]
Peru	8 563	8 838	9 690	10 206	12 649	14 120	17 329	27 720	31 233	30 961	30 822
Saint Kitts and Nevis [b]	45	56	66	65	78	72	89	96	110	154	156 [c]
Saint Vincent and the Grenadines [b]	55	61	53	51	75	70	79	87	84	89	91 [c]
Saint Lucia [b]	79	89	94	107	133	116	135	154	143	169	163 [c]
Suriname	63	119	106	106	129	126	215	401	433	468	600 [d]
Trinidad and Tobago	1 405	1 876	1 924	2 258	2 993	4 787	6 777	7 053	9 830	9 097	8 811 [c]
Uruguay	2 823	3 100	772	2 087	2 512	3 078	3 091	4 121	6 360	6 965	7 100 [d]
Venezuela (Bolivarian Republic of)	20 471	18 523	14 860	21 366	24 208	30 368	37 440	34 286	43 127	28 992	30 167

Source: Economic Commission for Latin America and the Caribbean (ECLAC), on the basis of official figures from the International Monetary Fund (IMF) and national sources.

[a] Balance as of June.

[b] Does not include gold.

[c] Balance as of April.

[d] Balance as of May.

[e] Balance as of November.

Table A-18

LATIN AMERICA AND THE CARIBBEAN: STOCK EXCHANGE INDICES

(National indices to end of period, 31 December 2000=100)

	2000	2001	2002	2003	2004	2005	2006	2007	2008		2009	
									III	IV	I	II
Argentina	100	71	126	257	330	370	502	516	383	259	270	381
Brazil	100	89	74	146	172	219	291	419	325	246	268	337
Chile	100	109	92	137	166	181	248	281	254	219	229	285
Colombia	100	134	206	291	542	1 187	1 393	1 335	1 154	944	1 001	1 233
Costa Rica	100	113	117	104	88	96	169	193	209	177	114	116
Ecuador	100	130	195	178	216	272	353	329	341	349	342	302
Jamaica	100	117	157	234	390	362	348	374	353	277	273	280
Mexico	100	113	108	156	229	315	468	523	440	396	347	431
Peru	100	97	115	202	307	397	1 066	1 450	931	583	764	1 081
Trinidad and Tobago	100	98	124	157	243	242	220	222	241	191	186	176
Venezuela (Bolivarian Republic of)	100	96	117	325	439	299	765	555	556	514	640	653

Source: Economic Commission for Latin America and the Caribbean (ECLAC), on the basis of information from Bloomberg.

Table A-19

LATIN AMERICA AND THE CARIBBEAN: OVERALL REAL EFFECTIVE EXCHANGE RATES [a]

(Indices 2000=100, deflacted by CPI)

	2000	2001	2002	2003	2004	2005	2006	2007 [b]	2008 [b]	2009 [b c]
Latin America and the Caribbean [d]	**100.0**	**99.2**	**111.0**	**120.5**	**119.6**	**111.4**	**108.6**	**105.4**	**99.1**	**98.9**
Argentina	100.0	95.9	225.8	205.0	212.8	213.4	218.0	222.1	229.1	230.1
Bolivia (Plurinational State of)	100.0	101.1	95.5	104.2	109.5	116.9	119.3	117.9	105.9	91.0
Brazil	100.0	120.4	132.6	131.2	123.8	100.4	88.9	82.5	79.2	88.5
Chile	100.0	111.7	109.4	114.7	108.5	103.2	100.9	102.5	101.7	107.2
Colombia	100.0	104.2	105.7	119.6	107.1	96.7	97.8	85.7	83.0	93.6
Costa Rica	100.0	97.5	98.6	104.4	106.0	107.3	106.1	103.5	100.0	97.2
Cuba [e]	100.0	90.5	94.1	99.8	106.1	105.4	112.3	115.1	125.9	...
Dominica	100.0	100.3	101.6	104.2	108.0	110.9	113.2	116.8	119.1	114.7
Dominican Republic [f]	100.0	96.5	98.6	131.4	125.6	87.5	95.7	95.9	98.5	101.0
Ecuador	100.0	70.7	61.8	60.3	61.6	64.7	65.3	68.1	68.7	63.0
El Salvador	100.0	99.7	99.7	100.2	98.9	101.0	101.4	102.7	103.7	98.5
Guatemala	100.0	96.3	88.6	88.8	85.7	79.3	76.9	76.3	72.2	72.2
Honduras	100.0	97.1	96.9	98.5	100.9	100.6	98.0	97.8	94.4	86.8
Jamaica	100.0	101.7	101.2	116.9	113.6	104.4	104.8	108.5	101.8	112.2
Mexico	100.0	94.4	94.0	104.5	108.3	104.6	104.7	105.8	108.1	126.0
Nicaragua	100.0	101.2	103.3	106.9	107.7	108.4	107.0	110.9	105.4	102.3
Panama	100.0	103.1	101.2	103.2	108.4	111.0	112.7	114.3	112.2	105.5
Paraguay	100.0	102.8	106.5	112.5	106.4	118.7	106.5	95.5	83.7	90.0
Peru	100.0	98.1	95.8	99.8	99.9	101.1	104.0	104.1	100.3	96.8
Trinidad and Tobago	100.0	94.5	91.1	91.9	93.6	91.0	89.1	87.6	83.0	74.8
Uruguay	100.0	101.4	118.4	150.5	152.5	134.1	128.3	127.0	116.0	115.9
Venezuela (Bolivarian Republic of)	100.0	95.3	125.1	141.1	139.5	141.0	132.4	118.6	96.6	76.4

Source: Economic Commission for Latin America and the Caribbean (ECLAC), on the basis of official figures from the International Monetary Fund (IMF) and national sources.

[a] Annual averages. A country's overall real effective exchange rate index is calculated by weighting its real bilateral exchange rate indices with each of its trading partners by each partner's share in the country's total trade flows in terms of exports and imports. The extraregional real effective exchange rate index excludes trade with other Latin American and Caribbean countries. A currency depreciates in real effective terms when this index rises and appreciates when it falls.

[b] Preliminary figures, weighted by trade in 2006.

[c] January-May average.

[d] Simple average of the extraregional real effective exchange rate for 20 countries.

[e] Preliminary figures. Yearly calculation by ECLAC, based on consumer price data and nominal exchange rates provided by the National Statistical Office of Cuba.

[f] Owing to lack of data, the period 2002-2009 has been weighted using trade figures for 2001.

Table A-20
LATIN AMERICA AND THE CARIBBEAN: PARTICIPATION RATE
(Average annual rates)

			2000	2001	2002	2003	2004	2005	2006	2007	2008 [a]
Latin America and the Caribbean [b]		**Total**	**59.3**	**59.7**	**59.5**	**59.7**	**59.9**	**60.0**	**60.0**	**60.8**	**61.2**
		Female	**44.9**	**45.7**	**45.6**	**46.6**	**46.7**	**47.0**	**47.2**	**48.0**	**48.6**
		Male	**74.5**	**74.4**	**74.1**	**73.6**	**73.9**	**73.7**	**73.6**	**74.6**	**74.6**
Argentina [c]	Urban areas	Total	56.6	56.0	55.8	60.1	60.3	59.9	60.3	59.5	58.8
		Female	43.4	42.6	43.3	49.2	49.0	48.3	49.0	47.7	47.2
		Male	71.7	71.4	70.3	72.9	73.2	73.2	73.3	73.0	72.0
Bolivia (Plurinational State of)	National total	Total	62.4	67.8	64.6	67.6	64.9	...	...	...	...
		Female	53.7	60.2	56.3	60.1	57.2	...	...	...	...
		Male	71.8	75.9	73.2	75.4	73.4	...	...	...	...
Brazil [c]	Six metropolitan areas	Total	58.0	56.4	56.7	57.1	57.2	56.6	56.9	56.9	57.0
		Female	45.2	43.9	43.9	47.8	48.3	47.7	48.1	48.5	48.7
		Male	72.7	71.0	70.5	67.7	67.3	66.7	66.8	66.5	66.5
Chile	National total	Total	54.4	53.9	53.7	54.4	55.0	55.6	54.8	54.9	56.0
		Female	35.6	35.0	35.0	36.6	38.1	39.2	38.5	39.1	41.0
		Male	74.0	73.4	73.0	73.0	72.3	72.6	71.7	71.4	71.8
Colombia	Thirteen metropolitan areas	Total	63.5	64.4	64.8	65.0	63.6	63.3	62.0	61.8	62.6
		Female	54.8	55.5	55.3	56.9	54.9	54.9	53.5	53.5	54.0
		Male	73.8	74.6	74.7	74.2	73.3	72.8	71.6	71.2	72.1
Costa Rica	National total	Total	53.6	55.8	55.4	55.5	54.4	56.8	56.6	57.0	56.7
		Female	35.0	38.6	38.2	38.5	36.8	40.4	40.7	41.6	41.7
		Male	72.8	73.7	73.2	73.3	72.9	73.9	73.5	73.2	72.5
Cuba	National total	Total	70.1	70.9	71.0	70.9	71.0	72.1	72.1	73.7	74.7
		Female	53.9	53.7	53.9	54.2	54.4	55.6	56.7	59.3	60.2
		Male	84.9	86.7	86.6	86.0	86.1	87.0	86.0	86.7	87.8
Dominican Republic	National total	Total	55.2	54.3	55.1	54.7	56.3	55.9	56.0	56.1	55.6
		Female	40.6	40.0	42.1	41.0	43.7	43.1	43.6	43.2	43.5
		Male	70.4	69.2	68.3	68.6	69.2	68.8	68.6	69.3	67.9
Ecuador	Urban total	Total	57.3	63.1	58.3	58.2	59.1	59.5	59.1	61.3	60.1
		Female	45.0	52.5	46.7	47.0	47.9	48.6	47.7	50.9	49.6
		Male	70.3	74.0	70.2	69.8	70.8	70.9	71.2	72.5	71.3
El Salvador [d]	National total	Total	52.2	53.3	51.2	53.4	51.7	52.4	52.6	62.1	62.7
		Female	38.7	38.5	38.0	40.4	38.0	39.5	40.4	40.7	47.3
		Male	67.7	69.2	65.8	68.3	66.5	67.4	67.0	81.0	81.4
Honduras	National total	Total	...	52.5	51.7	50.0	50.6	50.9	50.7	50.7	51.0
		Female	...	34.7	32.5	33.0	32.7	33.2	33.5	33.3	34.4
		Male	...	71.8	72.3	68.4	70.0	70.0	69.7	70.1	69.3
Jamaica [e]	National total	Total	63.4	63.0	65.8	64.4	64.3	64.2	64.7	64.8	65.4
		Female	54.2	53.6	57.3	55.4	55.8	55.5	56.4	56.5	57.5
		Male	72.8	73.0	74.7	73.7	73.3	73.3	73.5	73.6	73.8
Mexico	Urban areas	Total	58.7	58.1	57.8	58.3	58.9	59.5	60.7	60.7	60.4
		Female	41.4	40.9	40.6	41.5	42.9	44.1	45.8	46.2	46.1
		Male	78.0	77.3	76.9	76.8	76.7	76.9	77.6	77.3	76.7
Nicaragua	National total	Total	53.8	57.5	...	53.7	53.1	53.8	51.4	51.1	53.3
		Female	...	40.2	...	...	...	39.4	...	...	...
		Male	...	75.6	...	...	...	69.2	...	...	...
Panama	National total	Total	59.9	60.5	62.6	62.8	63.3	63.6	62.6	62.7	63.9
		Female	41.6	41.7	45.1	45.9	46.6	47.4	45.8	46.8	47.2
		Male	78.8	79.5	80.1	79.9	80.6	80.3	79.9	79.3	81.3
Paraguay	National total	Total	63.7	59.2	61.2	59.8	63.4	61.8	60.1	60.8	61.7
		Female	49.0	45.5	45.8	45.7	50.4	48.6	46.1	48.0	47.9
		Male	78.9	73.3	76.9	74.3	76.6	75.1	74.0	73.9	75.8
Peru	Metropolitan Lima	Total	63.4	65.5	62.9	63.2	62.3	62.5	64.0	63.5	66.4
		Female	51.4	55.9	51.8	54.2	49.9	52.3	53.4	51.7	56.4
		Male	76.8	76.1	75.3	72.9	75.6	73.4	75.4	76.1	77.0
Uruguay	Urban total	Total	59.7	60.8	59.3	58.1	58.5	58.5	60.9	62.7	62.6
		Female	49.3	51.0	49.4	48.9	48.7	49.5	51.9	53.7	54.3
		Male	71.9	72.2	70.7	69.0	70.0	69.3	71.7	73.6	72.7
Venezuela (Bolivarian Republic of)	National total	Total	64.6	66.5	68.7	69.3	68.5	66.3	65.4	64.9	64.7
		Female	47.3	50.9	54.3	55.5	54.5	51.5	50.6	50.0	50.1
		Male	81.9	82.0	83.5	83.0	82.6	81.2	80.4	79.9	79.4

Source: Economic Commission for Latin America and the Caribbean (ECLAC), on the basis of official figures.
[a] Preliminary figures.
[b] The data relating to the different countries are not comparable owing to differences in coverage and in the definition of the working age population. The regional series are simple averages of national data (excluding Nicaragua and the Plurinational State of Bolivia) and include adjustments for lack of information and changes in methodology.
[c] New measurements have been used since 2003; the data are not comparable with the previous series.
[d] New measurements have been used since 2007; the data are not comparable with the previous series.
[e] New measurements have been used since 2002; the data are not comparable with the previous series.

Table A-21

LATIN AMERICA AND THE CARIBBEAN: OPEN URBAN UNEMPLOYMENT

(Average annual rates)

		2000	2001	2002	2003	2004	2005	2006	2007	2008 [a]
Latin America and the Caribbean [b]		**10.4**	**10.2**	**11.0**	**11.0**	**10.3**	**9.1**	**8.6**	**7.9**	**7.4**
Argentina [c]	Urban areas	15.1	17.4	19.7	17.3	13.6	11.6	10.2	8.5	7.9
Bahamas [d]	National total	...	6.9	9.1	10.8	10.2	10.2	7.6	7.9	12.1
Barbados [d]	National total	9.2	9.9	10.3	11.0	9.8	9.1	8.7	7.4	8.1
Belize [d]	National total	11.1	9.1	10.0	12.9	11.6	11.0	9.4	8.5	8.2
Bolivia (Plurinational State of)	Urban total	7.5	8.5	8.7	9.2	6.2	8.1	8.0	7.7	7.0
Brazil [e]	Six metropolitan areas	7.1	6.2	11.7	12.3	11.5	9.8	10.0	9.3	7.9
Chile	National total	9.7	9.9	9.8	9.5	10.0	9.2	7.7	7.1	7.8
Colombia [d]	Thirteen metropolitan areas	17.3	18.2	17.6	16.7	15.4	13.9	13.0	11.4	11.5
Costa Rica	Urban total	5.3	5.8	6.8	6.7	6.7	6.9	6.0	4.8	4.8
Cuba	National total	5.4	4.1	3.3	2.3	1.9	1.9	1.9	1.8	1.6
Dominican Republic [d]	National total	13.9	15.6	16.1	16.7	18.4	18.0	16.2	15.6	14.1
Ecuador [d]	Urban total [f]	14.1	10.4	8.6	9.8	9.7	8.5	8.1	7.4	6.9
El Salvador [g]	Urban total	6.5	7.0	6.2	6.2	6.5	7.3	5.7	5.8	5.5
Guatemala	Urban total	...	...	5.4	5.2	4.4	...	...	...	...
Honduras	Urban total	...	5.9	6.1	7.6	8.0	6.5	4.9	4.0	4.1
Jamaica [d]	National total	15.5	15.0	14.2	11.4	11.7	11.3	10.3	9.8	10.6
Mexico	Urban areas	3.4	3.6	3.9	4.6	5.3	4.7	4.6	4.8	4.9
Nicaragua	Urban total	7.8	11.3	11.6	10.2	9.3	7.0	7.0	6.9	8.0
Panama [d]	Urban total	15.2	17.0	16.5	15.9	14.1	12.1	10.4	7.8	6.5
Paraguay	Urban total	10.0	10.8	14.7	11.2	10.0	7.6	8.9	7.2	7.4
Peru	Metropolitan Lima	8.5	9.3	9.4	9.4	9.4	9.6	8.5	8.4	8.4
Suriname	National total	14.0	14.0	10.0	7.0	8.4	11.2	12.1	...	...
Trinidad and Tobago [d]	National total	12.2	10.8	10.4	10.5	8.4	8.0	6.2	5.6	4.9 [h]
Uruguay	Urban total	13.6	15.3	17.0	16.9	13.1	12.2	11.4	9.6	7.9
Venezuela (Bolivarian Republic of)	National total	13.9	13.3	15.8	18.0	15.3	12.4	10.0	8.4	7.4

Source: Economic Commission for Latin America and the Caribbean (ECLAC), on the basis of official figures.

[a] Preliminary figures.

[b] The data for Argentina and Brazil have been adjusted to reflect changes in methodology in 2003 and 2002, respectively.

[c] New measurements have been used since 2003; the data are not comparable with the previous series.

[d] Includes hidden unemployment.

[e] New measurements have been used since 2002; the data are not comparable with the previous series.

[f] Up to 2003, the figures refer to Cuenca, Guayaquil and Quito.

[g] New measurements have been used since 2007; the data are not comparable with the previous series.

[h] Average of the March, June and September data.

Table A-22

LATIN AMERICA AND THE CARIBBEAN: EMPLOYMENT RATE [a]

(Average annual rates)

		2000	2001	2002	2003	2004	2005	2006	2007	2008 [b]
Latin America and the Caribbean [c]		**52.8**	**52.5**	**52.1**	**52.5**	**53.1**	**53.6**	**54.2**	**54.8**	**55.1**
Argentina [d]	Urban areas	49.0	47.4	45.9	0.0	0.0	0.0	0.0	0.0	0.0
Bolivia (Plurinational State of)	Urban total	51.9	55.4	53.0	54.9	55.0	51.2	54.0	52.7	...
Brazil [d]	Six metropolitan areas	53.8	52.9	52.6	...	...	...	...	...	...
Chile	National total	49.1	48.6	48.4	49.3	49.5	50.4	50.5	51.0	51.7
Colombia	Thirteen metropolitan areas	52.6	52.7	53.4	54.2	53.8	54.5	54.0	54.8	55.3
Costa Rica	National total	50.8	52.4	51.8	51.8	50.9	53.0	53.3	54.4	53.9
Cuba	National total	66.3	68.0	68.6	69.2	69.7	70.7	70.7	72.4	73.6
Dominican Republic	National total	47.6	45.8	46.2	45.4	46.0	45.9	46.9	47.4	47.7
Ecuador	Urban total	52.1	56.2	52.9	51.5	53.5	54.4	54.3	56.8	56.0
El Salvador [e]	National total	48.7	49.8	48.0	49.7	48.2	48.3	49.2	58.1	59.0
Honduras	National total	...	50.3	49.7	47.4	48.6	48.6	49.0	49.2	49.4
Jamaica	National total	53.4	53.5	54.0	57.1	56.8	57.0	58.0	58.6	58.5
Mexico	Urban areas	56.8	56.0	55.5	55.6	55.8	56.7	57.9	57.8	57.5
Nicaragua	National total	50.6	51.0	...	49.5	49.6	50.8	48.8	48.6	50.1
Panama	National total	51.8	52.0	54.1	54.6	55.9	57.3	57.2	58.7	60.3
Paraguay	National total	59.0	54.7	54.6	55.0	58.8	58.2	55.4	57.4	58.2
Peru	Metropolitan Lima [f]	59.7	60.5	62.0	61.1	61.6	60.7	61.8	63.0	62.4
Trinidad and Tobago	National total	53.8	53.8	54.6	55.2	57.8	58.6	59.9	59.9	60.2 [g]
Uruguay	Urban total	51.6	51.4	49.1	48.3	50.9	51.4	53.9	56.7	57.7
Venezuela (Bolivarian Republic of)	National total	55.5	57.6	57.8	56.8	58.1	58.1	58.9	59.5	59.9

Source: Economic Commission for Latin America and the Caribbean (ECLAC), on the basis of official figures.

[a] Employed population as a percentage of the working-age population.

[b] Preliminary figures.

[c] Weighted average adjusted for lack of information and changes in methodology.

[d] New measurements have been used since 2003; the data are not comparable with the previous series.

[e] New measurements have been used since 2007; the data are not comparable with the previous series.

[f] For 2000, the figures refer to the urban total.

[g] Average of the March, June and September data.

Table A-23

LATIN AMERICA AND THE CARIBBEAN: FORMAL EMPLOYMENT INDICATORS

(Indices 2000=100)

	2000	2001	2002	2003	2004	2005	2006	2007	2008 [a]
Argentina [b]	100.0	101.0	93.1	96.2	107.0	118.7	129.6	139.8	147.7
Brazil [c]	100.0	102.9	101.6	104.2	109.5	115.7	121.3	127.5	135.6
Chile [b]	100.0	101.6	103.4	105.9	109.6	118.2	125.7	136.7	146.2
Costa Rica [d]	100.0	97.6	104.0	106.9	110.9	116.1	123.9	134.4	144.3
El Salvador [d]	100.0	101.7	100.9	102.5	104.9	108.6	113.9	119.8	123.3
Guatemala [d]	100.0	102.2	104.9	105.5	108.9	110.4	113.0	118.2	118.1
Jamaica [e]	100.0	98.0	97.4	96.3	97.9	99.0	100.2	101.5	...
Mexico [d]	100.0	99.5	98.6	98.2	99.6	102.8	107.7	112.2	114.5
Nicaragua [d]	100.0	101.8	101.0	103.7	112.9	123.2	136.2	148.8	159.9
Panama [f]	100.0	95.5	89.7	95.7	99.4	108.5	117.6	124.1	128.3
Peru [e]	100.0	98.1	98.1	99.8	102.5	107.1	115.0	124.3	134.7
Uruguay [d g]	100.0	97.7	92.1	93.9	99.8	110.7	120.5	130.9	141.0

Source: Economic Commission for Latin America and the Caribbean (ECLAC), on the basis of official figures.

[a] Preliminary figures.
[b] Dependent workers paying into pension schemes.
[c] Workers covered by social and labour legislation.
[d] Workers with social security coverage.
[e] Workers of medium-sized and large firms.
[f] Private workers with social security coverage. From 2007, workers of small, medium-sized and large businesses.
[g] Employment positions generating social security contributions.

Table A-24

LATIN AMERICA: VISIBLE UNDEREMPLOYMENT INDICATORS

(Percentage of employed)

	2000	2001	2002	2003	2004	2005	2006	2007	2008 [a]
Argentina [b]	17.1	18.9	24.0	20.7	17.5	14.2	12.5	10.4	9.5
Brazil [c]	...	...	4.1	5.0	4.6	3.7	4.1	3.6	3.1
Chile [d]	6.1	7.1	6.2	6.5	8.4	8.5	8.5	8.0	9.0
Colombia [e]	14.2	16.3	16.8	15.3	15.2	13.8	11.9	10.0	9.1
Costa Rica [f]	10.5	11.3	12.3	15.2	14.4	14.6	13.5	11.5	10.5
Ecuador [g]	16.1	12.6	10.2	9.8	8.1	7.3	6.3	10.8	9.9
El Salvador [h]	3.7	3.8	4.3	4.8	4.5	6.2	4.9	5.3	6.3
Honduras [i]	...	4.0	4.9	6.3	7.1	7.4	5.6	4.4	3.6
Mexico [j]	...	...	...	...	...	7.5	6.9	7.2	6.9
Panama [k]	...	...	...	...	4.4	4.6	3.4	2.7	2.1
Paraguay [l]	9.1	8.3	9.5	8.8	8.3	7.5	5.6	5.8	6.6
Peru [m]	12.3	12.8	11.8	9.8	9.6	9.5	9.4	9.5	8.9
Uruguay [k]	11.9	15.3	18.4	19.3	15.8	17.1	13.6	12.8	17.2

Source: Economic Commission for Latin America and the Caribbean (ECLAC), on the basis of official figures.

[a] Preliminary figures.
[b] Employed persons who work less than 35 hours per week and wish to work more hours; total urban areas.
[c] Employed persons who work less than 40 hours per week and wish to work more hours; six metropolitan areas.
[d] Employed persons who work less than 35 hours per week and who wish to work more; national total; third quarter of each year. The figures up to 2005 and since 2006 are not directly comparable since the sample changed.
[e] Employed persons who work less than 48 hours per week and wish to work more hours; 13 metropolitan areas.
[f] Employed persons who work less than 47 hours per week and wish to work more hours; national total.
[g] Employed persons who work less than 40 hours per week and wish to work more hours. Up to 2006, Cuenca, Guayaquil and Quito; since 2007, urban national.
[h] Employed persons who work less than 40 hours per week and wish to work more hours; total urban areas. New measurements have been used since 2007; the data are not comparable with the previous series.
[i] Employed persons who work less than 36 hours per week and wish to work more hours; total urban areas.
[j] Employed workers wishing to work more than their current job permits, national total.
[k] Employed persons who work less than 40 hours per week and wish to work more hours; total urban areas.
[l] Employed persons who work less than 30 hours per week and wish to work more hours; total urban areas.
[m] Employed persons who work less than 35 hours per week and wish to work more hours; metropolitan Lima.

Table A-25

LATIN AMERICA AND THE CARIBBEAN: TREND IN REAL AVERAGE WAGES

(Average annual index, 2000=100)

	2000	2001	2002	2003	2004	2005	2006	2007	2008 [a]
Argentina [b]	100.0	99.2	85.4	83.8	92.2	99.0	107.8	117.6	127.9
Bolivia (Plurinational State of)	100.0	105.8	109.3	111.1	114.1	110.0	101.2	98.4	...
Brazil [c]	100.0	95.1	93.1	84.9	85.5	85.2	88.2	89.5	91.4
Chile [d]	100.0	101.7	103.7	104.6	106.5	108.5	110.6	113.7	113.4
Colombia [b]	100.0	99.7	102.7	102.1	103.8	105.3	109.3	108.7	106.8
Costa Rica [e]	100.0	101.0	105.1	105.5	102.8	100.8	102.4	103.8	102.2
Cuba	100.0	96.2	105.1	107.8	114.6	129.5	144.5	143.1	140.5
Guatemala [e]	100.0	100.5	99.6	100.0	97.8	93.9	92.9	91.4	89.0
Mexico [b]	100.0	106.7	108.7	110.2	110.5	110.2	110.6	111.7	112.5
Nicaragua [e]	100.0	101.0	104.5	106.5	104.2	104.5	105.9	104.0	97.8
Panama [f]	100.0	98.8	95.8	95.3	94.5	93.4	95.3	96.2	95.4
Paraguay	100.0	101.4	96.3	95.6	97.2	98.2	98.8	101.1	100.3 [g]
Peru [h]	100.0	99.1	103.7	105.3	106.5	104.4	105.7	103.8	106.5 [g]
Uruguay	100.0	99.7	89.0	77.9	77.9	81.5	85.0	89.0	91.9
Venezuela (Bolivarian Republic of)	100.0	106.9	95.1	78.4	78.6	80.7	84.8	85.8	82.2

Source: Economic Commission for Latin America and the Caribbean (ECLAC), on the basis of official figures.
[a] Preliminary figures.
[b] Manufacturing. From 2005, registered private-sector workers.
[c] Workers covered by social and labour legislation. Since 2003, private sector only.
[d] General index of hourly wages.
[e] Average wages declared by workers covered by social security.
[f] Average wages declared by workers covered by social security. The variation in remunerations for 2007 relative to 2006 refers to workers in large, medium-sized and small enterprises.
[g] Figure for June.
[h] Private sector workers in the Lima metropolitan area.

Table A-26

LATIN AMERICA AND THE CARIBBEAN: REAL MINIMUM WAGE

(Indices 2000=100)

	2000	2001	2002	2003	2004	2005	2006	2007	2008 [a]
Argentina	100.0	101.1	81.3	84.0	129.8	171.1	193.2	219.6	253.3
Bolivia (Plurinational State of)	100.0	110.8	116.0	116.9	112.0	106.3	111.1	109.7	108.0
Brazil	100.0	109.8	114.3	117.4	121.4	128.5	145.3	154.8	160.8
Chile	100.0	103.8	106.8	108.3	111.3	113.4	116.3	118.5	118.3
Colombia	100.0	101.2	101.9	102.0	103.8	105.0	107.9	108.6	106.9
Costa Rica	100.0	100.2	99.5	99.2	97.6	97.8	99.5	100.8	99.5
Cuba	100.0	89.6	94.3	92.4	94.4	206.6	196.6	184.7	180.7
Dominican Republic	100.0	105.7	105.1	95.5	81.2	96.4	89.6	93.8	87.7
Ecuador	100.0	111.5	112.5	119.3	122.2	125.9	130.0	135.1	146.7
El Salvador	100.0	96.4	94.6	96.7	95.3	91.1	90.5	92.7	92.9
Guatemala	100.0	108.3	108.6	117.3	117.6	115.9	119.6	117.7	105.7
Haiti	100.0	88.4	80.5	107.5	91.7	79.6	70.0	64.8	56.2
Honduras	100.0	102.5	104.6	113.6	114.5	121.2	127.4	130.9	131.1
Mexico	100.0	100.4	101.2	100.4	99.1	99.0	99.0	98.3	96.2
Nicaragua	100.0	102.1	105.9	109.2	113.5	118.1	128.5	131.6	141.6
Panama	100.0	107.0	105.8	106.5	107.5	104.5	108.1	106.3	109.2
Paraguay	100.0	103.7	102.9	105.8	102.4	104.4	106.7	103.9	101.3
Peru	100.0	101.2	101.0	102.2	106.9	105.1	112.0	111.7	114.5
Uruguay	100.0	98.7	88.7	77.7	77.5	131.9	153.2	159.6	176.9
Venezuela (Bolivarian Republic of)	100.0	100.0	94.5	83.3	92.7	103.7	113.9	114.4	107.1

Source: Economic Commission for Latin America and the Caribbean (ECLAC), on the basis of official figures.
[a] Preliminary figures.

Table A-27

LATIN AMERICA AND THE CARIBBEAN: MONETARY BASE

(End-of-year balances as percentages of GDP)

	2000	2001	2002	2003	2004	2005	2006	2007	2008
Antigua and Barbuda	11.6	13.3	13.6	16.4	15.7	15.6	15.0	13.3	11.9
Argentina	5.3	4.5	9.3	12.1	11.3	10.5	11.7	11.9	10.3
Bahamas	6.5	7.2	7.6	8.2	10.3	8.6	7.8	9.0	8.5
Barbados	11.0	12.7	18.3	20.1	13.7	12.9	13.0	16.2	15.2
Belize	11.9	11.9	10.3	10.3	10.9	11.5	13.2	13.2	13.8
Bolivia (Plurinational State of)	7.9	8.3	8.2	8.5	8.3	10.2	12.2	16.9	18.5
Brazil	4.0	4.1	5.0	4.3	4.6	4.7	5.1	5.6	5.1
Chile	4.1	4.2	4.2	4.1	4.1	4.4	4.5	4.3	4.8
Colombia	5.5	5.5	6.1	6.2	6.4	6.8	7.1	7.5	6.9
Costa Rica	5.9	5.2	5.1	5.4	5.5	6.1	6.4	7.2	7.0
Cuba	28.2	32.2	32.5	27.8	31.6	31.6	26.0	23.6	30.2
Dominica	12.6	12.7	18.9	17.7	15.2	15.1	17.2	16.9	13.8
Dominican Republic	8.5	9.3	8.3	12.6	8.6	9.1	9.0	8.9	8.5
Ecuador	1.6	1.4	1.2	1.1	1.2	1.5	1.4	1.7	2.5
El Salvador	13.0	11.8	9.9	11.6	10.4	9.9	9.3	10.2	10.4
Grenada	14.1	15.9	18.2	18.1	25.9	16.9	17.2	18.5	16.5
Guatemala	9.2	9.5	10.0	9.8	10.0	10.2	11.1	10.9	9.7
Guyana	22.9	24.4	26.2	27.5	27.7	29.5	27.6	25.0	24.7
Haiti	17.4	19.9	22.0	24.0	22.7	21.1	20.0	19.4	18.6
Honduras	9.7	8.3	8.5	8.4	9.1	8.9	9.6	11.2	11.2
Jamaica	8.9	8.2	7.6	7.5	7.3	7.1	7.4	7.3	6.8
Mexico	3.5	3.5	3.8	4.0	4.0	4.1	4.4	4.4	4.8
Nicaragua	5.5	6.1	6.3	7.3	7.5	7.8	8.7	9.4	8.4
Panama	...	0.9	6.0	6.0	5.6	5.2	4.9	5.2	4.4
Paraguay	8.5	8.4	8.8	9.7	9.8	9.2	9.2	10.5	10.9
Peru	3.0	3.2	3.4	3.5	3.9	4.5	4.6	5.3	6.0
Saint Kitts and Nevis	15.7	16.6	18.9	16.7	19.6	16.3	18.2	18.8	18.4
Saint Vincent and the Grenadines	17.3	18.4	15.4	15.3	14.9	14.4	14.5	15.4	14.1
Saint Lucia	11.0	13.3	13.3	14.1	15.7	13.0	13.7	14.2	14.0
Suriname	30.6	24.8	21.1	15.4	15.0	12.4	13.9	15.8	16.3
Trinidad and Tobago	8.2	8.8	8.1	6.6	5.7	7.1	6.8	6.7	9.2
Uruguay	3.9	3.9	4.1	4.2	3.9	4.9	4.5	5.5	4.5
Venezuela (Bolivarian Republic of)	7.3	7.3	7.1	8.4	7.8	7.6	11.3	13.1	12.4

Source: Economic Commission for Latin America and the Caribbean (ECLAC), on the basis of official figures.

Table A-28

LATIN AMERICA AND THE CARIBBEAN: MONEY SUPPLY (M3) [a]

(End-of-year balances as percentages of GDP)

	2000	2001	2002	2003	2004	2005	2006	2007	2008
Antigua and Barbuda	77.2	77.2	80.1	92.0	92.9	93.1	91.4	88.3	90.7
Argentina	29.6	24.9	21.9	24.9	24.7	25.8	25.8	26.1	22.3
Bahamas	62.7	64.3	63.3	65.5	69.8	69.4	69.6	74.7	77.9
Barbados	78.8	83.2	96.8	95.1	105.1	108.1	110.8	119.2	112.9
Belize	58.0	59.7	57.0	55.7	59.1	59.6	62.0	68.0	70.9
Bolivia (Plurinational State of)	51.5	52.9	49.4	47.7	42.3	43.0	42.4	47.8	46.5
Brazil [b]	24.1	24.7	26.9	24.3	25.4	27.1	27.9	30.1	37.1
Chile	53.1	54.2	54.6	48.8	50.3	53.3	53.2	58.2	69.6
Colombia [c]	28.9	29.1	28.6	28.3	29.5	31.0	31.9	33.4	35.4
Costa Rica	33.4	33.8	36.3	37.1	42.6	44.0	44.3	43.8	46.8
Cuba [d]	36.8	39.0	40.6	37.7	38.0	46.6	38.6	37.2	40.6
Dominica	64.3	70.4	79.8	78.1	76.3	77.6	80.2	81.4	81.7
Dominican Republic	24.3	27.9	28.5	36.8	27.8	27.7	25.2	25.7	24.0
Ecuador	25.6	24.2	23.4	20.3	21.7	23.0	24.0	25.9	27.5
El Salvador	46.3	44.9	42.0	40.2	39.2	37.2	38.0	40.9	42.4
Grenada	85.0	95.6	98.9	97.2	117.1	98.2	97.3	100.2	100.8
Guatemala	30.3	32.1	31.7	33.5	34.0	35.7	37.8	37.1	35.4
Guyana	65.7	69.7	70.9	73.8	73.3	75.2	78.5	75.1	78.0
Haiti	37.6	38.7	45.4	47.8	42.5	42.1	37.9	35.8	33.9
Honduras	41.2	44.8	46.5	47.2	49.2	50.8	55.0	56.5	51.4
Jamaica	34.6	34.9	35.2	33.8	34.1	33.2	32.5	33.7	29.9
Mexico	39.1	43.3	44.4	45.6	45.0	48.6	49.5	50.4	54.8
Nicaragua	37.5	37.4	40.0	41.8	43.0	41.3	39.4	41.2	37.5
Panama	80.6	85.6	80.9	79.5	78.3	78.0	86.1	88.9	...
Paraguay	31.7	35.3	31.9	29.1	28.3	27.5	26.8	30.0	33.1
Peru	25.4	26.1	26.1	24.7	24.0	25.8	24.3	26.9	30.3
Saint Kitts and Nevis	87.4	86.0	89.2	92.3	101.8	97.1	98.4	104.5	110.7
Saint Vincent and the Grenadines	70.3	70.3	71.0	69.1	72.3	72.7	69.9	67.2	66.4
Saint Lucia	61.8	66.7	67.2	68.3	70.1	74.6	83.4	84.7	89.7
Suriname	68.2	65.0	55.8	51.0	56.0	47.5	49.3	54.9	57.1
Trinidad and Tobago	37.4	40.3	40.9	32.2	33.3	35.2	35.5	35.8	38.3
Uruguay	71.1	89.9	86.0	79.6	64.8	58.0	56.5	48.8	54.5
Venezuela (Bolivarian Republic of) [e]	20.4	19.1	18.2	23.0	21.8	23.3	30.3	31.3	28.8

Source: Economic Commission for Latin America and the Caribbean (ECLAC), on the basis of official figures.

[a] According to the ECLAC definition, this corresponds to M1 plus savings and time deposits in national currency plus foreign-currency deposits.

[b] According to the country's definition, this corresponds to M1 plus special interest-bearing deposits, savings deposits and securities issued by deposit institutions.

[c] According to the country's definition, this also includes deposits of entitites in liquidation and, since 2001, term deposit certificates of special entities and demand deposits of non-bank entities.

[d] Refers to M2 (M1 plus fixed-term deposits).

[e] Does not include foreign-currency deposits.

Table A-29

LATIN AMERICA AND THE CARIBBEAN: FOREIGN-CURRENCY DEPOSITS

(End-of-year balances as percentages of GDP)

	2000	2001	2002	2003	2004	2005	2006	2007	2008
Antigua and Barbuda	5.4	4.3	6.1	5.3	6.1	5.8	7.5	9.0	8.2
Argentina	16.8	16.5	0.7	1.4	1.7	2.0	2.3	2.6	2.7
Bahamas	1.6	1.6	1.5	1.7	1.6	2.1	2.2	2.7	2.7
Barbados	6.3	8.3	12.5	10.7	10.7	16.4	11.3	19.9	14.1
Bolivia (Plurinational State of)	44.3	45.0	41.7	39.4	33.1	30.9	26.7	23.9	20.3
Chile	5.1	6.3	5.9	5.4	4.9	4.7	4.7	4.8	9.1
Costa Rica	13.3	14.7	16.0	16.2	21.6	21.7	20.8	18.2	22.0
Dominican Republic	0.1	0.0	0.0	0.1	0.0	0.0	0.0	0.0	0.0
Dominica	1.4	2.2	3.2	1.4	1.7	1.3	1.3	1.1	1.6
Grenada	5.9	6.6	6.7	7.4	7.0	6.8	5.0	7.4	7.2
Guatemala	0.1	1.4	2.0	2.8	3.7	3.9	4.2	4.7	4.8
Haiti	11.7	13.1	17.6	20.0	16.6	18.0	15.6	15.2	14.8
Honduras [a]	9.8	11.6	12.4	12.5	13.6	13.4	13.8	14.0	13.3
Jamaica	8.4	8.7	9.8	11.1	11.3	10.5	9.5	11.0	9.8
Mexico	1.3	1.7	1.5	1.2	1.4	1.5	1.4	1.3	1.4
Nicaragua	24.6	25.0	27.9	28.4	28.6	27.8	25.8	27.0	25.6
Paraguay	16.2	19.9	18.4	14.8	13.1	11.7	10.6	10.7	12.8
Peru	17.7	17.4	17.1	15.3	13.2	14.1	12.4	12.4	14.2
Saint Kitts and Nevis	28.0	25.4	24.9	27.0	28.8	28.3	30.8	32.1	26.7
Saint Vincent and the Grenadines	1.0	0.8	1.0	1.0	2.3	1.2	2.3	2.6	2.3
Saint Lucia	0.4	0.7	1.3	1.6	1.8	2.7	8.4	4.3	5.8
Suriname	24.9	25.4	21.7	23.9	27.5	22.6	23.6	26.3	26.4
Trinidad and Tobago	10.2	9.1	9.8	6.0	8.4	7.3	8.6	8.7	10.6
Uruguay	60.2	80.0	77.4	70.3	56.0	47.6	45.3	36.4	42.2

Source: Economic Commission for Latin America and the Caribbean (ECLAC), on the basis of official figures.

[a] Term deposits in foreign currency.

Table A-30

LATIN AMERICA AND THE CARIBBEAN: DOMESTIC CREDIT TO THE PRIVATE SECTOR

(End-of-year balances as percentages of GDP)

	2000	2001	2002	2003	2004	2005	2006	2007	2008 [a]
Antigua and Barbuda	73.8	72.9	77.2	76.9	71.9	74.9	76.0	75.2	77.9
Argentina	23.9	20.8	15.3	10.8	10.5	11.7	13.0	14.5	13.6
Bahamas	63.5	66.8	66.4	66.4	67.9	70.7	75.8	82.5	86.1
Barbados	51.2	51.0	55.7	51.4	58.4	68.1	72.5	72.6	73.5
Belize	41.2	44.6	47.8	51.5	53.5	54.0	55.8	61.2	62.3
Bolivia (Plurinational State of)	58.5	53.2	51.1	47.8	42.1	39.3	34.8	34.0	31.1
Brazil	33.8	32.5	32.5	31.8	32.0	37.0	43.8	52.2	62.2
Chile	66.0	65.6	65.9	62.7	62.3	64.3	63.7	69.8	80.0
Colombia	23.8	22.3	20.6	19.8	19.6	20.2	23.1	26.0	27.6
Costa Rica	21.0	23.5	25.4	26.5	26.7	29.4	31.1	36.6	41.7
Cuba [b]	...	...	...	...	...	9.2	15.0	21.0	23.4
Dominica	62.9	62.3	63.9	60.2	59.5	60.1	62.9	61.4	63.4
Dominican Republic	21.1	24.5	26.5	26.8	18.0	17.5	17.2	19.0	17.9
Ecuador	31.1	26.6	20.7	19.8	21.1	22.8	23.9	24.9	27.2
El Salvador	0.0	40.2	44.5	42.3	42.1	42.3	42.5	42.1	40.8
Grenada	78.4	81.2	80.6	75.9	81.2	74.5	81.6	86.8	91.8
Guatemala	19.8	20.6	20.0	20.4	20.9	23.2	27.1	30.0	29.1
Guyana	44.9	43.3	42.4	33.7	31.0	31.8	33.7	33.7	37.8
Haiti	16.0	15.6	18.4	17.7	15.4	15.7	14.2	13.6	13.2
Honduras	34.1	36.7	36.1	37.7	38.5	39.7	45.2	52.7	50.9
Jamaica	7.6	8.3	10.0	12.5	13.3	14.1	15.8	18.2	19.8
Mexico	15.7	12.9	14.3	14.0	13.2	14.5	16.9	18.4	17.4
Nicaragua	0.0	17.7	19.6	22.9	25.4	29.3	33.7	39.3	37.6
Panama	101.9	108.6	90.4	87.1	85.1	87.1	88.4	92.0	89.7
Paraguay [c]	4.2	4.0	4.2	3.6	2.9	2.6	2.2	1.9	1.6
Peru	31.9	30.4	30.1	28.7	27.0	28.7	28.6	33.1	34.0
Saint Kitts and Nevis	79.0	75.2	72.4	79.0	80.8	79.4	79.5	84.9	83.4
Saint Vincent and the Grenadines	66.6	66.0	64.2	62.0	59.6	57.6	58.6	60.0	57.4
Saint Lucia	79.3	93.7	92.5	84.5	86.4	93.1	106.6	129.4	133.8
Suriname	9.7	11.0	18.3	19.6	21.7	20.6	22.1	25.6	32.0
Trinidad and Tobago	29.2	28.3	30.0	25.9	26.6	26.9	25.7	27.5	28.3
Uruguay	54.8	65.0	72.0	44.5	29.7	20.1	25.6	24.2	27.8
Venezuela (Bolivarian Republic of)	10.5	11.6	9.6	8.6	10.7	12.7	...	...	...

Source: Economic Commission for Latin America and the Caribbean (ECLAC), on the basis of official figures.

[a] Preliminary figures.

[b] Includes credit, services and agricultural production cooperative production units, private farmers and individuals.

[c] Credit granted to the private sector by the banking sector.

Table A-31

LATIN AMERICA AND THE CARIBBEAN: REPRESENTATIVE LENDING RATES

(Annual average of annualized monthly rates)

	2000	2001	2002	2003	2004	2005	2006	2007	2008
Antigua and Barbuda [a]	...	...	...	...	...	11.2	10.7	10.3	10.1
Argentina [b]	11.1	26.5	53.0	19.1	6.8	6.2	8.6	11.1	19.5
Bahamas [c]	...	...	...	12.0	11.2	10.3	10.0	10.6	11.0
Barbados [b]	...	...	...	7.6	7.4	8.5	10.0	10.4	9.7
Belize [d]	16.0	15.5	14.8	14.4	13.9	14.2	14.2	14.3	14.2
Bolivia (Plurinational State of) [e]	...	13.7	10.9	9.1	8.2	8.2	7.8	8.2	8.9
Brazil [f]	41.9	41.1	44.4	49.8	41.1	43.7	40.0	34.5	38.8
Chile [g]	18.7	16.7	14.4	13.0	11.0	13.5	14.4	13.6	15.2
Colombia [h]	18.8	20.7	16.3	15.2	15.1	14.6	12.9	15.4	17.2
Costa Rica [i]	28.1	26.7	26.8	26.2	23.4	24.0	22.7	17.3	16.7
Cuba [j]	...	...	...	9.6	9.7	9.8	9.4	9.1	9.0
Dominica [a]	...	...	...	...	...	9.9	9.5	9.2	9.1
Dominican Republic [b]	23.6	20.0	21.3	27.8	30.3	21.4	15.7	11.7	16.0
Ecuador [k]	15.2	15.5	14.1	12.6	10.2	8.7	8.9	10.1	9.8
El Salvador [l]	10.7	9.6	7.1	6.6	6.3	6.9	7.5	7.8	7.9
Grenada [a]	...	...	...	...	...	10.0	9.8	9.7	9.5
Guatemala [a]	20.9	19.0	16.9	15.0	13.8	13.0	12.8	12.8	13.4
Guyana [b]	17.2	17.3	17.3	16.6	16.6	15.1	14.9	14.1	13.9
Haiti [m]	25.1	28.6	25.5	30.7	34.1	27.1	29.5	31.2	23.3
Honduras [a]	26.8	23.8	22.7	20.8	19.9	18.8	17.4	16.6	17.9
Jamaica [n]	32.9	29.4	26.1	25.1	25.1	23.2	22.0	22.0	22.3
Mexico [o]	16.9	12.8	8.2	6.9	7.2	9.9	7.5	7.6	8.7
Nicaragua [p]	18.1	18.6	18.3	15.5	13.5	12.1	11.6	13.0	13.2
Panama [q]	10.3	10.6	9.2	8.9	8.2	8.2	8.1	8.3	8.2
Paraguay [r]	26.8	28.3	34.3	30.5	21.2	15.3	16.6	14.6	14.6
Peru [s]	...	...	22.3	20.2	18.7	17.9	17.1	16.5	16.7
Saint Kitts and Nevis [a]	...	...	...	...	...	9.9	9.2	9.3	8.6
Saint Vincent and the Grenadines [a]	...	...	...	...	...	9.6	9.7	9.6	9.5
Saint Lucia [a]	...	...	...	...	...	10.4	10.5	9.9	9.2
Suriname [o]	29.0	25.7	22.2	21.0	20.4	18.1	15.7	13.8	12.2
Trinidad and Tobago [b]	16.5	15.6	13.4	11.0	9.4	9.1	10.2	10.5	12.3
Uruguay [t]	32.1	38.1	116.4	56.6	26.0	15.3	10.7	10.0	13.1
Venezuela (Bolivarian Republic of) [u]	24.5	24.8	38.4	25.7	17.3	15.6	14.6	16.7	22.8

Source: Economic Commission for Latin America and the Caribbean (ECLAC), on the basis of official figures.

[a] Weighted average lending rates.
[b] Prime lending rate.
[c] Interest rate on loans and overdrafts, weighted average.
[d] Rate for personal and business loans, residential and other construction; weighted average.
[e] Nominal dollar rate for 60-91-day banking operations.
[f] Preset lending rate for legal persons.
[g] Lending rate for 90-360-day periods, non-adjustable operations.
[h] Total lending rate of the system (weighted average of all lending rates).
[i] Average rate of the financial system for loans in national currency.
[j] Corporate lending rate in convertible pesos.
[k] Benchmark dollar lending rate.
[l] Basic lending rate for up to 1 year.
[m] Average of minimum and maximum lending rates.
[n] Average lending rate.
[o] Lending rate published by the International Monetary Fund.
[p] Weighted average of the weekly lending rate for loans in national currency in the system.
[q] Interest rate on 1-year trade credit.
[r] Weighted average of effective lending rates in national currency, not including overdrafts or credit cards.
[s] Average lending rate, constant structure.
[t] Business credit, 30-367 days.
[u] Average rate for loan operations for the six major commercial banks.

Table A-32

LATIN AMERICA AND THE CARIBBEAN: CONSUMER PRICES

(Percentage variation December–December)

	2000	2001	2002	2003	2004	2005	2006	2007	2008	2009 [a]
Latin America and the Caribbean [b]	**9.0**	**6.1**	**12.2**	**8.5**	**7.4**	**6.1**	**5.0**	**6.4**	**8.4**	**5.6**
Antigua and Barbuda	...	...	2.5	1.8	2.8	2.5	0.0	5.2	2.3	...
Argentina	-0.7	-1.5	41.0	3.7	6.1	12.3	9.8	8.5	7.2	5.5 [c]
Bahamas	1.0	2.9	1.9	2.4	1.9	1.2	2.3	2.8	4.6	4.3 [d]
Barbados	3.8	-1.2	0.9	0.3	4.3	7.4	5.6	4.7	7.3	7.3 [e]
Belize	0.6	1.1	2.3	2.6	3.1	4.2	3.0	4.1	6.4	1.5 [e]
Bolivia (Plurinational State of)	3.4	0.9	2.5	3.9	4.6	4.9	4.9	11.7	11.8	2.1
Brazil	6.0	7.7	12.5	9.3	7.6	5.7	3.1	4.5	5.9	4.8
Chile	4.5	2.6	2.8	1.1	2.4	3.7	2.6	7.8	7.1	1.9
Colombia	8.8	7.6	7.0	6.5	5.5	4.9	4.5	5.7	7.7	3.8
Costa Rica	10.2	11.0	9.7	9.9	13.1	14.1	9.4	10.8	13.9	8.2
Cuba [g]	-2.3	-1.4	7.3	-3.8	2.9	3.7	5.7	2.8	-0.1	0.9 [f]
Dominica	1.1	1.1	0.5	2.8	0.8	2.7	1.8	6.0	2.0	...
Dominican Republic	9.0	4.4	10.5	42.7	28.7	7.5	5.0	8.9	4.5	0.3
Ecuador	91.0	22.4	9.4	6.1	1.9	3.1	2.9	3.3	8.8	4.5
El Salvador	4.3	1.4	2.8	2.5	5.4	4.3	4.9	4.9	5.5	0.2
Grenada	3.4	-0.7	2.3	1.2	2.5	6.2	1.7	7.4	5.2	...
Guatemala	5.1	8.9	6.3	5.9	9.2	8.6	5.8	8.7	9.4	0.6
Guyana	5.8	1.5	6.0	...	...	8.2	4.2	14.1	6.4	...
Haiti	19.0	8.1	15.2	35.8	19.1	15.4	10.3	10.0	10.2	-1.0
Honduras	10.1	8.8	8.1	6.8	9.2	7.7	5.3	8.9	10.8	5.4
Jamaica	6.1	8.7	7.3	14.1	13.7	12.9	5.8	16.8	16.9	9.0
Mexico	9.0	4.4	5.7	4.0	5.2	3.3	4.1	3.8	6.5	5.7
Nicaragua	9.9	4.7	4.0	6.6	8.9	9.6	10.2	16.2	12.7	3.1 [c]
Panama	0.7	0.0	1.9	1.5	1.5	3.4	2.2	6.4	6.8	2.5 [c]
Paraguay	8.6	8.4	14.6	9.3	2.8	9.9	12.5	6.0	7.5	2.0
Peru	3.7	-0.1	1.5	2.5	3.5	1.5	1.1	3.9	6.7	3.1
Saint Kitts and Nevis	...	...	1.7	3.1	1.7	6.0	7.9	2.1	7.6	...
Saint Vincent and the Grenadines	0.4	5.5	-0.7	0.5	1.7	3.9	4.8	8.3	8.7	...
Saint Lucia	1.4	-0.2	0.4	2.7	...	...	...	6.8	3.8	...
Suriname	76.2	...	...	...	...	15.8	4.7	8.3	9.4	0.8 [f]
Trinidad and Tobago	5.6	3.2	4.3	3.0	5.6	7.2	9.1	7.6	14.5	10.3 [c]
Uruguay	5.1	3.6	25.9	10.2	7.6	4.9	6.4	8.5	9.2	6.5
Venezuela (Bolivarian Republic of)	13.4	12.3	31.2	27.1	19.2	14.4	17.0	22.5	31.9	27.4

Source: Economic Commission for Latin America and the Caribbean (ECLAC), on the basis of official figures.

[a] Twelve-month variation to June 2009.

[b] The only English-speaking Caribbean countries included are Barbados, Jamaica and Trinidad and Tobago.

[c] Twelve-month variation to May 2009.

[d] Twelve-month variation to March 2009.

[e] Twelve-month variation to February 2009.

[f] Twelve-month variation to April 2009.

[g] Refers to national-currency markets.

Table A-33

LATIN AMERICA AND THE CARIBBEAN: WHOLESALE PRICES

(Percentage variation December–December)

		2000	2001	2002	2003	2004	2005	2006	2007	2008	2009 [a]
Argentina	WPI	2.4	-3.4	113.7	2.0	7.9	10.6	7.2	14.6	8.8	5.6
Brazil	IPA-DI	12.1	11.9	35.4	6.3	14.7	-1.0	4.3	9.4	9.8	1.2
Chile	WPI	7.9	3.1	10.4	-1.0	7.8	3.2	7.9	14.0	22.7	6.5
Colombia	PPI	14.9	9.0	3.8	10.2	5.2	3.0	5.3	1.3	9.0	5.3
Costa Rica	IND-PPI	10.2	8.6	8.4	11.0	17.7	12.1	13.7	14.6	23.5	11.0
Ecuador	PPI	64.9	-5.6	17.7	4.5	4.3	21.6	7.2	18.2	-28.3	-30.9
El Salvador	IPRI	4.9	-4.8	4.9	-0.6	13.0	6.9	0.6	13.9	-6.0	-14.6 [b]
Mexico	NPPI	6.4	1.3	9.2	6.8	8.0	3.4	7.3	5.4	7.8	4.2
Peru	WPI-NP	3.8	-2.2	1.7	2.0	4.9	3.6	1.3	5.2	8.8	-0.2
Uruguay	IPP-PN	9.5	3.8	64.6	20.5	5.1	-2.2	8.2	16.1	6.4	-0.1
Venezuela (Bolivarian Republic of)	IPM -IVA	15.8	10.2	49.4	48.4	23.1	14.2	15.9	17.2	32.4	29.7

Source: Economic Commission for Latin America and the Caribbean (ECLAC), on the basis of official figures.

[a] Twelve-month variation to May 2009.

[b] Twelve-month variation to April 2009.

Abbreviations:

WPI: Wholesale price index; IPA-DI: Wholesale price index-domestic availability (acronym in Portuguese); PPI: Producer price index; IND-PPI: Industrial producer price index; IPRI: Industrial price index; NPPI: National producer price index; WPI-NP: Wholesale price index, national products; PPI-NP: Producer price index, national products; WPI-VAT: Wholesale price index, includes value added tax.

Table A-34
LATIN AMERICA AND THE CARIBBEAN: PUBLIC-SECTOR BALANCE
(Percentages of GDP)

	Central government						Non-financial public sector					
	Primary balance			Overall balance			Primary balance			Overall balance		
	2006	2007	2008 [a]	2006	2007	2008 [a]	2006	2007	2008 [a]	2006	2007	2008 [a]
Latin America and the Caribbean (excl. Cuba)	**2.2**	**2.2**	**1.3**	**-0.0**	**0.3**	**-0.4**	**4.2**	**3.9**	**...**	**1.4**	**1.4**	**...**
Latin America and the Caribbean (inc. Cuba)	**2.0**	**2.0**	**0.9**	**-0.2**	**0.1**	**-0.7**	**4.2**	**3.9**	**...**	**1.4**	**1.4**	**...**
Argentina [b]	2.7	2.7	2.5	1.0	0.6	0.4	3.5	3.3	...	1.4	0.7	...
Bolivia (Plurinational State of) [c]	5.3	3.5	0.8	3.5	2.3	-0.0	6.3	3.0	4.1	4.5	1.7	3.2
Brazil [d]	2.1	2.3	2.5	-2.9	-1.9	-0.8	3.8	3.9	4.1	-2.9	-2.2	-1.5
Chile	8.4	9.4	5.8	7.7	8.8	5.3	12.4	11.8	...	11.3	10.8	...
Colombia [e]	0.1	1.0	0.9	-3.5	-2.7	-2.3	3.0	2.8	3.3	-0.8	-1.0	0.1
Costa Rica	2.7	3.7	2.4	-1.1	0.6	0.2	5.2	4.9	2.1	1.3	1.8	-0.1
Cuba	-2.0	-1.8	-5.3	-3.2	-3.2	-6.7	...	...	...	...	...	...
Dominican Republic [h]	0.3	1.4	-1.6	-1.1	0.1	-3.2	...	...	...	...	...	...
Ecuador	2.0	1.9	0.3	-0.2	-0.1	-1.2	5.4	4.0	-0.2	3.3	2.1	-1.6
El Salvador	2.0	2.2	1.7	-0.4	-0.2	-0.6	1.4	2.2	1.3	-1.1	-0.2	-1.0
Guatemala	-0.6	0.0	-0.3	-1.9	-1.4	-1.6	...	...	...	...	...	...
Haiti	0.8	-1.2	-0.9	-0.0	-1.6	-1.2	...	...	...	...	...	...
Honduras [f]	-0.1	-2.3	-1.7	-1.1	-2.9	-2.3	...	...	...	...	...	...
Mexico [g]	-0.3	-0.5	-0.2	-1.8	-2.0	-1.6	2.1	1.9	1.6	0.1	0.0	-0.1
Nicaragua	1.8	1.9	0.0	0.0	0.4	-1.2	2.5	2.8	0.4	0.7	1.3	-0.7
Panama	4.4	4.7	3.4	0.2	1.2	0.3	4.9	7.0	3.6	0.5	3.5	0.4
Paraguay [h]	1.5	1.8	3.3	0.5	1.0	2.6	...	3.9	4.2	2.3	2.8	3.4
Peru	3.2	3.5	3.6	1.5	1.8	2.2	4.0	4.9	3.7	2.1	3.1	2.1
Uruguay	3.2	2.1	1.7	-1.0	-1.6	-1.0	3.8	3.4	1.2	-0.5	-0.4	-1.6
Venezuela (Bolivarian Republic of)	2.1	4.5	0.1	0.0	3.0	-1.2	0.6	-1.0	-1.2	-1.5	-2.6	-2.6

Source: Economic Commission for Latin America and the Caribbean (ECLAC), on the basis of official figures.
[a] Preliminary figures.
[b] The central government coverage corresponds to national public administration. The non-financial public sector (NFPS) coverage corresponds to the non-financial public sector of Argentina.
[c] The central government coverage corresponds to general government.
[d] The central government coverage corresponds to the federal government. The figures are derived from the primary balance calculated "below-the-line" and nominal interest.
[e] The central government coverage corresponds to the central national government. The central government balance does not include the cost of financial restructuring.
[f] The central government coverage corresponds to the consolidated central government.
[g] The central government coverage corresponds to the federal government. The coverage of the non financial public sector refers to the public sector.
[h] The overall balance includes the residue.

Table A-35
LATIN AMERICA AND THE CARIBBEAN: CENTRAL GOVERNMENT FISCAL REVENUE
(Percentages of GDP)

	Total revenue			Current revenue			Capital revenue		
	2006	2007	2008 [a]	2006	2007	2008 [a]	2006	2007	2008 [a]
Latin America and the Caribbean (excl. Cuba)	**18.9**	**19.4**	**19.6**	**18.4**	**18.9**	**19.0**	**0.2**	**0.2**	**0.3**
Latin America and the Caribbean (inc. Cuba)	**20.1**	**20.8**	**20.9**	**19.5**	**20.1**	**20.3**	**0.3**	**0.3**	**0.3**
Argentina	17.2	18.2	19.3	17.0	18.1	19.2	0.2	0.1	0.1
Bolivia (Plurinational State of) [b]	32.7	32.7	32.7	30.8	31.1	31.5	1.8	1.6	1.2
Brazil	22.9	23.8	24.7	22.9	23.8	24.7	...	...	...
Chile [c]	25.8	27.5	26.4	25.8	27.5	26.4	0.0	0.0	0.0
Colombia [d]	14.7	15.0	15.7	13.4	13.5	13.6	1.2	1.5	2.1
Costa Rica	14.2	15.5	15.9	14.2	15.5	15.9	0.0	0.0	0.0
Cuba	43.2	46.0	45.9	41.7	43.7	44.1	1.5	2.3	1.8
Dominican Republic	16.1	17.7	15.9	15.9	17.3	15.7	0.0	0.0	0.0
Ecuador	16.5	18.5	26.2	16.5	18.5	26.2	0.0	0.0	0.0
El Salvador	14.4	14.6	14.7	14.2	14.3	14.4	0.0	0.0	0.0
Guatemala	12.7	12.9	12.1	12.7	12.9	12.1	0.0	0.0	0.0
Haiti	10.6	10.9	9.6	10.2	10.3	9.5	0.0	0.0	0.0
Honduras	18.1	19.1	19.3	16.6	17.5	17.2	0.0	0.0	0.0
Mexico	15.1	15.4	17.0	15.1	15.4	17.0	0.0	0.0	0.0
Nicaragua	22.7	23.3	21.9	18.8	19.6	19.0	0.0	0.0	0.0
Panama	18.6	19.5	19.7	18.5	19.2	18.3	0.1	0.1	1.1
Paraguay	18.3	17.6	18.3	18.2	17.2	17.9	0.1	0.0	0.0
Peru	17.6	18.2	18.3	17.4	18.1	18.2	0.1	0.1	0.1
Uruguay	21.2	20.3	19.4	21.2	20.3	19.4	0.0	0.0	0.0
Venezuela (Bolivarian Republic of)	29.6	28.9	24.7	29.6	28.9	24.7	0.0	0.0	0.0

Source: Economic Commission for Latin America and the Caribbean (ECLAC), on the basis of official figures.
[a] Preliminary figures.
[b] General government.
[c] Total revenue corresponds to revenue plus sales of physical assets.
[d] Total revenue includes special funds and incorporates accrued revenues.

Table A-36

LATIN AMERICA AND THE CARIBBEAN: CENTRAL GOVERNMENT FISCAL EXPENDITURE

(Percentages of GDP)

	Total expenditure			Current expenditure			Capital expenditure			Interest		
	2006	2007	2008 [a]	2006	2007	2008 [a]	2006	2007	2008 [a]	2006	2007	2008 [a]
Latin America and the Caribbean (excl. Cuba)	**18.9**	**19.2**	**20.0**	**15.4**	**15.3**	**15.7**	**3.5**	**3.9**	**4.3**	**2.2**	**2.0**	**1.7**
Latin America and the Caribbean (inc. Cuba)	**20.3**	**20.7**	**21.6**	**16.3**	**16.4**	**17.1**	**3.8**	**4.1**	**4.4**	**2.2**	**1.9**	**1.6**
Argentina	16.2	17.5	18.8	13.6	15.3	16.6	2.6	2.2	2.2	1.7	2.1	2.1
Bolivia (Plurinational State of) [b]	29.2	30.5	32.7	18.9	18.7	21.8	10.4	11.7	10.9	1.8	1.3	0.8
Brazil	25.7	25.7	25.6	21.4	21.1	20.7	4.3	4.6	4.9	4.9	4.2	3.3
Chile [c]	18.1	18.7	21.1	15.1	15.4	17.3	3.0	3.2	3.8	0.7	0.6	0.5
Colombia [d]	18.1	17.6	18.1	16.5	15.8	15.8	1.5	1.8	2.3	3.6	3.7	3.2
Costa Rica	15.3	14.9	15.7	14.3	13.6	13.5	0.9	1.3	2.2	3.8	3.1	2.2
Cuba	46.4	49.2	52.6	33.6	38.3	43.1	9.1	8.3	7.2	1.2	1.4	1.4
Dominican Republic	17.2	17.6	19.6	13.0	13.0	14.4	4.2	4.6	5.1	1.4	1.2	1.6
Ecuador	16.7	18.7	27.4	12.7	12.9	16.1	4.0	5.7	11.3	2.3	2.0	1.5
El Salvador	14.8	14.8	15.3	12.2	12.3	12.6	2.6	2.6	2.7	2.4	2.4	2.3
Guatemala	14.7	14.3	13.7	9.4	9.5	9.2	5.3	4.8	4.5	1.4	1.5	1.4
Haiti	10.6	12.4	10.8	9.7	9.8	8.6	0.9	2.6	2.1	0.8	0.3	0.3
Honduras	19.2	21.9	21.7	16.0	17.9	17.1	3.3	4.1	4.7	1.0	0.6	0.6
Mexico [e]	16.9	17.3	18.7	14.0	14.4	15.1	2.8	3.0	3.5	1.5	1.4	1.4
Nicaragua	22.7	22.9	23.1	19.3	19.2	20.3	3.5	3.7	2.8	1.8	1.5	1.2
Panama	18.4	18.3	19.5	15.9	14.2	13.9	2.5	4.1	5.6	4.2	3.5	3.1
Paraguay	17.8	16.7	15.7	13.7	12.9	12.8	4.2	3.8	2.9	1.0	0.8	0.6
Peru	16.1	16.4	16.1	14.1	14.2	13.8	2.0	2.1	2.4	1.8	1.6	1.4
Uruguay	22.1	21.8	20.4	20.7	20.3	18.7	1.4	1.5	1.7	4.1	3.6	2.7
Venezuela (Bolivarian Republic of) [f]	29.6	25.8	25.8	22.5	19.9	19.9	6.7	5.8	5.8	2.1	1.5	1.3

Source: Economic Commission for Latin America and the Caribbean (ECLAC), on the basis of official figures.
[a] Preliminary figures.
[b] General government.
[c] Total expenditure refers to expenditure plus investment, capital transfers and fixed capital consumption.
[d] Includes accrued expenditure and floating debt.
[e] Current expenditure, capital expenditure and interest correspond to federal government expenditure.
[f] Total expenditure includes extrabudgetary.

Table A-37

LATIN AMERICA AND THE CARIBBEAN: CENTRAL GOVERNMENT TAX BURDEN INCLUDING SOCIAL SECURITY CONTRIBUTIONS

(Percentages of GDP)

	2000	2001	2002	2003	2004	2005	2006	2007	2008 [a]
Latin America and the Caribbean (exc. Cuba)	**15.1**	**15.4**	**15.3**	**15.5**	**16.0**	**16.7**	**17.2**	**17.9**	**17.8**
Latin America and the Caribbean (inc. Cuba)	**15.7**	**15.9**	**15.9**	**16.1**	**16.4**	**17.3**	**17.9**	**18.3**	**18.2**
Argentina [b]	21.5	20.9	19.9	23.4	26.4	26.8	27.4	29.1	30.6
Bolivia (Plurinational State of) [b]	17.9	17.0	17.3	17.2	19.0	20.4	19.8	20.1	21.7
Brazil [b]	30.4	31.3	31.9	31.4	32.2	33.3	33.5	34.7	35.5
Chile	17.7	18.1	18.0	17.3	17.0	18.3	18.3	20.2	20.1
Colombia	12.5	14.1	13.9	14.0	14.7	14.9	15.6	15.6	15.5
Costa Rica	12.3	13.2	13.2	13.3	13.3	13.6	14.0	15.2	15.6
Cuba	27.5	25.9	26.6	26.9	23.3	28.7	30.0	27.7	25.2
Dominican Republic	11.3	13.1	13.0	12.0	12.8	14.6	15.0	16.0	15.0
Ecuador	11.6	13.3	14.1	12.9	12.8	13.0	13.9	14.3	16.5
El Salvador	12.4	12.3	13.0	13.3	13.3	14.1	15.0	15.0	14.6
Guatemala	10.9	11.1	12.2	11.9	11.8	11.5	12.1	12.3	11.6
Haiti	7.9	7.4	8.2	8.8	8.9	9.7	10.2	10.3	9.5
Honduras	14.3	16.6	15.4	15.5	15.5	15.7	16.2	17.5	15.9
Mexico	11.0	11.7	12.0	11.6	10.3	10.1	9.9	10.3	9.4
Nicaragua	17.5	16.0	16.8	18.6	19.3	20.3	21.3	22.1	21.7
Panama	16.0	15.2	14.8	14.6	14.4	14.3	15.7	16.5	16.5
Paraguay	12.0	12.0	11.2	11.3	12.9	13.0	13.1	12.6	13.7
Peru	14.1	14.3	13.8	14.5	14.7	15.2	16.7	17.2	17.4
Uruguay	22.5	22.4	21.5	21.4	21.6	22.6	23.4	23.0	23.3
Venezuela (Bolivarian Republic of)	13.6	12.2	11.2	11.9	13.3	15.9	16.3	17.0	14.2

Source: Economic Commission for Latin America and the Caribbean (ECLAC), on the basis of official figures.
[a] Preliminary figures.
[b] General government.

Table A-38

LATIN AMERICA AND THE CARIBBEAN: CENTRAL GOVERNMENT TAX BURDEN AND COMPOSITION OF TAX REVENUES

(Percentages of GDP)

	Total		Income tax and capital gains tax		Property tax		Other direct taxes		General goods and services taxes	
	2007	2008 [a]	2007	2008 [a]	2007	2008 [a]	2007	2008 [a]	2007	2008 [a]
Latin America and the Caribbean (exc. Cuba)	**17.9**	**17.8**	**4.8**	**4.8**	**0.7**	**0.7**	**0.0**	**0.0**	**6.5**	**6.6**
Latin America and the Caribbean (inc. Cuba)	**18.3**	**18.2**	**4.7**	**4.8**	**0.7**	**0.7**	**0.1**	**0.0**	**7.0**	**7.0**
Argentina [b]	29.1	30.6	5.4	5.3	3.2	3.2	0.0	0.0	10.4	10.6
Bolivia (Plurinational State of) [b]	20.1	21.7	3.3	4.0	1.3	1.2	0.0	0.0	9.2	10.0
Brazil [b]	34.7	35.5	7.5	8.2	2.9	2.0	0.5	0.3	12.8	13.5
Chile	20.2	20.1	8.4	7.3	...	...	0.0	0.0	7.9	8.9
Colombia	15.6	15.5	5.6	5.1	1.0	1.3	0.0	0.0	5.4	5.7
Costa Rica	15.2	15.6	3.9	4.4	0.6	0.6	0.0	0.0	5.9	6.0
Cuba	27.7	25.2	3.9	3.6	...	...	0.3	0.4	16.8	15.0
Dominican Republic	16.0	15.0	4.0	3.7	1.0	1.1	0.0	0.0	4.9	4.7
Ecuador	14.3	16.5	2.8	4.4	0.2	0.2	0.0	0.0	5.5	5.4
El Salvador	15.0	14.6	4.6	4.5	0.1	0.1	0.0	0.0	6.8	6.6
Guatemala	12.3	11.6	3.3	3.3	0.0	0.0	0.0	0.0	5.9	5.5
Haiti	10.3	9.5	1.8	1.8	0.0	0.0	0.1	0.0	3.0	2.9
Honduras	17.5	15.9	5.1	4.9	0.2	0.2	0.0	0.0	6.1	6.1
Mexico	10.3	9.4	4.7	5.1	0.2	0.2	0.0	0.0	3.7	3.8
Nicaragua	22.1	21.7	5.5	5.7	0.0	0.0	0.0	0.0	7.6	7.3
Panama	16.5	16.5	4.8	4.8	0.6	0.5	0.2	0.2	2.2	2.3
Paraguay	12.6	13.7	2.0	2.2	0.0	0.0	0.0	0.0	5.7	6.4
Peru	17.2	17.4	7.2	6.9	0.3	0.3	0.0	0.0	5.8	6.6
Uruguay	23.0	23.3	3.5	4.6	1.3	1.0	0.0	0.0	8.7	8.4
Venezuela (Bolivarian Republic of)	17.0	14.2	7.7	5.9	0.6	0.9	0.0	0.0	5.7	4.7

	Specific goods and services tax		Tax on trade and International transactions		Other indirect taxes		Other taxes		Social security contributions	
	2007	2008 [a]	2007	2008 [a]	2007	2008 [a]	2007	2008 [a]	2007	2008 [a]
Latin America and the Caribbean (exc. Cuba)	**1.8**	**1.4**	**1.3**	**1.3**	**0.0**	**0.0**	**0.2**	**0.4**	**2.6**	**2.7**
Latin America and the Caribbean (inc. Cuba)	**1.8**	**1.4**	**1.3**	**1.2**	**0.0**	**0.0**	**0.3**	**0.4**	**2.7**	**2.7**
Argentina [b]	1.7	1.7	3.4	4.4	0.0	0.0	0.4	0.4	4.5	5.1
Bolivia (Plurinational State of) [b]	3.2	3.0	1.1	1.2	0.0	0.0	0.3	0.4	1.8	1.8
Brazil [b]	1.6	1.5	0.5	0.6	0.1	0.1	0.5	0.5	8.5	8.8
Chile	1.5	1.3	0.4	0.3	0.0	0.0	0.7	0.7	1.3	1.5
Colombia	0.3	0.3	1.0	0.9	0.0	0.0	0.2	0.2	2.2	2.0
Costa Rica	3.3	1.0	1.2	1.2	0.0	0.0	0.1	2.1	0.3	0.3
Cuba	1.4	1.3	0.0	0.0	0.0	0.0	1.1	1.0	4.1	3.9
Dominican Republic	4.2	3.9	1.7	1.6	0.0	0.0	0.0	0.0	0.1	0.1
Ecuador	0.5	0.9	1.5	1.5	0.0	0.0	0.0	0.1	3.9	4.0
El Salvador	0.8	0.7	1.0	0.8	0.0	0.0	0.0	0.3	1.6	1.6
Guatemala	1.3	1.1	1.1	0.9	0.4	0.4	0.2	0.1	0.3	0.3
Haiti	0.8	0.5	3.0	2.8	0.0	0.0	1.7	1.5	...	...
Honduras	3.7	2.5	1.2	1.1	0.0	0.0	0.0	0.0	1.3	1.1
Mexico	-0.0	-1.4	0.3	0.3	0.0	0.0	0.1	0.2	1.3	1.3
Nicaragua	3.9	3.7	1.0	1.0	0.0	0.0	0.0	0.0	4.0	4.1
Panama	1.1	1.0	1.8	1.8	0.0	0.0	0.2	0.2	5.7	5.8
Paraguay	2.1	1.9	1.4	1.5	0.0	0.0	0.2	0.4	1.2	1.3
Peru	1.3	1.0	0.7	0.5	0.2	0.1	0.2	0.2	1.6	1.8
Uruguay	2.3	1.7	1.3	1.0	0.0	0.0	0.0	0.4	5.9	6.2
Venezuela (Bolivarian Republic of)	0.7	0.9	1.5	1.1	0.0	0.0	0.0	0.0	0.9	0.8

Source: Economic Commission for Latin America and the Caribbean (ECLAC), on the basis of official figures.

[a] Preliminary figures.

[b] General government.

Table A-39

LATIN AMERICA AND THE CARIBBEAN: CENTRAL GOVERNMENT GROSS PUBLIC DEBT

(Percentages of GDP)

	2000	2001	2002	2003	2004	2005	2006	2007	2008 [a]
Latin America and the Caribbean	**43.2**	**45.5**	**58.4**	**57.5**	**50.9**	**42.8**	**35.8**	**29.9**	**28.0**
Argentina [b]	45.0	53.7	145.9	138.2	126.4	72.8	63.6	55.7	48.3
Bolivia (Plurinational State of) [c]	60.7	72.7	77.5	86.8	81.1	75.6	49.8	37.1	33.8
Brazil [d]	29.9	31.6	37.9	34.0	31.0	30.9	31.0	31.4	25.2
Chile [e]	13.6	14.9	15.7	13.0	10.7	7.3	5.3	4.1	5.2
Colombia [f]	32.9	39.0	44.0	43.9	40.0	39.6	37.6	32.9	33.5
Costa Rica	42.4	43.2	43.6	41.3	41.0	37.5	33.3	27.6	24.9
Dominican Republic	...	...	...	...	...	22.0	20.4	18.4	20.0
Ecuador	73.3	56.9	50.3	45.8	40.8	35.9	29.4	27.5	23.7
El Salvador [c]	27.2	30.7	35.2	37.2	38.1	37.6	37.5	34.5	33.4
Guatemala [c]	19.0	20.2	18.4	20.9	21.4	20.8	21.7	21.4	20.2
Haiti [g]	43.8	46.2	60.2	57.5	46.7	44.1	35.6	32.2	37.6
Honduras	55.6	53.9	55.5	60.7	59.6	44.7	28.7	17.3	19.4
Mexico [h]	21.2	20.5	21.9	22.1	20.8	20.3	20.7	21.2	24.7
Nicaragua	113.0	109.9	133.7	137.7	100.6	92.6	68.7	42.4	38.2
Panama [i]	65.5	70.1	69.0	66.6	69.6	65.1	60.3	53.2	44.6
Paraguay	32.6	41.1	59.2	44.4	38.0	31.4	23.8	16.9	15.3
Peru	45.2	44.2	45.7	47.4	41.8	38.2	31.3	27.2	24.8
Uruguay	30.6	40.1	94.4	90.2	71.4	64.2	57.2	48.2	46.2
Venezuela (Bolivarian Republic of) [j]	26.8	30.4	42.4	46.3	38.1	32.8	23.9	19.3	14.0

Source: Economic Commission for Latin America and the Caribbean (ECLAC), on the basis of official figures.

[a] Preliminary figures.

[b] National public administration. As from 2005, does not include debt not presented for swap.

[c] Does not include publicly guaranteed private debt.

[d] Net public debt. Federal government and central bank.

[e] Consolidated.

[f] Central national government.

[g] Does not include public sector commitments to commercial banks.

[h] Federal government.

[i] Does not include domestic floating debt.

[j] Non-financial public sector.

Table A-40

LATIN AMERICA AND THE CARIBBEAN: NON-FINANCIAL PUBLIC-SECTOR GROSS PUBLIC DEBT

(Percentages of GDP)

	2000	2001	2002	2003	2004	2005	2006	2007	2008 [a]
Latin America and the Caribbean	**48.8**	**51.0**	**65.4**	**63.8**	**57.0**	**48.9**	**41.2**	**33.9**	**32.2**
Argentina [b]	53.1	64.8	184.4	156.9	143.3	87.6	76.3	66.7	59.3
Bolivia (Plurinational State of) [c]	65.8	76.7	80.2	89.5	83.9	78.3	52.6	40.0	36.7
Brazil [d]	47.7	50.8	59.6	53.7	49.3	46.7	45.0	44.3	37.0
Chile [e]	18.6	20.2	22.1	19.5	16.0	13.0	10.6	0.1	12.1
Colombia [f]	39.5	42.9	49.5	46.7	42.4	38.9	36.0	32.3	31.9
Costa Rica	41.8	43.2	45.1	45.6	46.9	42.9	38.4	31.9	29.9
Dominican Republic [j]	...	...	...	...	...	...	...	19.0	20.8
Ecuador [c]	81.7	62.7	54.3	49.2	43.7	38.6	32.0	30.0	25.8
El Salvador [c]	30.0	33.6	38.6	40.3	40.5	39.7	39.7	36.6	35.7
Guatemala [c]	21.2	21.7	19.6	22.0	22.4	21.5	21.9	21.6	20.5
Haiti [g]	49.1	50.7	66.5	63.5	51.1	47.5	38.1	34.5	39.6
Honduras	55.4	53.5	55.1	59.9	59.4	44.8	30.0	18.2	18.5
Mexico [h]	25.3	24.1	25.7	26.1	24.2	23.0	22.7	23.0	27.2
Nicaragua	114.7	111.3	134.1	138.0	100.7	92.8	69.1	43.3	39.3
Panama	66.5	71.1	69.4	67.0	70.4	66.2	61.0	53.7	45.2
Paraguay	35.3	44.0	63.0	46.9	41.7	32.8	24.8	19.9	18.3
Peru [i]	45.2	44.2	45.7	47.4	41.8	38.2	31.3	27.2	24.8
Uruguay	34.4	44.7	101.4	96.1	75.5	67.4	60.4	51.4	49.4
Venezuela (Bolivarian Republic of)	26.8	30.4	42.4	46.3	38.1	32.8	23.9	19.3	14.0

Source: Economic Commission for Latin America and the Caribbean (ECLAC), on the basis of official figures.

[a] Preliminary figures.

[b] Up to 2002 the figures refer to national public-sector debt plus provincial debt. From 2003 on, the figures are consolidated.

[c] Refers to the external debt of the non-financial public-sector and central-government domestic debt.

[d] Net public debt. Public sector.

[e] Consolidated.

[f] Consolidated non-financial public sector.

[g] Does not include public sector commitments to commercial banks.

[h] Includes public sector external debt and federal government domestic debt.

[i] Includes local and regional government debt owed to Banco de la Nación.

[j] Public sector.

Table A-41

LATIN AMERICA AND THE CARIBBEAN: SUBNATIONAL GOVERNMENT FISCAL INDICATORS

(Percentages of GDP)

		2000	2001	2002	2003	2004	2005	2006	2008 [a]
Argentina	**Provinces**								
	Total revenue	11.5	11.2	10.4	11.3	12.8	13.4	13.5	13.9
	Total expenditure	12.6	13.5	10.9	10.9	11.8	13.1	13.4	14.0
	Primary balance	-0.5	-1.5	-0.0	0.9	1.4	0.7	0.5	0.2
	Overall balance	-1.2	-2.4	-0.5	0.4	1.0	0.3	0.1	-0.1
	Public debt	7.5	11.2	21.9	18.8	16.8	14.8	12.8	11.0
Bolivia (Plurinational State of)									
	Regional governments								
	Total revenue	6.3	7.8	8.2	7.7	8.6	10.4	12.7	13.0
	Total expenditure	6.4	7.9	7.9	9.6	8.1	8.2	10.8	11.8
	Primary balance	0.1	0.1	0.5	0.4	0.7	2.4	2.1	1.3
	Overall balance	-0.1	-0.2	0.3	0.4	0.6	2.2	1.9	1.1
	Public debt	1.0	0.9	1.1	1.2	1.5	1.5	1.2	1.1
Brazil	**States and municipalities**								
	Total revenue	12.9	12.9	12.8	12.3	12.3	12.8	12.9	13.2
	Total expenditure	12.2	12.7	12.7	12.0	11.9	12.3	12.5	12.5
	Primary balance [b]	0.2	0.3	0.3	0.6	0.7	0.7	0.6	0.9
	Overall balance [b]	-0.4	-0.4	-0.4	-0.1	0.1	0.0	-0.1	0.4
	Public debt	15.7	17.6	19.8	18.6	18.1	16.3	15.4	14.4
Chile	**Municipalities**								
	Total revenue	3.2	3.2	3.3	3.1	2.7	2.9	2.7	2.7
	Total expenditure	3.3	3.2	3.3	3.1	2.8	2.8	2.5	2.6
	Primary balance	-0.1	0.0	0.0	0.0	-0.0	0.2	0.2	0.1
	Overall balance	-0.1	0.0	0.0	0.0	-0.0	0.2	0.2	0.1
Colombia	**Departments and municipalities**								
	Total revenue	6.8	6.9	7.5	7.8	7.8	8.7	8.6	8.5
	Total expenditure	7.3	6.9	7.4	7.5	7.1	8.4	8.8	9.0
	Primary balance	-0.1	0.3	0.4	0.5	0.9	0.4	-0.1	-0.3
	Overall balance	-0.5	-0.0	0.1	0.3	0.7	0.3	-0.3	-0.5
	Public debt	3.2	3.6	3.3	2.5	1.8	1.7	1.5	1.6
Costa Rica	**Local governments**								
	Total revenue	0.8	0.9	0.8	0.8	0.8	0.8	0.9	0.9
	Total expenditure	0.7	0.8	0.8	0.8	0.8	0.8	0.8	0.9
	Primary balance	0.1	0.1	0.1	0.1	0.0	-0.0	0.1	0.0
	Overall balance	0.1	0.0	0.0	0.1	-0.0	-0.1	0.0	-0.0
Cuba	**Local governments**								
	Total revenue	15.0	15.9	17.3	17.5	17.9	20.8	21.3	21.3
	Total expenditure	15.0	15.9	17.3	17.5	17.9	20.8	21.3	21.3
	Primary balance	0.0	0.0	0.0	0.0	0.0	0.0	0.0	0.0
	Overall balance	0.0	0.0	0.0	0.0	0.0	0.0	0.0	0.0
Ecuador	**Town councils and municipalities**								
	Total revenue	2.8	3.9	4.0	3.7	4.3	3.9	4.1	6.6
	Total expenditure	2.1	3.3	3.8	3.3	4.2	3.6	4.1	4.0
	Primary balance	0.6	0.6	0.2	0.3	0.1	0.3	0.1	2.7
	Overall balance	0.6	0.6	0.2	0.3	0.1	0.3	0.0	2.6
Mexico	**State governments and federal district**								
	Total revenue	7.1	7.7	7.7	8.0	7.8	8.2	8.4	8.4
	Total expenditure	7.1	7.8	7.9	7.9	7.6	8.1	8.2	8.3
	Primary balance	0.1	0.0	-0.1	0.1	0.2	0.2	0.3	0.1
	Overall balance	-0.0	-0.0	-0.2	0.0	0.1	0.1	0.2	0.0
	Public debt	1.5	1.6	1.7	1.6	1.5	1.6	1.6	1.8
Paraguay	**Provincial governments**								
	Total revenue	0.4	0.4	0.3	0.3	0.5	0.5	0.5	0.5
	Total expenditure	0.4	0.4	0.2	0.3	0.5	0.5	0.5	0.4
	Primary balance	-0.0	0.0	0.0	-0.0	0.0	-0.0	-0.0	0.1
	Overall balance	-0.0	0.0	0.0	-0.0	0.0	-0.0	-0.0	0.1
Peru	**Local governments**								
	Total revenue	2.1	2.1	2.1	2.2	2.3	2.5	2.7	3.7
	Total expenditure	2.1	2.1	2.1	2.1	2.2	2.2	2.7	2.6
	Primary balance	0.1	0.1	0.1	0.2	0.1	0.3	0.1	1.1
	Overall balance	0.0	-0.0	0.1	0.1	0.1	0.3	0.1	1.1

Source: Economic Commission for Latin America and the Caribbean (ECLAC), on the basis of official figures.

[a] Preliminary figures.

[b] The primary and overall balances do not include financial resources (credit operations and disposal of assets).

NACIONES UNIDAS
UNITED NATIONS

CEPAL
ECLAC

Publicaciones de la CEPAL / *ECLAC publications*

Comisión Económica para América Latina y el Caribe / *Economic Commission for Latin America and the Caribbean*
Casilla 179-D, Santiago de Chile. E-mail: publications@cepal.org
Véalas en: www.cepal.org/publicaciones
Publications may be accessed at: www.eclac.org

Revista CEPAL / *CEPAL Review*

La Revista se inició en 1976 como parte del Programa de Publicaciones de la Comisión Económica para América Latina y el Caribe, con el propósito de contribuir al examen de los problemas del desarrollo socioeconómico de la región. Las opiniones expresadas en los artículos firmados, incluidas las colaboraciones de los funcionarios de la Secretaría, son las de los autores y, por lo tanto, no reflejan necesariamente los puntos de vista de la Organización.

La *Revista CEPAL* se publica en español e inglés tres veces por año.

Los precios de suscripción anual vigentes para 2009 son de US$ 30 para la versión en español y de US$ 35 para la versión en inglés. El precio por ejemplar suelto es de US$ 15 para ambas versiones. Los precios de suscripción por dos años (2008-2009) son de US$ 50 para la versión en español y de US$ 60 para la versión en inglés.

CEPAL Review first appeared in 1976 as part of the Publications Programme of the Economic Commission for Latin America and the Caribbean, its aim being to make a contribution to the study of the economic and social development problems of the region. The views expressed in signed articles, including those by Secretariat staff members, are those of the authors and therefore do not necessarily reflect the point of view of the Organization.

CEPAL Review is published in Spanish and English versions three times a year.

Annual subscription costs for 2009 are US$ 30 for the Spanish version and US$ 35 for the English version. The price of single issues is US$ 15 in both cases. The cost of a two-year subscription (2008-2009) is US$ 50 for Spanish-language version and US$ 60 for English.

Informes periódicos institucionales / *Annual reports*

Todos disponibles para años anteriores / *Issues for previous years also available*

- *Balance preliminar de las economías de América Latina y el Caribe, 2008, 184 p.*
  ***Preliminary Overview of the Economies of Latin America and the Caribbean, 2008**, 176 p.*
- *Estudio económico de América Latina y el Caribe, 2007-2008, 152 p.*
  ***Economic Survey of Latin America and the Caribbean, 2007-2008**, 146 p.*
- *Panorama de la inserción internacional de América Latina y el Caribe, 2007. Tendencias 2008, 160 p.*
  ***Latin America and the Caribbean in the World Economy, 2007. 2008 Trends,** 148 p.*
- *Panorama social de América Latina, 2008*, 262 p.
  ***Social Panorama of Latin America, 2008**, 256 p.*
- *La inversión extranjera directa en América Latina y el Caribe*, 2008, 160 p.
  ***Foreign Direct Investment of Latin America and the Caribbean, 2008**, 156 p.*
- *Anuario estadístico de América Latina y el Caribe* / ***Statistical Yearbook for Latin America and the Caribbean*** (bilingüe/*bilingual*), 2007, 434 p.

Libros de la CEPAL

103 *L'Amérique latine et les Caraïbes au seuil du troisième millénaire*, 2009, 138 p.
102 *Migración interna y desarrollo en América Latina entre 1980 y 2005*, Jorge Rodríguez y Gustavo Busso, 2009, 272 p.
101 *Claves de la innovación social en América Latina y el Caribe*, Adolfo Rodríguez Herrera y Hernán Alvarado Ugarte, 2009, 236 p.
100 *Envejecimiento, derechos humanos y políticas públicas*, Sandra Huenchuan (ed.), 2009, 232 p.
99 *Economía y territorio en América Latina y el Caribe. Desigualdades y políticas*, 2009, 212 p.
98 *La sociedad de la información en América Latina y el Caribe: desarrollo de las tecnologías y tecnologías para el desarrollo*, Wilson Peres y Martin Hilbert (eds.), 2009, 388 p.

97 *América Latina y el Caribe: migración internacional, derechos humanos y desarrollo,* Jorge Martínez Pizarro (ed.), 2008, 375 p.
96 *Familias y políticas públicas en América Latina: una historia de desencuentros,* Irma Arriagada (coord.), 2007, 424 p.
95 *Centroamérica y México: políticas de competencia a principios del siglo XXI,* Eugenio Rivera y Claudia Schatan (coords.), 2008, 304 p.
94 *América Latina y el Caribe: La propiedad intelectual después de los tratados de libre comercio,* Álvaro Díaz, 2008, 248 p.
93 *Tributación en América Latina. En busca de una nueva agenda de reformas,* Oscar Cetrángolo y Juan Carlos Gómez-Sabaini (comps.), 2007, 166 p.
92 *Fernando Fajnzylber. Una visión renovadora del desarrollo en América Latina,* Miguel Torres Olivos (comp.), 2006, 422 p.
91 *Cooperación financiera regional,* José Antonio Ocampo (comp.), 2006, 274 p.
90 *Financiamiento para el desarrollo. América Latina desde una perspectiva comparada,* Barbara Stallings con la colaboración de Rogério Studart, 2006, 396 p.
89 *Políticas municipales de microcrédito. Un instrumento para la dinamización de los sistemas productivos locales. Estudios de caso en América Latina,* Paola Foschiatto y Giovanni Stumpo (comps.), 2006, 244 p.
88 *Aglomeraciones en torno a los recursos naturales en América Latina y el Caribe: Políticas de articulación y articulación de políticas,* 2006, 266 p.
87 *Pobreza, desertificación y degradación de los recursos naturales,* César Morales y Soledad Parada (eds.), 2006, 274 p.

Copublicaciones recientes / *Recent co-publications*

EnREDos. Regulación y estrategias corporativas frente a la convergencia tecnológica, Marcio Wohlers y Martha García-Murillo (eds.), CEPAL/Mayol, Colombia, 2009.

Desafíos y oportunidades de la industria del software en América Latina, Paulo Tigre y Felipe Silveira Marques (eds.), CEPAL/Mayol, Colombia, 2009.

¿Quo vadis, *tecnología de la información y de las comunicaciones?,* Martin Hilbert y Osvaldo Cairó (eds.), CEPAL/Mayol, Colombia, 2009.

***O Estruturalismo latino-americano,* Octavio Rodríguez, CEPAL/Civilização Brasileira, 2009.**

***L'avenir de la protection sociale en Amérique latine. Accessibilité, financement et solidarité,* CEPALC/Eska, France, 2009.**

Fortalecer los sistemas de pensiones latinoamericanos. Cuentas individuales por reparto, Robert Holzmann, Edward Palmer y Andras Uthoff (eds.), CEPAL/Mayol, Colombia, 2008.

Competition Policies in Emerging Economies. Lessons and Challenges from Central America and Mexico, Claudia Schatan and Eugenio Rivera Urrutia (eds.), ECLAC/Springer, USA, 2008.

Estratificación y movilidad social en América Latina. Transformaciones estructurales en un cuarto de siglo, Rolando Franco, Arturo León y Raúl Atria (coords.), CEPAL/Lom, Chile, 2007.

Economic growth with equity. Challenges for Latin America, Ricardo Ffrench-Davis and José Luis Machinea (eds.), ECLAC/Palgrave Macmillan, United Kingdom, 2007.

Mujer y empleo. La reforma de la salud y la salud de la reforma en Argentina, María Nieves Rico y Flavia Marco (coords.), CEPAL/Siglo XXI, Argentina, 2006.

El estructuralismo latinoamericano, Octavio Rodríguez, CEPAL/Siglo XXI, México, 2006.

Gobernabilidad corporativa, responsabilidad social y estrategias empresariales en América Latina, Germano M. de Paula, João Carlos Ferraz y Georgina Núñez (comps.), CEPAL/Mayol, Colombia, 2006.

Desempeño económico y política social en América Latina y el Caribe. Los retos de la equidad, el desarrollo y la ciudadanía, Ana Sojo y Andras Uthoff (comps.), CEPAL/Flacso-México/ Fontamara, México, 2006.

Política y políticas públicas en los procesos de reforma de América Latina, Rolando Franco y Jorge Lanzaro (coords.), CEPAL/Flacso-México/Miño y Dávila, México, 2006.

Finance for Development. Latin America in Comparative Perspective, Barbara Stallings with Rogério Studart, ECLAC/Brookings Institution Press, USA, 2006.

Los jóvenes y el empleo en América Latina. Desafíos y perspectivas ante el nuevo escenario laboral, Jürgen Weller (ed.), CEPAL/Mayol Ediciones, Colombia, 2006.

Condiciones y políticas de competencia en economías pequeñas de Centroamérica y el Caribe, Claudia Schatan y Marcos Ávalos (coords.), CEPAL/Fondo de Cultura Económica, México, 2006.

Aglomeraciones pesqueras en América Latina. Ventajas asociadas al enfoque de cluster, Massiel Guerra (comp.) CEPAL/Alfaomega, Colombia, 2006.

Reformas para América Latina después del fundamentalismo neoliberal, Ricardo Ffrench-Davis, CEPAL/Siglo XXI, Argentina, 2006.

Coediciones recientes / *Recent co-editions*

El envejecimiento y las personas de edad. Indicadores sociodemográficos para América Latina y el Caribe, CEPAL/UNFPA, 2009.

Espacios iberoamericanos: la economía del conocimiento, CEPAL/SEGIB, Chile, 2008.

Hacia la revisión de los paradigmas del desarrollo en América Latina, Oscar Altimir, Enrique V. Iglesias, José Luis Machinea (eds.), CEPAL/SEGIB, Chile, 2008.

Por uma revisão dos paradigmas do desenvolvimento na América Latina, Oscar Altimir, Enrique V. Iglesias, José Luis Machinea (eds.), CEPAL/SEGIB, Chile, 2008.

Hacia un nuevo pacto social. Políticas económicas para un desarrollo integral en América Latina, José Luis Machinea y Narcís Serra (eds.) CEPAL/CIDOB, España, 2008.

Espacios iberoamericanos: comercio e inversión, CEPAL/SEGIB, Chile, 2007.
Espaços Ibero-Americanos: comércio e investimento, CEPAL/SEGIB, Chile, 2007.
Visiones del desarrollo en América Latina, José Luis Machinea y Narcís Serra (eds.), CEPAL/CIDOB, España, 2007.
Cohesión social: inclusión y sentido de pertenencia en América Latina y el Caribe, CEPAL/SEGIB, Chile, 2007.
Social Cohesion. Inclusion and a sense of belonging in Latin America and the Caribbean, ECLAC/SEGIB, Chile, 2007.
Espacios Iberoamericanos, CEPAL/SEGIB, Chile, 2006.
Espaços Ibero-Americanos, CEPAL/SEGIB, Chile, 2006.

Cuadernos de la CEPAL

93 *Privilegiadas y discriminadas. Las trabajadoras del sector financiero*, Flavia Marco Navarro y María Nieves Rico Ibáñez (eds.), 2009, 300 p.
92 *Estadísticas para la equidad de género: magnitudes y tendencias en América Latina*, Vivian Milosavljevic, 2007, 186 p.
91 *Elementos conceptuales para la prevención y reducción de daños originados por amenazas naturales*, Eduardo Chaparro y Matías Renard (eds.), 2005, 144 p.
90 *Los sistemas de pensiones en América Latina: un análisis de género*, Flavia Marco (coord.), 2004, 270 p.
89 *Energía y desarrollo sustentable en América Latina y el Caribe*. Guía para la formulación de políticas energéticas, 2003, 240 p.
88 *La ciudad inclusiva*, Marcello Balbo, Ricardo Jordán y Daniela Simioni (comps.), CEPAL/Cooperazione Italiana, 2003, 322 p.
87 ***Traffic congestion. The problem and how to deal with it***, Alberto Bull (comp.), 2004, 198 p.

Cuadernos estadísticos de la CEPAL

36 *Clasificaciones estadísticas internacionales incorporadas en el Banco de Datos de Comercio Exterior de América Latina y el Caribe de la CEPAL (Revisión 3)*. Solo disponible en CD, 2008.
35 *Resultados del Programa de Comparación Internacional para América del Sur.* Solo disponible en CD, 2007.
34 *Indicadores económicos del turismo.* Solo disponible en CD, 2006.
33 *América Latina y el Caribe. Balanza de pagos 1980-2005.* Solo disponible en CD, 2006.
32 *América Latina y el Caribe. Series regionales y oficiales de cuentas nacionales, 1950-2002.* Solo disponible en CD, 2005.
31 *Comercio exterior. Exportaciones e importaciones según destino y origen por principales zonas económicas. 1980, 1985, 1990, 1995-2002.* Solo disponible en CD, 2005.
30 *Clasificaciones estadísticas internacionales incorporadas en el banco de datos del comercio exterior de América Latina y el Caribe de la CEPAL*, 2004, 308 p.

Observatorio demográfico *ex Boletín demográfico* / ***Demographic Observatory** formerly* ***Demographic Bulletin*** (bilingüe/*bilingual*)

Edición bilingüe (español e inglés) que proporciona información estadística actualizada, referente a estimaciones y proyecciones de población de los países de América Latina y el Caribe. Incluye también indicadores demográficos de interés, tales como tasas de natalidad, mortalidad, esperanza de vida al nacer, distribución de la población, etc.

El Observatorio aparece dos veces al año, en los meses de enero y julio. Suscripción anual: US$ 20.00. Valor por cada ejemplar: US$ 15.00.

Bilingual publication (Spanish and English) proving up-to-date estimates and projections of the populations of the Latin American and Caribbean countries. Also includes various demographic indicators of interest such as fertility and mortality rates, life expectancy, measures of population distribution, etc.

The Observatory appears twice a year in January and July. Annual subscription: US$ 20.00. Per issue: US$ 15.00.

Notas de población

Revista especializada que publica artículos e informes acerca de las investigaciones más recientes sobre la dinámica demográfica en la región, en español, con resúmenes en español e inglés. También incluye información sobre actividades científicas y profesionales en el campo de población.

La revista se publica desde 1973 y aparece dos veces al año, en junio y diciembre.

Suscripción anual: US$ 20.00. Valor por cada ejemplar: US$ 12.00.

Specialized journal which publishes articles and reports on recent studies of demographic dynamics in the region, in Spanish with abstracts in Spanish and English. Also includes information on scientific and professional activities in the field of population.

Published since 1973, the journal appears twice a year in June and December.

Annual subscription: US$ 20.00. Per issue: US$ 12.00.

Series de la CEPAL

Comercio internacional / Desarrollo productivo / Desarrollo territorial / Estudios estadísticos y prospectivos / Estudios y perspectivas (Bogotá, Brasilia, Buenos Aires, México, Montevideo) / ***Studies and Perspectives*** (The Caribbean, Washington) / *Financiamiento del desarrollo / Gestión pública / Informes y estudios especiales / Macroeconomía del desarrollo / Manuales / Medio ambiente y desarrollo / Mujer y desarrollo / Población y desarrollo / Políticas sociales / Recursos naturales e infraestructura / Seminarios y conferencias.*

Véase el listado completo en: www.cepal.org/publicaciones / *A complete listing is available at*: www.cepal.org/publicaciones

كيفية الحصول على منشورات الأمم المتحدة

يمكن الحصول على منشورات الأمم المتحدة من المكتبات ودور التوزيع في جميع أنحاء العالم . استعلم عنها من المكتبة التي تتعامل معها أو اكتب إلى : الأمم المتحدة ، قسم البيع في نيويورك أو في جنيف .

如何购取联合国出版物

联合国出版物在全世界各地的书店和经售处均有发售。请向书店询问或写信到纽约或日内瓦的联合国销售组。

HOW TO OBTAIN UNITED NATIONS PUBLICATIONS

United Nations publications may be obtained from bookstores and distributors throughout the world. Consult your bookstore or write to: United Nations, Sales Section, New York or Geneva.

COMMENT SE PROCURER LES PUBLICATIONS DES NATIONS UNIES

Les publications des Nations Unies sont en vente dans les librairies et les agences dépositaires du monde entier. Informez-vous auprès de votre libraire ou adressez-vous à : Nations Unies, Section des ventes, New York ou Genève.

КАК ПОЛУЧИТЬ ИЗДАНИЯ ОРГАНИЗАЦИИ ОБЪЕДИНЕННЫХ НАЦИЙ

Издания Организации Объединенных Наций можно купить в книжных магазинах и агентствах во всех районах мира. Наводите справки об изданиях в вашем книжном магазине или пишите по адресу: Организация Объединенных Наций, Секция по продаже изданий, Нью-Йорк или Женева.

COMO CONSEGUIR PUBLICACIONES DE LAS NACIONES UNIDAS

Las publicaciones de las Naciones Unidas están en venta en librerías y casas distribuidoras en todas partes del mundo. Consulte a su librero o diríjase a: Naciones Unidas, Sección de Ventas, Nueva York o Ginebra.

Las publicaciones de la Comisión Económica para América Latina y el Caribe (CEPAL) y las del Instituto Latinoamericano y del Caribe de Planificación Económica y Social (ILPES) se pueden adquirir a los distribuidores locales o directamente a través de:

Publicaciones de las Naciones Unidas
2 United Nations Plaza, Room DC2-853
Nueva York, NY, 10017
Estados Unidos
Tel. (1 800)253-9646 Fax (1 212)963-3489
E-mail: publications@un.org

Publicaciones de las Naciones Unidas
Sección de Ventas
Palais des Nations
1211 Ginebra 10
Suiza
Tel. (41 22)917-2613 Fax (41 22)917-0027

Unidad de Distribución
Comisión Económica para América Latina y el Caribe (CEPAL)
Av. Dag Hammarskjöld 3477, Vitacura
7630412 Santiago
Chile
Tel. (56 2)210-2056 Fax (56 2)210-2069
E-mail: publications@cepal.org

Publications of the Economic Commission for Latin America and the Caribbean (ECLAC) and those of the Latin American and the Caribbean Institute for Economic and Social Planning (ILPES) can be ordered from your local distributor or directly through:

United Nations Publications
2 United Nations Plaza, Room DC2-853
New York, NY, 10017
USA
Tel. (1 800)253-9646 Fax (1 212)963-3489
E-mail: publications@un.org

United Nations Publications
Sales Sections
Palais des Nations
1211 Geneva 10
Switzerland
Tel. (41 22)917-2613 Fax (41 22)917-0027

Distribution Unit
Economic Commission for Latin America and the Caribbean (ECLAC)
Av. Dag Hammarskjöld 3477, Vitacura
7630412 Santiago
Chile
Tel. (56 2)210-2056 Fax (56 2)210-2069
E-mail: publications@eclac.org

Impresión: GraficAndes